WITHDRAWN

WRITING PARIS

SUNY series in
Latin American and Iberian Thought and Culture

Jorge J. E. Gracia, editor

Writing Paris

❖

*Urban Topographies of Desire
in Contemporary Latin American Fiction*

MARCY E. SCHWARTZ

STATE UNIVERSITY OF NEW YORK PRESS

Published by
State University of New York Press, Albany

© 1999 State University of New York

For information, address State University of New York Press,
State University Plaza, Albany, NY 12246

Production by Laurie Searl
Marketing by Anne M. Valentine

Library of Congress Cataloging-in-Publication Data

Schwartz, Marcy E., 1958–
    Writing Paris : urban topographies of desire in contemporary Latin American fiction / Marcy E. Schwartz.
        p.   cm. — (SUNY series in Latin American and Iberian thought and culture)
    Includes bibliographical references (p.   ) and index.
    ISBN 0-7914-4151-2 (alk. paper). — ISBN 0-7914-4152-0 (pbk. : alk. paper)
    1. Spanish American fiction—20th century—History and criticism.
2. Paris (France)—In literature.   I. Title.   II. Series.
PQ7082.N7S385   1999
863—dc21   98-8711
                                                                                       CIP

10 9 8 7 6 5 4 3 2 1

For Rick, Albertine, and Samantha;

and in memory of my mother,

Celia Jean Handler Schwartz

Contents

Illustrations

Acknowledgments

I am indebted to a great number of individuals who have contributed to the research and writing of this book, and to my development as a scholar. This project began as a doctoral dissertation under the committed, rigorous, and generous guidance of Sara Castro-Klarén. Well beyond the dissertation, her collegiality has been a source of meaningful intellectual stimulation.

I am grateful to my colleagues in the Department of Spanish and Portuguese at Rutgers University for their support and stimulation. I am also thankful to Rutgers for a semester's sabbatical leave granted by the Faculty of Arts and Sciences during the last phase of writing this book, and to the university for a Research Council grant.

I express immense gratitude to the following colleagues for generously reading and commenting on earlier versions of chapters in this book: Sara Castro-Klarén, Carlos Alonso, Aníbal González, Jorge Schwartz, Frank Dauster, Susana Rotker, Tom Stephens, Jorge Marcone, Margo Persin, Dámaris Otero-Torres, Laura Beard, Gerard Aching, Santiago Juan-Navarro, José Antonio Mazzotti, and César Ferreira. For research logistics and bibliography, I also thank George Lerner, Danièle Angel, Ricardo Oré, and Peter Klarén. For help with acquiring and documenting visual materials, I am grateful to Ana María Escallón, Daniel Balderston, Cecilia Hare, and Margo Persin.

How much sooner or later this book would have been completed without the most enriching company of my family is beyond my prediction. I cannot adequately express my gratitude to my husband, Rick Shain, for his reading, editing, historical insight, rigor with the manuscript, and confidence in my work. I owe much of my productivity and happiness to his humor and the joy of parenting our daughters together. I thank Samantha and Albertine for being proud of me, and for the jewels of their lives in mine.

Additionally, I am grateful to Antonio Seguí and Liliana Porter (and the Monique Knowlon Gallery) for the generous contribution of their illustrations. I gratefully acknowledge permission from the editors of *Monographic Review/Revista Monográfica* to reprint material in the Introduction and in chapter 1 that originally appeared in Volume XII (1996). A previous version of chapter 4 was originally published in *Los mundos de Alfredo Bryce Echenique* (© 1994), reprinted with the permission of the publisher of the Pontificia Universidad Católica del Perú and the editors. I also gratefully acknowledge permission to reprint material from the following: P. Boulat/*Life* magazine (© Time Inc.) for the photograph of Julio Cortázar by the late Pierre Boulat; Anagrama Press for permission to quote from *De Pe a Pa: de Pekín a París* (© 1986 by Luisa Futoransky); the Carmen Balcells Literary Agency for permission to quote from *La vida exagerada de Martín Romaña* (© 1981 by Alfredo Bryce Echenique), *Cuentos completos* (© 1994 by Julio Cortázar), and for permission to reproduce Cortázar's drawing and notes from *Cuaderno de bitácora* (© 1983).

Figure 1.1
"La Tour Eiffel" 1981 by Antonio Seguí

Born in 1934 in Córdoba, Argentina, Seguí has resided in Paris since 1963. This drawing is among a series of over a dozen works from the early 1980s of Parisian architecture.

Introduction

❖

The City As Text and Paris As Fiction

A column celebrating Parisian artistic and intellectual life appeared regularly in the late nineteenth century in the Chilean daily *La Epoca*. The detailed chronicles, written by Pedro Balmaceda Toro under the pseudonym A. de Gilbert, covered current Parisian salons and exhibits, personalities and fashion, cafés and receptions. Although he presented himself as a sophisticated participant in Parisian intellectual life, Balmacedo Toro devised his accounts from secondhand sources and gossip. In fact, he had never been to Paris. His fabrication and his readers' vicarious fascination typify Paris's inscription into Latin American writing. His column provided an avenue for an impostor *flâneur* in an invented Paris.[1]

This book is not about Paris, but about the Paris inscribed in Latin American narrative. A large corpus of Latin American writing since independence inhabits Paris as both a poetic and politicized space for the cultural imaginary. No other city has provided such a consistent literary destination from Latin America. While some of those texts are based on actual visits by their writers, many more, like Balmacedo Toro's chronicles, invent a desired Paris. Beyond biographical itineraries, Paris is evoked by writers and intellectuals as a metaphor for a broad spectrum of culturally bound desires. Latin American urban culture has designated Paris as an idealized, hegemonic cultural center that serves as a model for European modernity. The spectrum of social and cultural connotations associated with Paris offers alternatives to local and national conventions. The city summons such diverse images as bohemian lifestyles, social prestige, sensuous Parisian streets, and revolutionary politics. Latin American writing constructs Paris out of this constellation of aesthetic, class, and gendered projections. The chapters that follow examine the foundations of those projections and their contemporary transformations.

1

The persistence of Paris in contemporary writing reveals a city whose design is not limited to a geographical reference and whose narrative function is not confined to a static setting. Paris as a fictional construct grows out of a wider context of urban cultural politics. Writing and the assertion of a literate cultural praxis are at the foundation of urban development in Latin America. Angel Rama traces that writing culture in *La ciudad letrada* from the colonial period through contemporary experience. The modern conception of "urbanness" in Latin America has been drawn largely from European models, a dependence that still provokes vehement debates over cultural identity. The contest between the rural and the urban resonates with a number of other cultural and political tensions. While cities universally represent cosmopolitanism versus the countryside's particularism, in a postcolonial region such as Latin America this structural cleavage is intensified. In the ongoing process of defining Latin America, the relationship between the country and the city parallels the underlying tension between the local and the international. While these terms do not begin to account for sociological realities, the urban and the rural still operate as cultural categories. Urban constructs like Paris in Latin American writing attest to the ever-increasing interpenetration of the local and the global, and make suspect Latin America's divisive conceptual categorizations.[2]

These urban-rural tensions underlie the problematic nature of the troubled categories of "European" and "American" associations which the narratives discussed in this book emphasize. Paris as an imagined, fictional city in Latin American writing provides a site for the struggles and complexities of urban identity on this side of the Atlantic. Established European modes of visual, verbal, and ideological expression have had a consistent role in determining urban culture in Latin America, and in writing a Latin American Paris. This Paris is one of the crucial characters in modern narrative that, more than a physical space of street grids and geographical coordinates, portrays the textual field of cultural ideals where a community's "energías deseantes acerca del mundo" coalesce (Rama, *Ciudad* 77). Urban culture in the Americas habitually engages Paris as it grapples with European cultural domination. The modernist turn toward Paris, from the Spanish American *modernista* movement beginning in the late nineteenth century to the North American "Lost Generation" of the 1920s and 1930s, is emblematic of the Americas' search for cultural identification outside the newer nations' colonial roots.

"Postcolonial" in this context does not refer to a historical moment of overcoming colonialism, but rather, as Mignolo asserts, to a critical position with regard to its legacies ("Occidentalización" 29, n. 3). Recognition of cultural transplantedness abounds in colonial culture in linguistic manifestations, political strategies, and religious observance. Since independence, continued transnational circumstances generate cultural practices that indicate an enduring sense of displacement. Narrative fiction is one of these practices that, according to Sara Castro-Klarén, has been the genre of Latin American written expression that most thoroughly explores this postcolonial dimension (Zevallos-Aguilar interview 971). Fictional spaces circumscribe the uneasy alliance between regional Latin American places and distant but imposing foreignness. Paris as a narrativized zone of Euro-American confrontations then forms one of the battlegrounds of postcolonial critique. Fiction maps the French capital into what Mignolo calls Latin America's *zona fronteriza,* "[donde] se produce la tensión entre lo que se considera propio y lo que se considera ajeno" ("Posoccidentalismo" 681). In these texts, language and cultural projection collide in discourse that blurs the fine lines between familiarity and otherness, longing and resistance.[3]

This book illustrates the contradictions of Paris's incorporation into contemporary fiction as a city redesigned by the postcolonial imagination. When writers expose Paris as an embodiment of elaborate cultural fantasies, they activate a fictional urban construct to debate the perpetuity of European cultural norms and economic dependence despite the end of overseas rule. This debate hovers around the contradictory images of exotic otherness and affirming familiarity. One side presents Paris from the perspective of the imaginary constructions of an *other,* extra-European place evoked during the late medieval period that crystallized during the age of European expansion. Just as common, however, is the image of Paris as an accessible and familiar realm of opportunity. Contemporary postcolonial writing reformulates those spatial relations in the process of reactivating and relocating the cultural imagination.

Paris as a projection of these ambivalent cultural contentions only confirms J. Jorge Klor de Alva's argument that Latin America never experienced "colonialism" and therefore has never reached a truly *post*colonial stage. Rather than European dominance over indigenous populations, Iberian expansion into what came to be identified as Latin America consisted of transplanted Europeans trying to refashion European society in a new place. Klor de Alva considers colonial reality a resettlement process where Europeans

and *criollos* searched for "a way to be European in America" (12).
Fictional versions of Paris are extensions of a foundational Euro-
vision that determined much of urban cultural conceptualization.
In the following chapters, the term *postcolonial* will refer to this
alternative experiment in nation building (different from, for example, the postcolonial projects of former British and French territories in Southeast Asia and Africa). This project defines
"postcolonial" as a critical position for rearticulating Latin America's
geohistorical relationships through their continuing cross-Atlantic
intersections. Paris in contemporary Latin American fiction still
functions as an enduring "template" of the region's Europeanizing
legacy.[4]

The historical underpinnings of this fictionalization of Paris in
Latin American writing help account for the contradictory images
of the city that still persist in contemporary texts. Since the Enlightenment, educated Latin Americans transfered their attention
away from colonial sources in search of new political, economic,
and aesthetic models. The urban *criollo* administrations developed
their own commerce, particularly with the United States and Brit-
ain, and an expanding demand for Latin American resources abroad
further disassociated the colonies from Spain and Portugal. Many
of the European modernization advances in the eighteenth century
bypassed Iberia due to its cultural conservativism that maintained
an agrarian economy. The colonies recognized in the rest of Europe
a promise of modernity from which Spain and Portugal were ex-
cluded. The *criollo* elite in new Latin American cities looked to
Paris to resolve their doubly marginalized position with respect to
Iberia and northern Europe.[5]

> Paris passa a representar o modelo por excelência da
> Cosmópolis, *axis mundi* sobre o qual gravitarão as "mini"
> ou "subcosmópolis" . . . a funcionar como caldo de cultura
> para o encontro e fermentaçao das novas idéias. (Schwartz,
> *Vanguarda* 5)

For Latin Americans, Paris embodied the essence of humanistic
modernity that rendered Iberian cultures anachronistic.

Rather than "independence" from Europe, the movement toward freedom from Spanish dominance reflected the new nations
of Latin America shifting their international alliances, particularly
in the cultural and economic realms, from Iberia to France, England, and the new United States.[6] The Anglo-American Revolu-

tion of 1776 provided a successful ideological example of self-determination along with new commercial oppportunities.[7] Models for urban modernization in Latin America drew from British technological advances as well as from French political philosophy. Despite the Inquisition's censorship, French political and philosophical publications circulated among the Latin American educated elite. While the impact of Enlightenment philosophy and the French Revolution were certainly not direct causes of independence, they did provide "an indispensable source from which leaders drew to justify, defend, and legitimize their actions" (Lynch 33). The British industrial revolution of the late eighteenth century only fueled the creole appetite for modernity. A combination of international tensions such as the strain on European alliances and the competition for markets intersected in Latin America with ethusiastic support for Anglo-American independence, French revolutionary thought, and British urban industrialism.

For Latin American independence movements, this conjunction between political thought and urban technological modernity was a powerful confluence. In the principal radical political movements in France, revolution and urbanization have always been vitally interconnected as well. From the storming of the Bastille in 1789 to the Commune in 1871, and even the student revolts in May 1968, revolution has utilized urban space for the transmission of its message and for social and political symbolism.[8] As Priscilla Parkhurst Ferguson remarks in her study of Paris and revolutionary movements, the process of revolution involves the "complex interaction of political identity, social setting, and cultural practice" (2). The political symbolism of neighborhoods and monuments, the iconic architecture of national institutions, and the accessibility of public street demonstrations all attest to the city's co-participation in social movements. Latin American writing takes Paris as a metonym for revolution and northern European modernization and recreates the city's image as a pattern for America's political and cultural development. Paris as a dual symbol of modernity and political freedom, the city's longest-lasting role, persists in contemporary fiction from Latin America.

Latin America's problematic early independence period reveals more of the contradictions but also some of the justifications for its association with Paris and French culture. The facade of a unified Christian culture was not sufficient to mask the challenge of America's heterogeneous, multicultural society. The diversity of its immigrants and the lack of social integration among *criollos,*

Africans, and indigenous peoples created disjunctures at home that provoked nation builders to seek foreign models and solutions. Carlos Alonso calls the contradictory incorporation and rejection of both indigenous and foreign cultures Latin America's "rhetorical predicament." Paris as a written textual presence is one of many rhetorical stances (along with the autochthonous posture of regional writing that Alonso studies) that grows out of Latin America's cultural crisis of seeking to belong within modernity.[9] Latin America's philosophical and cultural affinities with France but political rejection of its control over the Spanish monarchy also encapsulate Latin America's conflictive relationship with its colonial powers' northern neighbor. The French invasion of Mexico in the 1860s was similarly a transnational affair that sought to establish a Mexican empire under European protection. Internal political factions, such as the liberals versus the conservatives in Mexico in the mid-nineteenth century, often translated into coalitions that represented national versus foreign interests. It is clear, however, that despite France's imperial activity in the region, Latin America's Europeanizing projection consistently drew from Paris as its model for political thought, high culture, and modern urbanity.[10]

These Parisian models, from art and literature to architecture and city planning, fed the concept of a modern "lettered" city where artistic fulfillment and cultural potential were achieved through writing. Rama designates these urban spaces of writing as the *ciudad letrada* and the *ciudad escrituraria*. An essential component of Paris's modelling of cultural standards for Latin America consisted of written paradigms for physically designing new urban centers. A New World conception of city space strove to tame the wild forces of uncharted territory. Latin American intellectuals sought models for urban structures patterned in Paris as the concrete representation of a modern cultural elite. Early city planning relied especially on French models, such as the planning strategies of Georges Eugène Haussmann (1809–91) (see Hardoy).

From the early nineteenth century, increased literacy, publishing, journalism, religious and governmental bureaucracy, and educational programs constituted a dominant writing culture in the most active Latin American cities. From the 1830s into the first quarter of the twentieth century, publishing and journalism boomed in urban centers like Mexico, Rio de Janeiro, Buenos Aires, and Lima. They became the international cultural ports for the rest of the region through literacy and writing. The correlation among dominant elite sectors of the population, urban space, and writing determines extensive components of national cultural identity and its international projection, or what Néstor García Canclini calls the "patrimonio en el que se define y elabora lo propio de cada nación" (*Consumidores* 32–33). This "writing culture" has drawn Paris's presence into Latin American urban identity from early independent thought through contemporary literary movements.[11] The fact that only a small but powerful elite determines and closely identifies with this written "patrimony" accounts for the volatile reactions it provokes. The texts considered in this book respond to that supposed collective heritage, and attempt to revise it.

While the centrality of Paris in Latin American aesthetic and intellectual life is often considered a nineteenth- and early twentieth-century phenomenon, contemporary writing still acknowledges and confronts Paris as a locus of international cultural power. Recent fiction stages Paris as a cultural space for exposing Latin America's postcolonial bind and contests the city's established social and cultural hierarchy. Contemporary narrative questions Paris's privileged status within Latin American urban culture, often rejecting the French capital's image of prestige and the promise of sexual freedom. Many texts attack the city's traditional social resonance through the juxtaposition of political alternatives. Variations on the Latin American projection of Paris revise its gender, social class, and ideological and aesthetic stratification. Recent fiction casts Paris as a transnational market for literature as a commodity, a haven for conflicted revolutionaries, and a catalyst for language and behaviors that defy conventional gender norms.

This book examines narrative texts by Julio Cortázar (1914–1984), Manuel Scorza (1928–1986), Alfredo Bryce Echenique (1939–), and Luisa Futoranksy (1939–) as transformations of previous literary generations' conceptualizations of Paris. Their writing insists on exposing Paris, invading Paris, and exploiting Paris. These writers gain entrance to a male-oriented destination previously reserved for the socially elite. They open Paris as an exploratory zone for women, revolutionaries, anarchists, and exiles who rewrite the bohemian aesthete's Parisian literary experience. Bryce Echenique maps Paris's class-determined zones through his character's attempt to graph conflicting social class hierarchies. Paris houses the underworld of prostitutes and criminals (Cortázar), as well as the secretive political world of revolutionaries and fugitives (Scorza). Futoransky makes Paris the imaginary and geographical destination of exile that further deterritorializes transnational Latin Americans. These subtexts underscore the social and ideological contradictions inherent in the

Latin American construct of Paris that contemporary narrative refutes and amends. The city figures as an erotic force, a sign of social
prestige, and a hegemonic center for cultural production.

The urban narratives under consideration in this study employ
the city's spatial grid along with its local and external connotations
in order to map out their stories. Paris is not only a thematic or
geographical allusion, nor simply an episode in intellectual biogra-
phies. It is built into narratives as a cultural construct to provide
an urban framework for both spatial organization and cultural projection. As fictions come to occupy a named city, Michel de Certeau
explains, the place tends to shed reminders of a concrete referent.
In fiction, the meaning of cities' proper names shifts:

> . . . these words operate in the name of an emptying-out
> and wearing-away of their primary role. They become
> liberated spaces that can be occupied. A rich indetermi-
> nation gives them, by means of a semantic rarefaction,
> the function of articulating a second, poetic geography on
> top of the geography of the literal, forbidden or permitted
> meaning. (de Certeau 105)

Paris's significance as a geographical referent diminishes in Latin
American writing because of its reemergence as a cluster of cultural
and political assumptions. In Latin America's urban semiotics, Paris
is composed of a reservoir of images, legends, allusions, and values
that embody aesthetic, sociopolitical, and sexual projections.

Contemporary Latin American writing uses Paris to problematize ideological positions. The city's symbolism simultaneously
heralds revolution and denounces Eurocentric domination. Paris
performs in Latin American fiction as a social space that is not
only a source of social and cultural expectations but also is a protagonist and an agent of the action. Social space is part of "the terrain
of political practice," where interactive social operations create a
dynamic place rather than a static setting (Ross 8, 35).[12] These texts
include student demonstrations and international revolutionary
movements that infiltrate the city's streets and neighborhoods. The
issues of emigration from Latin America to France with the inevitable encounters with racism and classism also politicize the city's
relationship with fictional characters. The traditional Parisian social class segregation in housing, employment, and education frequently charts the urban space of Latin American fiction. More
than a destination for political exiles or voluntary cultural expatri-

ates, Paris in fiction participates in the intricacies of social identification. The city signals this differential and relative positionality for Europe in Latin American writing and thought. Contemporary fiction reinvents Paris as a response to Western hegemony in the context of modern Latin America.

The expression of Latin American desire for Paris continually entangles the sexual, the social, and the political. A shift in contemporary Latin American fiction transforms previous representations of Parisian erotic pursuits and gender relationships. Narratives of the first half of the century, such as Ricardo Güiraldes's *Raucho* and Sebastián Salazar Bondy's *Pobre gente de París*, portray male intellectuals in search of sexual freedom along Paris's seamy streets. More recent writers parody these erotic fantasies, now literary common places, to exploit them as pretexts for transmitting very different political and aesthetic messages. Where earlier itineraries to Paris from Latin America masked sexual fantasy with the pursuit of new political philosophy or intellectual expansion, contemporary writing uses the body and sexuality as metaphors for Europe's political and cultural domination. Cortázar's short fiction borrows from the convention of the woman/city as labyrinthine mystery to graft his narrative quest for alternative modes of reality. Scorza parodies the encounter between Latin American men and French women in a metafictional turn that renders the love story ironically banal in order to subvert its cultural and political foundations. Futoransky's woman protagonist muddles through Paris burdened with the same gendered conventions. She attempts to defy them, but ends up a victim of her own middle-aged, cross-cultural self-consciousness. The discourses of power and bodily inscription collaborate in a topography of desire.

Latin American fiction incorporates Paris into a metaphysics of place that positions the city both intertextually and philosophically. In a move to further dislocate the fictional from the geographical, these texts use Paris as a site where readings converge and ideologies collide. Cortázar manipulates Paris in his fiction of juxtaposed territories in which characters travel or write to the "other side" in search of an expansive ontological experience. His stories use Parisian interstitial spaces—subway trains, highways, bridges, arcades—to highlight transitional placelessness. Futoranksy positions Paris as a synthesis for her philosophical intertextuality where Buddhist and Yiddish citations mingle with her character's *porteño* childhood memories. Scorza's novel concludes with a dialogue in Paris where the characters debate over the viability of

Marxism for effective transnational social and political change. The city provides a place for grounding metaphysical and philosophical consideration.

Paris in these novels and short stories becomes a terrain for aesthetic experimentation that transmits the texts' sociopolitical and philosophical messages. Bilingualism, neologisms, semiotic twists, temporal and spatial disorientation, metafictionality, and self-consciousness in the narration serve to accent Paris's ubiquitous presence. The texts resist the city's history of cultural domination through their narrative and linguistic innovations that challenge cultural models and regional stereotypes. To subvert urban authority, these narratives exploit fragmentation in citations and multiple narrators that defy unified structure. Scorza's sensationalized jungle scenes parody Europe's commercial appropriation of the developing world. Bryce Echenique's protagonist invents a personalized language to combat the challenges of unfamiliar linguistic and cultural territory. Contemporary writing composes an atlas of Latin America's readings from and about Paris. Futoransky's "reading" of the city layers contemporary visual and printed Paris onto the expected Latin American images of the city. Along with Parisian architecture and geography, these writers incorporate graffiti, subway maps, commercial signs, popular song lyrics, and local journalism to barrage their disoriented protagonists in the process of deciphering a foreign place. Simultaneously a metatext and a palimpsest, the written city reveals its scriptural scaffolding.

Exploring the historical and discursive apparatus of Paris in twentieth-century Latin American narrative uncovers the cultural politics of contemporary literary expression. In the context of increasingly global interactions, the Latin American intellectual and artistic relationship with Paris is a vital component in New World cultural identification. Paris, for many twentieth-century writers, has been the locus of the problematic relationship between Latin America and Europe in articulating urban culture. Latin American fiction inscribes Paris in the region's transcultural negotiations with sociolinguistic, ideological, aesthetic, and erotic impact. This book confirms the global resonance of Latin American writing in novels and short stories that continues to assert their cultural politics through place. The Latin American construct of Paris emerges in contemporary fiction to challenge the Europeanizing cultural phantoms that linger in the collective urban imagination.

CHAPTER ONE

Desiring Paris

❖

The Latin American Conception
of the Lettered City, 1840 to 1960

> Y el mundo vierte sobre París su vasta corriente como en la
> concavidad maravillosa de una gigantesca copa de oro. Vierte
> su energía, su entusiasmo, su aspiración, su ensueño, y París
> todo lo recibe y todo lo embellece cual con el mágico influjo
> de un imperio secreto.
>
> Rubén Darío, *Peregrinaciones*

> Aller à Paris, c'est pour nous un retour.
>
> —Alicia Dujovne Ortiz, *Buenos Aires*

The epigraphs above frame Paris's contradictions for Latin America.
Expectations of the city that range from the fantastic to the familiar encompass a social spectrum that extends from the elite diplomat to the marginal bohemian. The depictions of Paris vacillate
between images of orgiastic decadence and ennobling tradition. The
city is heralded as an artistic and erotic utopia, but it also is re-
proached for its destructive effect on naive visitors. These contradictions in Latin American imagery for Paris expose some of the
conflicts at the core of urban identity.

This chapter traces the social, aesthetic, and erotic roles of
Paris in shaping Latin American urban consciousness. From
Sarmiento through the *modernistas* and regional writers, Latin
American writing has manipulated a cluster of conflicting desires
associated with Paris. Intellectuals and writers draw on varying

combinations of these desires to satisfy the region's political motives, aesthetic models, and gender paradigms during particular historical periods. Since the early independence period, *criollo* culture has had to confront and define itself with European urban models in its continuing attempt to determine political and aesthetic boundaries. The Paris written into Latin American cultural consciousness has emerged from this persistent confrontation.

Writing that praises Paris from a vantage point of New World fabrication and yearning reveals tensions that are more complex than the psychological commonplace of expectation followed by disappointment. Idealizations and disenchantments cancel each other out, collapsing the oppositions, in writing whose very exaggeration reveals its ambivalence. The Paris constructed in Latin America has political, semiotic, and aesthetic components that intensify the psychological. In particular, class associations cast the city as an expansive and interactive social space. Beyond the cosmopolitan mingling of classes prescribed in the modern urban realm (see Ross), the city's imaginative possibilities for those across the Atlantic extend to a broad scope of otherwise disparate groups. Competing images of sexuality, status, and style undermine the Latin American version of Parisian hierarchies. The interplay of these concurrent and sometimes competing pressures destabilizes Paris's imagined Latin American foundation. With this array of itineraries, invented Paris entices readers to embark on the *viaje a Europa* but leaves its vicarious travellers to sort out conflicting propaganda.

PARIS AS PRESTIGE: SARMIENTO

Paris as a modern, urban model found one of its first narrative voices in Domingo Faustino Sarmiento. Sarmiento is known for his Eurocentric vision for Latin America's early nation building. His travel writings (*Viajes 1845–1847*), illustrate his search for Latin American cultural identity outside of Argentina in descriptions of his visits to Europe, North Africa, and the United States. *Viajes* presents his romanticized perspective of Europe in which Paris metonymically represents Europe and is emblematic of "civilization." His travel writings form the foundation of the aesthetically and intellectually seductive "viaje a Europa" that elite Latin Americans considered socially essential. Mary Louise Pratt considers Sarmiento an infiltrator in his region's "cultural Mecca" (*Imperial*

Eyes 191). David Viñas calls the legendary trip to Europe a search for privileged aesthetic sanctification and glutonous consumption (see his "El viaje a Europa" in *De Sarmiento a Cortázar* 129–99). When Sarmiento announces that he has arrived in the "Francia de nuestros sueños," he invokes a collective dream that is a space for consuming European goods.[1]

Sarmiento's writing creates a hierarchical relationship between Paris and Latin America. Paris is perfection and harmony, the artistic and organizational model that inspires Latin American progress. Foreigners are supposed to conform and adapt to Parisian behaviors. Outsiders must learn how to *flâner*, how to wander, observe and take in the spectacle of "la encantada vida de Paris" (116). Although he eventually designated the United States' public education system as the solution to Argentina's cultural and political problems, his faith in the French as models for world culture was unfaltering:

> El francés de hoi es el guerrero mas audaz, el poeta mas ardiente, el sabio mas profundo, el elegante mas frívolo, el ciudadano mas celoso, el jóven mas dado a los placeres, el artista mas delicado, i el hombre mas blando en su trato con los otros. Sus ideas i sus modas, sus hombres i sus novelas, son hoi el modelo i la pauta de todas las otras naciones. (142)

Sarmiento's enumeration couples "novelas" with "hombres," as though Frenchmen engender books in a logical succession. He commends the French for their confident discretion, and his adjectives acclaim their energetic enthusiasm and intensity.

The working-class popular traditions of French urban life seem to attract Sarmiento as much as its high culture refinements.[2] Sarmiento paradoxically honors the French for their orderly and delicate taste, as well as for their spontaneous frivolity. Paris's image in his writing overflows the rigid structures he also admires to include the city's public street dances. He praises the neighborhood street festivals, such as the *fête* of Montmartre or the festivities of Bastille Day that celebrate another side of the City of Light.

Paris for Sarmiento embodies the contradictory forces of civilizing "order" and romantic "freedom," a pervasive tension throughout his writing.[3] He associates institutional organization and efficiency with the French and their capital, along with impetuousness and social mobility. He calls Paris a *torbellino*, a *prisma*, and a *santuario*, a range of images that discloses the multiplicity of roles the city plays. Sarmiento ardently hopes to acquire the French appearance and behavior that he associates with higher social class. He calls this process the foreigner's "rudo aprendizaje . . . por ensayar sus dedos torpes en este instrumento de que sólo aquellos insignes artistas arrancan inagotables armonías" (165). Arrival in Paris implies having ascended to an intellectual and artistic haven, and to have left behind the earthy materiality of Latin America. "Hay regiones demasiado altas, cuya atmósfera no pueden respirar los que han nacido en las tierras bajas. . . ." (6). Paris represents a corrective mold for Latin American institutions, behavior, and style. A number of Latin American statesmen and literary historians throughout the nineteenth century looked to France for political and aesthetic models.[4] Like Sarmiento, these political and literary figures incorporated Paris's promise of distinction into their New World cultural and political visions.

MODERNISTA DESIRE

In the continual Latin American dialogue with European models, the French capital plays a dialogical role in the assertion of a local aesthetic. During the last half of the nineteenth century, the romantic novel and its sentimental landscapes reposition the literary scene in the renewed emphasis on home ground. An affirmation of the countryside asserted an American emotional geography and downplayed the European colonial past.[5] However, postindependence nationalistic fervor began to wane. The withdrawal of French imperialist activity in Latin America in the last quarter of the nineteenth century cleared the way for reexploring Paris. By the 1880s, Paris resurfaced in its role of distinction, elegance, and sensuality.

Memoirs, chronicles, and essays from the *modernista* period embellish Sarmiento's Paris of social prestige, expanding into the realm of the sensual and sexual. The *modernistas* stress the city's refinement and voluptuousness.

> Una Atenas que fuera Citeres . . . y algunas veces Lesbos: tal definía París sin pensar que es indefinible. Al cabo de algunos años se le comprende más, lo que equivale a decir que se le quiere mejor. Al confuso entusiasmo de bárbaro, sucede una helena y lúcida devoción. (García Calderón, *Frivolamente* vi)

This fragment from one of Ventura García Calderón's collections of Parisian chronicles associates Paris with classical permanence, mystical devotion, and erotic fantasy. The "barbarous" observer in the aforementioned passage experiences Paris beyond words and concepts. The city's undefinability resists logical linguistic description, and thus it pertains to the realm of the senses and impressions.

These early twentieth-century laudatory appraisals of Paris echo Sarmiento's pervasive *afrancesado* attitude toward Latin American culture. The Paris drawn by these Latin American sketches communicates a culmination of style and class that contrasts with home: "A ejemplo de tus parques civilizados que obedecen a una oculta geometría, quiero mondar cada mañana el alma bárbara" (García Calderón, *Cantilenas* 17). Once again, Paris is praised for its institutional structures and civilizing geometric creations. All of these chroniclers compare Paris to Athens, Rome, and Alexandria, identifying it as a seat of Western civilization.

The Latin American yearning for Paris forms part of the growing urban sensibility of modernity. A specific genre emerged for capturing the vitality and sensuality of the period's artistic and cultural world capital. Between the 1880s and the 1920s, the modern *crónica* became instrumental in disseminating a codified *modernista* aesthetics of Paris.[6] The prose poems recount events in the city, fragments of a trip, and scenic impressions to capture a modern, urban state of mind. Related to the French journalistic "chronique" of the nineteenth century, a sort of Parisian *artículo de costumbres*, the *crónica* allows for the lyrical subjectivity of the narrative voice. A response to the popularity of travel diaries during the period, the *crónica* employs many of the tropes of travel writing. The genre also registers the boost in mechanical efficiency of the industrial revolution that encouraged concise literary forms. An avid Latin American readership at home anticipated these poetic and sensual bulletins as necessary supplements to their vicarious eroticism involving Paris.

The *crónica* flourished in journalistic venues both in France and in Latin America. In his discussion on Latin American journalism in Paris during this period, Marc Cheymol asserts that modern Latin American literature is founded in the journalistic fervor of Paris during the "Années Folles." Both Darío and Enrique Gómez Carrillo edited journals in Paris printed in Spanish. The prominent French journals on Latin America published in Paris, such as *Revue de l'Argentine* and *Revue de L'Amérique Latine*, "ont été à la fois le reflet et le moteur de l'évolution des lettres hispanoaméricaines ... une sorte de tribune où cette littérature a pu prendre

conscience d'elle-même" (Cheymol, "Les Revues"). This vigorous
journalistic production reached beyond the expatriate community,
as readership about Paris in Latin America remained strong. Darío's
column, "Parisiana," appeared in *La Nación* in Buenos Aires, and
Nestor Vitor contributed frequent columns entitled "Cartas de Paris"
and "O Mundo, de Paris" for Brazilian dailies (Vitor 87–140); Pedro
Balmacedo Toro wrote a regular column for the Chilean daily *La
Epoca* without ever visiting Paris.[7] The Parisian chronicles also
were collected and successfully published as books, such as Darío's
Parisiana, published in 1908.[8]

Enrique Gómez Carrillo, the most widely published Latin
American *modernista* chronicler in Paris in the early twentieth
century, announced the *crónica's* aesthetic mission in poetic dec-
larations. He stated that travel narratives should record sensations
and insisted on an artistic, subjective but sensory (rather than
autobiographical) reportage:

> Por mi parte, yo no busco nunca en los libros de viaje el
> alma de los países que me interesan. Lo que busco es algo
> más frívolo, más sutil, más positivo: la sensación. Todo
> viajero artista, en efecto, podría titular su libro: *Sen-
> saciones* ... el cuadro lejano es una imagen interpretada
> por un visionario. (*Páginas* 7)

This stylistic prescription announces the travel narrative's inten-
tions: to paint a verbal picture of a subjective encounter with a
new place. As though he were writing a spiritual diary, the narrator
should "exhale, en una prosa sensible y armoniosa, las sensaciones
de su alma" (12). These texts evoke the nineteenth century *flâneur*,
the Baudelairian urban drifter. The wandering narrators of the
modernista chronicles assume the role of "machines recording
sensations" (García Calderón, *Frivolamente* 36). This new genre
was expected to fill in the emotional and sensorial void in urban,
mechanized surroundings.

Paris dominated the chronicle where Latin American narrators
recounted events such as the 1900 World's Fair, art exhibitions, and
fashion debuts. Paris headed up sections not only in travel books but
in Darío's prose poems and short tales, in fanciful literary and artistic
reviews. In Gómez Carrillo's anthology *Páginas escogidas*, the first
section is called "En Europa." It begins with a short essay, "La psicología
del viajero," which identifies travel to Paris as the trip of all trips.
Paris is representative here of all European or Western civilization.

The *modernistas* approached Paris as the foreign, unfamiliar other with the "saudade utópico pelo desconhecido."[9] Paris held magnetic powers over artists and intellectuals, who converted "her" into lover, siren, sanctuary, classical goddess, or bewitching enchantress.

In modernista prose about Paris, the city's modern image always promises sensuality and erotic potential. During this period of Spanish American cultural affirmation, the *modernista* gaze on Paris might seem contradictory to the movement's advocacy of political and cultural autonomy. However, in the logic of these texts, the possibility of sexual freedom reverses their dependence on a Europeanizing urban aesthetic. Ventura García Calderón calls Paris "the seductive paradise we dream of in our twenties, evoking a youthful mood of erotic adventure" ("Pour quoi . . ." 22). In his chronicles, he strives to communicate Paris's sensual sublimity where, for him, women are never over thirty years old (*Frivolamente* 111). The chronicles recommend Paris as the site for sexual initiation of young Latin American men.

Paris becomes personalized, possessed, loved, and coveted in all of these desire-filled chronicles. These narrators often fuse the lover and the mistress in order to merge illicit sexual experimentation with the emotional domain of romance. Paris is cast as the metaphorical lover for a collective generation of male fantasies: "[d]e todo el viaje y de todos los viajes, *tú* constituyes en verdad *nuestro* único placer infinito . . ." (Gómez Carrillo 17, emphasis added). Darío declares, "mi madre y mi nodriza es Francia la dulce" (*Peregrinaciones* 410). In his preface to *Prosas profanas*, he exclaims, "mi esposa es de mi tierra; mi querida, de París" (11). Paris is admired, yearned for, adorned with words. At a distance, the city is nostalgically remembered until the anticipated return:

> La separación ha aumentado en nuestra alma el amor por
> ti. Encontrándonos de nuevo en tu seno, experimentamos
> la febril alegría de la mujer enamorada que, después de
> una ausencia, se halla entre los brazos de su amante.
> (Gómez Carrillo 17)

Here Gómez Carrillo makes Paris the lover's haven, the return to the ultimate sensual experience. Paris was inscribed as the provider of missing erotic opportunities in Latin America. A chronicled version of someone else's trip provided the vicarious experimentation longed for at home.

The Europeanizing view of literary prestige persisted in urban centers in Latin America through the *modernista* movement and beyond. The journalistic dynamism of the "Années Folles" established Paris as *the* international literary capital to many Latin American urban intellectuals. Once writers had published at home, they were expected to prove themselves by publishing in Paris. A Latin American writer journeyed to the French capital, carrying with him his locally published work:

> No le han bastado a este hombre los elogios que en su tierra logró su obra. Necesita ahora los elogios de París. Necesita que, desde París, su gloria se refleje sobre el mundo. (Gache 37)

According to the legend of Paris's cultural command, its literary (or artistic) products radiated worldwide. Just as the city presumably lifted the erotic restraints of Latin American culture, so Paris as a literary capital was expected to break through artistic and literary borders as well.

Paris as an international literary capital offered Latin Americans contact not just with France but with the cultural activity of other expatriate artists. The transcultural nature of the literary capital was supposed to turn a vocation of letters into an imperative rather than a choice, making the writer's presence there "une *manière* qui lève les servitudes et les obstacles de l'entreprise littéraire" (Bessière in Brunel 185). To escape the role of the provincial, struggling writer at home, the Latin American intellectual came to Paris to be transformed into a citizen of the world who had transcended geographic and cultural boundaries.

In his introduction to an exhaustive study of Paris as a literary center, Pierre Brunel defines a literary capital as the "tête écrivante" that exerts "l'hégémonie de la parole" (1–2). Brunel characterizes a literary capital as a city that offers the activity of publishing, interviews, and meetings; a city with the infrastructure of media and cultural institutions; and a center that supports translations. It is a space that opens itself worldwide:

> la capitale littéraire est chef d'un lieu dont les frontières ne sont pas fixes.... Un domaine plus vaste se dessine qui peut même chercher à *s'étendre au monde entier*. (Brunel 3, emphasis added)

Paris is, in fact, where many first editions in Spanish were published just after the First World War. There were European publishers especially committed to Latin American literature. Garnier dedicated a large part of its publishing to authors in Spanish, including translations of French authors and original texts in Spanish. The entrance to the Garnier bookstore and publishing house was known as the "sublime puerta" to Latin Americans seeking literary success in France and distribution within Latin America (Needell, quoted in Hardoy and Morse 182). The Paul Ollendorff bookstore and publishing house in Paris almost entirely dedicated its business to publishing and distributing Hispanic writers in the early part of this century. These French publishers took advantage of the Latin American rejection of and disassociation from Spanish cultural models and industry. Literary entrepreneurs like Garnier and Ollendorff recognized an ignored market that they could develop at home and abroad. While publishers in Latin America continued to print European authors, perpetuating a dependence on European literary culture, European publishers were appropriating the production of Latin American letters.

The commonly fictionalized theme of Paris as an international literary or artistic capital (see chapter 3 on Manuel Scorza) not only drew many Latin Americans to Europe but also fueled the projects of urban modernity in Latin America itself. The literary capital expands the literate city that is already powerful locally and regionally into an extensive international network of publishing, advertising, and media contacts. It becomes a determiner of wider canons and discursive strategies and reigns over ever-broadening intellectual territory.[10] Travel to Paris, with its adjustments and sacrifices, is only a minute piece of the literary capital's story of cultural control. More vital than individual stories of success or failure, illusion and frustration, the *image* of Paris as a literary capital for Latin America retains its force. The realities and practicalities of the international literary market have been less significant to the Latin American construct of Paris than the illusory faith in its literary promise.

A FAILED UTOPIA

In a short article entitled "París y los escritores extranjeros," Darío discusses the intoxicating effect of Paris on international writers and describes their process of "parisinación." Even Darío admits that his Paris was a fantasy, and that he wrote more about Paris

from Latin America before he actually went there to live. He quotes
Tulio Cestero, a writer from the Dominican Republic, living in
Paris at the time, who described Paris as an inconquerable, fleeting
vision that, "a los que llegan fuertes, jóvenes, sanos, con la primavera
en el alma, París los devuelve enfermos, viejos, rotos" (OC v. 1,
467–68). Brutal artistic competition and social alienation begin to
wear away the city's glossy veneer.

Latin American writing in generations following the *modernistas*
accentuates the cruel reality behind Paris's glamorous facade. Narratives such as Ricardo Güiraldes's *Raucho* (1917) and Sebastián
Salazar Bondy's *Pobre gente de París* (1958) reveal the persistent
integration of the French capital into Latin American fiction in an
attempt to forge an aesthetic identity. These texts mix Paris's allure from afar with its ultimate disenchantment. Paris is transformed into a decadent and destructive agent, a change that parallels the shift from an aesthetic of pleasure and luxury toward a
revelation of urban modernity's high cost.

Although these texts span several decades and were written
from the perspective of different countries and regions in Latin
America, *Raucho* and *Pobre gente de París* similarly embrace the
illusion of Paris in order to uncover its seamy desolation. These
narratives accord French women the archetypical role of seductresses and prostitutes who exploit the protagonists' mythification
of Paris and orchestrate their disillusionment. *Raucho* is Güiraldes's
autobiographical novella that juxtaposes rural life on the Argentine
pampas with scenes in Paris. The city becomes the dialectical
counterpoint to the Latin American countryside in this prototype
for his later novel *Don Segundo Sombra* (1926).

The novella begins with Raucho's mother's death and his father's
decision to move his sons to his *estancia* for the consolation of the
pampa. Raucho is attracted to the *peones'* work and learns the
ways of the ranch before receiving any formal education. However,
when he does enter the *colegio*, he has already learned some French,
geography, and history. Every summer, while reacquainting himself
with rural life on the ranch, he reads French literature and dreams
of "civilizaciones modernas de las grandes capitales" (65). He begins to resent his isolation from the urban world, becomes ob-
sessed with Paris, and finally arranges to travel there. In Paris he
seeks to satisfy his erotic fantasies. He ultimately falls ill, weakened from his sexual exploits in the city-turned-devouring-mistress.
Only a reunion with the Argentine pampa can restore his physical
and spiritual health.

Sexuality monopolizes Raucho's Parisian (mis)adventure and saturates the novella's urban space:

> Un principio de cópula flota sobre las parejas de hombres y mujeres, o simplemente de mujeres, que se abandonan copa en mano sobre las banquetas, esbozando caricias truncas, que les electriza e impulsa a excesos. (100)

Güiraldes parodies the *modernistas'* emphasis on the sensual and evocation of the erotic in *Raucho* in the protagonist's exaggerated obsessions. Paris becomes a dangerous place where women and the city together destroy eager foreigners. The city is compared to a growing and debilitating cancer, and only the natural landscapes of home can halt its progression.

Raucho bridges the cultural politics of the *modernistas* with that of the *novela de la tierra* movement. Cristóbal Pera, in his chapter "Del París 'Artificial' a la América 'Natural,' " explores the shift from the *modernistas'* cosmopolitan sensibility to nationalistic localism. Paris comes to embody artificiality, disease, and death after a long generation of writing that only endowed it with the most lofty or pleasurably illicit opportunities.

> [E]ste desplazamiento en las imágenes que remiten a París está relacionado dialécticamente con la renovada vocación nacionalista que opone lo "nacional" a lo "cosmopolita," lo "natural" americano a lo "artificial" parisino, el poder "regenerador" de la naturaleza a la "enfermedad" que se incuba en las ciudades. (Pera 159)

Güiraldes writes *Raucho* into a polarity of cosmopolitan Paris versus Latin American natural spaces. The novel's structure relies on a continuum of rural male vigor and its inevitable depletion in the sexual excesses of the city.

The emergence of the *novela de la tierra* and popular *criollista* literature in Latin America coincide with this period of Paris's challenged prominence. With the threat of increasing intervention from the United States in the Caribbean and Central America, and the impact of modernization in the cities, a renewed interest in local topics surged. Increasing immigration from Europe, particularly into the Southern Cone, spurred *criollo* culture to affirm its own identity by rejecting foreign influence.[11] New literary forms and styles countered the idea of civilization that relied on foreign cultural standards and modern urbanization with a local, utopian vision based on the power and attraction of the countryside. Land became a cultural metaphor, *patria* and nature fused to form a referent of cultural origin.[12] The American landscape's untamed barbarism is idealized as the creative vitality necessary for changing social structures. The vastness of the plain in Rómulo Gallegos's *Doña Bárbara*, the *pampa* in Güiraldes's *Don Segundo Sombra*, and the consuming jungle in José Eustasio Rivera's *La vorágine* exalt South American natural environment as a determining influence on individual lives and national destinies.

However, these novels inscribe "civilization" on the other side of their nationalistic and naturalistic coin. While they display initial resistance to European aesthetic modeling, they merely recast it. Literacy, legality, territory documents, land ownership, and racial dominance represent the strategies of urban writing culture transferred to rural settings. Despite the apparent shift in emphasis from Europe to Latin America, both writers and characters maintained connections to European educational and legal centers of authority.[13] Güiraldes dressed his own *literato* image in two costumes: "el del aristócrata que enseñó en París a bailar el tango y el del gaucho con que fue más de una vez retratado" (Rodríguez-Alcalá 616). *Don Segundo Sombra* introduces the *gaucho letrado*, a synthesis of the city with the *interior*. Beatriz Sarlo identifies the novel as Güiraldes's nostalgic, utopian solution to the urban domain's severe incontinuities due to the region's influx of immigrants and to the process of urban modernization (*Una modernidad periférica* 31–43). Although Güiraldes seemed to steer away from Sarmiento's view that Latin American salvation lay in the Europeanization of local culture, he replaced it with his vision of the idealized, literate gaucho that he had to go to Paris to acquire.

Sebastián Salazar Bondy's *Pobre gente de París* contemporizes Raucho's Parisian debacle in a group of short stories about a generation of young Latin American artists and intellectuals in Paris and the sacrifices they make to realize their "viaje a Europa." In the nineteenth century, the voyage to Paris was only possible for the wealthy, urban elite in Latin America. The economic crisis of the early 1930s in Europe, and the subsequent devaluation of the French franc, suddenly made the elitist voyage to Paris possible for less affluent artists and intellectuals. A new generation from a more varied class background began to write its own version of Parisian bohemia. The post–World War II era continued to see a more artistically marginal and economically unstable community of Latin Americans gathered in Paris. Their writing also recorded the underside of the prestigious luxury dreamed of in America.

Salazar Bondy's title comes from a popular Peruvian song that evokes the struggle and poverty of foreigners trying to attain glory in Paris.[14] The main character and narrator of the frame story, Juan, arrives in Paris "henchido de pura emoción y tembloroso como a una cita de amor" (Salazar Bondy 11). A few months later, he confesses that "aun no podía decir que la ciudad tantas veces soñada me hubiera deparado alguna verdadera satisfacción" (9). It hurts his pride to admit that he has been the "víctima de un espejismo, de una pueril fantasmagoría" (9). Juan and his fellow artists face solitude and poverty in Paris. Their desperate desire to experience and find success in Paris shows them willing to travel to and stay in Paris at almost all cost, such as the young Venezuelan painter who sleeps with a military official in order to acquire a scholarship for study abroad. Once in Paris, the students degradingly collect and sell used paper and receive donations of old clothes from those who take pity on them.

French women in Paris are given the archetypical role of sex objects and seductresses in these stories. The young Latin American characters seek out these female figures—embodiments of their Parisianized erotic desire—who eventually contribute to their downfall. Juan pursues Caroline, who rents a room in the same boardinghouse. One day he finds her in bed with his rich uncle, who is visiting from Lima. Juan's naiveté never allowed him to see her before as a prostitute. The discovery of her prostitution leads to the final scene between Juan and another neighborhood prostitute. They are in a brothel where Juan will spend all of his money, and where he hears the familiar melancholy melody, "Pobre gente de París, no la pasa muy feliz . . ."[15]

Thus the collection of stories ends with a lament in Spanish about Paris. What had been "el sueño de los veinte años" (67) becomes a winding Parisian staircase, "una larga espiral de penumbras crecientes, los círculos, en verdad, de un estrecho infierno urbano" (45).[16] Suddenly there are no more miracles in Paris, as one of the stories' titles announces; both the first and last page of the collection mention failure. Paris, rather than being conquered and possessed, is a failed project. The city devours them all, consuming their savings, health, dignity, and sanity.[17]

The contemporary fiction analyzed in this book's subsequent chapters registers the tension between urban modernity as a European export and American cultural and social independence. The New World has been an enduring participant in what critics now commonly call "global culture," a sort of double-edged imperialism in which regions and nations mutually define one another. Frederick Buell, in *National Culture and the New Global System*, examines the complex relationship between the local and the global, particularly for developing countries in contemporary circumstances. He states that currently we are living in an era

> in which new nationalisms and ethnic fundamentalisms—ones that conceal their global sources—have sprung up side by side with a widespread movement dedicated to demystifying the ideology of national culture and foregrounding the international and intercultural relationships upon which it has in fact erected itself. (Buell 9)

The story of Paris in Latin American writing, or rather the story of a Latin American Paris, is permeated with the discrepancy of European dependency and fervent efforts toward cultural and political autonomy. The nationalism of the *novela de la tierra* movement, for example, was both nostalgically conservative and revolutionary. It emerged from the conflictive responses to modernity that Europe and the United States exerted over Latin America. This chapter has revealed Paris's role in nation-building projects and literary movements that play a role in the ongoing process of cultural definition.

Contesting colonial power through the importation of *another* set of European cultural norms prolonged a reliance on and allegiance to European tradition. Contemporary cultural movements confirm the persistence of imagined European urban space and its discursive power in Latin America. As a discouraged, armed Leftist states in Scorza's late 1970's novel, *La tumba del relámpago*, "[l]a rabia, el coraje, son de aquí, y las ideas son de allá" (235). More recent fiction from Latin America that explores displacement, exile, and transnationalism incorporates Paris in the continuing struggle for a cosmopolitan urban cultural identity.

This panoramic sketch of Paris written into Latin American conceptions of the urban, the modern, the culturally progressive, and the erotically liberating reveals the conflictual bargaining over cultural identity in a postcolonial situation. Even the texts that portray the disillusionment with Paris, such as Salazar Bondy's *Pobre gente de París* and Güiraldes's *Raucho*, employ the same operative categories of cultural self-affirmation. The "place" these texts narrate is rarely the referential Paris, France, but rather an imagined space that is a repository for cultural yearnings. Latin American urban centers, while conscious of their local and regional institutional power, have had to seek aesthetic and imaginative models from both near and far. The "global" nature of this imperialism of the imaginary operates in both directions. European and American spaces perpetuate mutual otherness to exploit one another in affirming an array of identities.

Latin American writing proposes a dynamic role for Paris in the process of cultural identification. The city functions as both an established aesthetic construct and an increasingly intertextualized field. Paris has been a storehouse as well as a catalyst for aesthetic and thematic experimentation, linguistic play and crosscultural citation. Latin American writing sketches Paris as a zone of exploration for reencountering and challenging American ideas of European urban space. The cultural imagination that generates this Paris charts new districts located neither in France nor in Latin America. Its readers roam distant boulevards to reinvent a Paris mapped onto transnational urban identity.

Chapter Two

The Interstices of Desire

———————— ❖ ————————

Paris As Passageway in Julio Cortázar's Short Fiction

Il me semble que je serais toujours bien là où je ne suis
pas . . .

—Baudelaire, *Le spleen de Paris*

Temeroso y exaltado a la vez, el viajero entra en la ciudad
con pasos de gato en territorio ajeno. Gato de sí mismo
embarcándose en su propio salto, afelpado sigilo de aventura
y deriva allí donde todo es nuevo, donde todo es otro.

—Cortázar, *Paris. Ritmos de una ciudad*

A large corpus of Cortazarian fiction inhabits or evokes Paris. His
frequent inclusion of Paris often is dismissed as a passive conse-
quence of his residence in France from 1951 until his death in
1984. More than an autobiographical detail, however, his personal
geography serves his writing as a location from which to examine
the cultural and political dimensions of Latin America's postcolonial
condition. Cortázar uses Paris and its traditional projection in
Argentina to problematize cosmopolitan cultural identity in Latin
America. He extrapolates from the ambivalent cultural relationship between Latin America and Europe a mode of writing that
accentuates the persistent tensions between embracing an autono-
mous "American" identity, independent of European models, and
espousing a cosmopolitan identity, constructed on Latin America's
urbane connections to European cultural centers. The stories relo-
cate the cosmopolitan versus the local debate at the core of Latin

American cultural identification onto European territory, to contest European domination (cultural, political, economic, and intellectual) of the New World on Old World ground.

Alongside Latin America's traditional Parisian projections, Cortázar's fiction politicizes the city as a stronghold of Western capitalist values and a repository of postcolonial alienation and marginalization. He uses his short fiction to critique colonialism as a global political and economic complex. As a Latin American who was born in Belgium and lived the last decades of his life as an expatriate in France, Cortázar gained a special transnational perspective on world politics. France's nineteenth-century colonial expansion in the Middle East, North Africa, and Southeast Asia made its capital a colonial and postcolonial center. Cortázar observed from Paris the Algerian independence struggle and the Vietnam conflict from the French retreat in the 1950s through the 1970s. Although he saves his most virulent political attacks (against, for example, international human rights abuses and the United States' intervention in Vietnam) for *Libro de Manuel*,[1] the Paris that guides much of his short fiction represents the core of France's imperial endeavors. Cortázar's Parisian maps circumscribe displaced Latin Americans who come to terms with their own transcultural identification in the heart of France's defeated empire.

Cortázar's fictional Paris simultaneously represents two "others," one sociopolitical and the other philosophical. The city functions as a source of European political and cultural hegemony, and not just with respect to Latin America. At the same time, Paris offers doorways into "other" experiences that expand the realms of possibility into erotic and metaphysical estrangement. These two orientations for Paris work together in Cortázar's stories to propose liberating social and aesthetic practices. His texts map detours around the restrictive conventions of a Western bourgeois lifestyle and contest European spatiotemporal constructs embedded in colonial structures. This chapter analyzes Paris in the short fiction to reveal Cortázar's manipulation of the urban to propose a metaphysically expansive aesthetic that challenges social and political structures.

Cortázar uses Paris as a zone for cultural and philosophical confrontation. His fascination with interstitial spaces appears in all of his writing. His short stories in particular, through their brevity and structure, capture the betweenness of experience. In an interview, Cortázar confesses his obsession with these spaces of transition and passage:

Figure 2.1

Julio Cortázar on the banks of the Seine (late 1960s). The river's bridges, their supports, and the cavernous areas they create along the banks demarcate Cortázar's fictional Parisian underworlds. Photograph by Pierre Boulat.

> J'ai toujours été obsédé par la notion des espaces clos qui
> deviennent des lieux de passage. C'est grâce a ces lieux de
> passage que l'on peut faire irruption dans un monde
> fantastique. Pour l'atteindre il a souvent été nécessaire de
> disponer d'un pont, d'un métro, d'un autobus, d'une
> voiture, autant d'espaces clos qui facilitent—pour des
> raisons inexplicables—la communication avec ce que
> j'appelle le fantastique. (Montalbetti 84)

His stories in Paris are the narrative analogues to urban architectural structures of connection. Cortázar's interstices expand to
include contradictions and intuition to allow for transgressing the
boundaries of rational thinking and the conventional limitations
on encounters with other human beings.

In Cortázar's interstices, the political and cultural meet with the
metaphysical to confound protagonists who are on transitional journeys. The short stories recount the narrative space between an initial moment of desire and its yearned-for consummation during which
the protagonist is challenged to depart from the norm. During this
movement toward the object of desire, the protagonist must sort
through conflicting or overlapping codes to further his search. In his
stories, Cortázar joins materiality and philosophy in fantastic con-
junctions that defy unitary codes of interpretation and exclusive
forms of action. The short story form, according to Cortázar, takes
a fragment of reality and explodes it, "una explosión que se abre a
una realidad más amplia" (quoted in Mora 44). His protagonists'
positions force them to question both social norms and ontological
understanding. Paris becomes Cortázar's stage for dramatizing the
narrow threshold between spaces, times, and experiences.

Cortázar's short fiction perpetuates a contemporary version of
the Parisian *flâneur* moving among metropolitan crowds in search
of alternative experiences. The stories presuppose a modern urban
sensibility that avoids detailed descriptions of the Parisian "landscape" to configure instead an architecture of ontological alternatives.[2] Cortázar uproots his *flâneurs* from the street and displaces
them in urban interstices such as windows and corridors to emphasize fantastic otherness and the betweenness of Latin American
urban cultural identity.

While surrealist discourse is the central intertextual source for
Paris in *Rayuela*,[3] Baudelaire's *Le spleen de Paris* is the central
intertext for the Paris of the short stories. *Spleen* establishes a narrative structure for the shocking and even uncanny experiences of
urban life. The prose poems portray dramatic encounters among

divergent social classes, an achronological sense of time, the remoteness of urban gazes, and the magic of distance.[4] The Baudelairian construct of Paris builds on the poetic in *Les fleurs du mal* to exploit the narrative in *Spleen*, allowing the city streets and buildings to furnish encounters with the "other." The urban material network generates, for example, those penetrating stares whose intensity delays the passage of time. *Spleen* presents urban experience in Paris as a ritualized and mystical hyperawareness that pushes the boundaries of consciousness to absorb the shocks.

The exaggeration of the visual, which emerges from Baudelaire's examination of a commodified culture, produces "a tension between a critique and a transformation" that Cortázar's fiction also exhibits.[5] Paris can be traced in Cortázar's fiction throughout the evolution of his political engagement as a space for attacking European bourgeois conventions and therefore making room for experimentation with alternative behaviors, transgressive practices, and revolutionary aesthetics. From his earlier and more aestheticist short stories to his later novel *Libro de Manuel* (1973), and stories such as "Recortes de prensa" (1980), Paris figures in the emerging articulation of his revolutionary politics.[6] Cortázar expands on Baudelaire's urban aesthetic to position Paris as a locus for fantastic connections.

Cortázar's plots in the short fiction physically intertwine with Paris's urban structures. Once again the spatial dimension is more complex and vital than the static backdrop of a setting. In these texts, Paris as cultural construct and Paris as engineered urban modernity intersect. Cortázar takes the story off of the streets and displaces the *flâneur* to other levels of the city where he encounters alternative realities. Paris in the short fiction often resembles the Paris of *Rayuela*, confirming the novel's portrayal of the city as an embodiment of idealized creativity and metafictional potential.[7] However, while the street scenes of *Rayuela*'s "rabdomancia" mock nineteenth-century realist narrative conventions, the short fiction exploits the fantastic by relocating the urban scenario in interstitial realms that highlight the passage between worlds. Always drawing on physical material constructions, usually architectural, all of the stories concerning Paris perform as narrative bridges. They rely on Parisian windows, arcades, and the subway to connect realms that would otherwise exclude their protagonists.

The stories reinforce Paris's role in the articulation of Cortázar's increasingly politicized narrative theory.[8] The characters become entangled in Paris's urban maze in allegories of modern alienation that resist restrictive sexuality and the European intellectual tradition. The protagonists experiment with games of chance, erotic

Figure 2.2
This drawing from the *Rayuela* manuscript (*Cuaderno de bitácora* ms. 35, p. 161) reveals Cortázar's concern with bridges and other architectural junctures as metaphors for cultural and metaphysical connections.

pursuits, and creative processes that rely on urban infrastructure but resist conventional rules. As Susana Jakfalvi declares in her edition of *Las armas secretas*, rather than an escape, Paris is "la ventana que permita al escritor latinoamericano la confrontación de sus ideales con los de la realidad en un país subdesarrollado" (16). These texts stretch beyond the self-reflexive mode to position Paris in transnational juxtaposition to its former colonies and to Latin America. The French capital in the stories exemplifies urban modernity, eroticism, metaphysical exploration, and the problematics of both colonialism and postcolonial cultural identity that straddle Europe and Latin America. The city is caught playing two roles for Third World expatriates in Europe: the seat of colonialism's defeat and the perpetuity of postcolonial cultural hegemony.

Cortázar's stories highlight Paris through localization of the plots in urban structures that represent movement and transition. The structure of these scenarios is elastic, almost fluid, in order to privilege connection to alternative realms of experience. While *Rayuela* uses the Seine, its banks and bridges as narrative borders, these stories construct bridges out of the city's infrastructure to span contradictory modes or lifestyles. Cortázar's use of bridges, the métro, and the arcades, as the following sections of this chapter demonstrate, reveals a reliance on architecture and engineering to structure his stories, both spatially and historically. Michel Foucault discusses the ways in which French urban modernity was constructed by engineers and technicians, rather than architects.

> It was not architects, but engineers and builders of bridges, roads, viaducts, railways, as well as the polytechnicians . . . who thought out space . . . the technicians or engineers of the three great variables—territory, communication, and speed. (*Foucault Reader* 244)

The movement and flexibility in Cortázar's Parisian stories narratively put into practice what Parisian modernity concretely engineered. The stories depend on the city's architecture for literal and allegorical referents to urban Latin America's conception of the modern.

Cortázar's Paris provides a transitional space where characters confront their conflicting selves ("El otro cielo," "El perseguidor"), where the past invades the present ("Cartas de mamá"), where means of transportation not only lead to destinations but also change destinies ("Cuello de gatito negro," "Manuscrito hallado en un bolsillo," "Autopista del sur"). The arcades, the subway system, and the north-south highway all function as bridges that connect fragments of possible realities. The bridges Cortázar proposes represent Paris as urban modernity, a transnational hub, and a place for aesthetic experimentation. He exploits Paris's imaginative capacity as connective tissue in stories that forcefully integrate the jumbled layers of postcolonial cultural identity. His stories repave the *autopista*, rerail the subway, and reerect the arcades, continually inaugurating the traversal from the familiar to the novel. His rendering of Paris, full of fantastic distortions, renovates the European city in order to reexamine Latin American postcoloniality through his stories' ontologically revolutionary urban planning.

WINDOWS

> Celui qui regarde du dehors à travers une fenêtre ouverte ne voit jamais autant de choses que celui qui regarde une fenêtre fermée. . . . Ce qu'on peut voir au soleil est toujours moins intéressant que ce qui se passe derrière une vitre. . . . Qu'importe ce que peut être la réalité placée hors de moi, si elle m'a aidé à vivre, à sentir que je suis et ce que je suis?
>
> —Baudelaire, *Le spleen de Paris*

"Las babas del diablo" is narrated from the photographer/ translator's studio, far above the city streets with a window viewing the sky. The story recounts the process of shooting, developing, and enlarging a photo recently taken in the small square at the tip of the Isle de la Cité. The narration juxtaposes the fixed image of a fleeting encounter between a man and woman in the enlarged print, with the movement of birds and clouds glimpsed through the window. Descriptions of the changing sky appear in brief parenthetical comments:

> Vamos a contarlo despacio, ya se irá viendo qué ocurre a medida que lo escribo. Si me sustituyen, si ya no sé qué decir, si se acaban las nubes y empieza alguna otra cosa (porque no puede ser que esto sea estar viendo continuamente nubes que pasan, y a veces una paloma), si algo de todo eso. . . . (*Cc* 1, 215)

These parenthetical asides form discursive windows in the narration as the narrator views the sky through the glass and interprets the photo he is enlarging. The private space of the studio and the enlargement provide a new perspective that alters the public street scene previously viewed through the camera lens. What the photographer/narrator shot as a potential sexual encounter between an older woman and an adolescent boy, the enlargement reveals as an exchange between the boy and a procuress for her male client. Glass panes in "Las babas del diablo" function as screens between events and their interpretations. They filter the light from the outside into the camera or studio, and distinguish the spontaneous process of shooting from the calculated procedure of developing.

As visually porous membranes, Parisian windows often serve Cortázar's fictions as entrances to and exits from realms that contradict conventional social norms. Windows in Paris deflect the stories from public street scenes and underscore the search for contemplation, intimacy, play, or escape. Windows, like the camera lens, provide portals to desirous encounters that result in multiple interpretations. These openings restrict passage more than doors or streets. As Lois Parkinson Zamora confirms,

> the window is not an opening onto the world: Roberto's ["Las babas del diablo" photographer's] window does not carry him beyond the confined space of his room, but on the contrary, completes that confinement. The window . . . is an unreal landscape, an artifice of the mind, offering no alternate or external reality even though it sustains the illusion of escape. ("Voyeur/Voyant" 52)

The ambiguity of glass, transparent yet enclosing, delicate yet restraining, contributes to Cortázar's construction of Paris as liminal and interstitial: as a passageway between alternative modes of behavior, different but coinciding historical times, and moments of metamorphosis. Glass transparency provides the first filter in "Axolotl" and reflects the first gazes in "Manuscrito hallado en un bolsillo." These are dangerous boundaries that invite voyeurism and promise transgression into forbidden sexual and existential territories.

The glass tanks in "Axolotl" confirm Paris as a place for encountering the other, expanding the self, and confronting postcolonial zones of thought and experience. The axolotls' magnetic hold on the narrator, like Paris's pull on Latin American intellectual elites, lures him into expanding his identity in order to challenge fundamental boundaries. The story relies on glass panes for the exchanged gazes into and out of the aquatic tanks of the Jardin des Plantes. These penetrating stares ultimately result in exchanged identities. The narrator's obsession with the axolotls draws him daily to their "world" reconfigured in the tanks. He stares at them and pursues through their glassy eyes a deep and powerful connection:

> Los ojos de los axolotl me decían de la presencia de una vida diferente, de otra manera de *mirar*. *Pegando mi cara al vidrio* (a veces el guardián tosía, inquieto) buscaba *ver mejor* los diminutos puntos áureos, *esa entrada al mundo* infinitamente lento y remoto de las criaturas rosadas. (*Cc* 1, 382, emphasis added)

The axolotls have no eyelids, the narrator informs, and their persistent gazes back and forth become consuming. The guard even calls attention to this visual consumption: "Usted se los come con los ojos," and the narrator insists that he is devoured by axolotls, "me devoraban lentamente por los ojos, en un canibalismo de oro" (*Cc* 1, 383).

The text emphasizes mutual incorporation by sight in the repetition of visual terms (eyes, sight, look, and gaze) and the insistence on the glass pane as the site of metamorphosis.[9]

> Mi cara estaba pegada al vidrio del acuario, mis ojos trataban una vez más de penetrar el misterio de esos ojos de oro sin iris y sin pupila. Veía muy de cerca la cara de un axolotl inmóvil junto al vidrio. Sin transición, sin sorpresa, vi mi cara contra el vidrio, en vez del axolotl vi mi cara contra el vidrio, la vi fuera del acuario, la vi del otro lado del vidrio. (*Cc* 1, 384)

This definitive passage turns the glass into a sort of mirror for encounters between parallel identities. The axolotl (animal-other), who in its natural state lives in Mexican lakes, here resides in Paris, while the man looking into this transplanted "foreign" realm maintains an ambiguous cultural identification. The protagonist could be posing as the European colonizer fascinated with the "other" and ready to jump into and appropriate the axolotls' exoticized world. However, the narration's Spanish implies, but never specifies, that he is a displaced Latin American in Europe.[10] What at first resembles a contemporary colonial encounter between a dominant (human) self and exotic "other" represents a mutual recognition of two colonized subjects displaced onto the colonizers' territory. Their affinities break through species differentiation to facilitate their exchange. The ambiguity suggests the dynamic of a two-way mirror that simultaneously incorporates the French gaze on Latin America and the Latin American gaze on Paris.

By the end of the story, the physical transformation is complete, yet the strong intuitive connection weakens. While Paris facilitates the meeting and the metamorphosis, it cannot ensure the narrators/ protagonist's desired depth of understanding. The narration concludes that "los puentes están cortados entre él y yo" (*Cc* 1, 384). The pronouns shift between the first person singular human narrator and the first person plural axolotls, finally assigning the third person to the human left outside of the glass tank. The subject still thinks like a human, and the only connection left to explore is through writing. "Ahora soy definitivamente un axolotl ... me consuela pensar que acaso va a escribir sobre nosotros" (*Cc* 1, 385). The two switch *places*, but the man-turned-axolotl remains isolated within his "human" mental constructs of urban writing culture.

"Axolotl" is not the only text that exploits Paris as a space for the observation of other species as a means of defying human limitations. In an analogous scene to "Axolotl" in *Rayuela*, the characters peer into the glass fish tanks of the bird and fish market on the Quai de la Mégisserie along the Seine. Here as well the characters attempt to penetrate visually the fish "world" in order to understand another species:

> [l]os mirábamos, jugando a acercar los ojos al vidrio, pegando la nariz, encolerizando a las viejas vendedoras armadas de redes de cazar mariposas acuáticas, y comprendíamos cada vez peor lo que es un pez.... (34)

The metaphor of the butterflies implies the transformation from air to water and suggests a connection or possible passage between realms. Mirrors even enter the picture, in the mention that "un pez solo en su pecera se entristece y entonces basta ponerle un espejo y el pez vuelve a estar contento...." Attributing emotions to tropical fish furthers the suggestion of metamorphosis that "Axolotl" advances and problematizes.

These scenes of obsessive gazing through glass tanks in order to contemplate otherness engage Paris locales as interstitial zones. In "Axolotl," the public park with its small zoo provides an intermediary space between the organized, structured European cityscape and the extra-European wilderness. The Jardin des Plantes, designed in 1636 as a royal experimental garden for rare and medicinal plants, functions like a natural encyclopedia of vegetation and animal life. It is an institution of the imperial enterprise in its gathering, cataloging, and exoticizing of colonial flora for local curiosity.[11] The garden is organized into four sections divided by two crossing paths that display trees, evergreen bushes, and common and tropical plants. The park is still loyal to its original scientific purpose, with plaques designating the species of each plant and several buildings added in the late nineteenth century that serve as botanical greenhouses and natural history museums.

The zoo setting at the Jardin des Plantes underscores the postcolonial critique of "Axolotl," confirmed by the park's history.

The park's Muséum d'Histoire Naturelle supported the Jardin's encyclopedic, scientific aims since the early nineteenth century. The museum awarded academic grants to travelling naturalists to study and gather specimens to enrich the museum's collections. In the late nineteenth century, when the museum was in competition for funding with increasingly prestigious university science programs, the faculty contrived a mission in colonial research. They bolstered "tropical" research as a means to validate their scientific reputation in anticipation of the Colonial Exhibition and the Universal Exhibition held in Paris in 1889.[12] The apogee of French colonialism in the late nineteenth century, including the exploitation of tropical resources for "knowledge" at home, historically coincides with Spain's colonial collapse. Cortázar subtly draws attention to the Latin American postcolonial shift away from Spain and toward France with this implicit comparison.

The axolotls in the Muséum of the Jardin des Plantes are Mesoamerican animal samples, specimens of colonial collectionism, repeatedly exploited by European expansionist missions. In the shared gazes between man and beast in Cortázar's story, both are displaced victims of a prolonged colonial and postcolonial situation. The narrator's origins, despite his initial human form, seem familiar; however, as already mentioned, the story actually never identifies him. The axolotls' remote origins and habitat are given away in their Nahuatl phoneme that reveals Mexican roots.[13] Their larva state underscores their mutable development and the story's theme of metamorphosis. In Paris, the human pursues an intuited connection to the past that entraps him, and the animal remains caged by a variety of European colonial enterprises.

The fantastic transposition in a zoo is indicative of Cortázar's exploitation of Paris as a site for challenging the limitations of conventional existence that simultaneously expose Latin America's postcolonial situation. A description of the Jardin des Plantes in a photographic and historic study of Paris's public parks confirms Cortázar's choice for the fantastic setting of "Axolotl." Its diversity of buildings and purposes encompassing domains from the vegetable to the animal, from prehistoric remains to live zoo animals, creates "un lieu éminemment onirique, où le rationnel rejoint le fantastique ... dans un espace qui échappe à la ville qu'on y aura vite oubliée, une parenthèse miraculeuse" (Lévêque *Jardins de Paris* 61). The narrator thinks he begins to comprehend the axolotls, "su voluntad secreta, abolir el espacio y el tiempo con una inmovilidad indiferente" (*Cc* 1, 382), but their inner world remains foreign to him. The exchange of identities only partially works, and thus the fantastic shift coincides with the postcolonial predicament. The protagonist changes form but not substance, trades bodies but not minds. Both man and animal remain locked into the colonial paradigm that their respective estrangement in France glaringly mirrors back to them. Awareness and affinity are not sufficient to break their cultural and intellectual incarceration.[14]

The relationship with the "other" in Cortázar's Paris fiction consistently deploys the transparent yet distorted image in the glass to problematize the postcolonial perspective. Windows in Paris serve in Cortázar's stories to reflect another Western prison house: the inscription of gender difference. Male erotic pursuits are filtered through windows that demarcate encounters with the feminine as fantastic passage into separate worlds. Cortázar's construction of woman directly serves his narrative aims as his male protagonists graft their projections of the feminine onto their pursuits of alternative experiences. He taps the Paris construct's gendered roles in order to recast them. His stories take the naive foreigner's sexual initiation expectations of Paris and incorporate them in a new narrative package. Diverting the reader's attention with clichés of Parisian sexual pursuits, the stories manipulate the tropes of erotic fantasy as a means of transporting the protagonist to other realms of experience.

Windows often announce gender differentiation in these stories of fantastic passage and social critique. Women are divided, refracted, and fragmented by the story and its Paris gaze. That women generally appear reflected in window panes or behind glass reveals their association with otherness in the texts. La Maga's association with windows, glass, and mirrors reveals similar gender displacement in *Rayuela*. In the novel's first chapter, Horacio addresses la Maga in his narration, "fuiste siempre un espejo terrible, una espantosa máquina de repeticiones" (10). The day he meets la Maga, he follows her to "cruzar continuamente de una vereda a otra para mirar las cosas más insignificantes en las vitrinas apenas iluminadas. . . ." (11). In chapter 2, Horacio describes her reflected *image* as she admires her body in the mirror as being more irresistible than her physical presence (15). Horacio's desperate search for la Maga, who has disappeared, fuels much of the narration, just as the male protagonists in the short fiction tread the Parisian paths toward fantasized and fantastic erotic encounters.

Analytical writing on mirrors and gender frequently stresses fragmentation of the self and a search for unification against the decentering obstacles of male-dominated discourse.[15] Luce Irigaray's theories on the mirror and the lack of definition for woman in Western culture are revealing for interpreting Cortázar. In *Ce sexe qui n'en est pas un*, Irigaray critiques the "prevalence of the gaze" in male eroticism. This visual aggression relegates woman to "only a more or less complacent facilitator for the working out of man's fantasies" (*New French Feminisms* 100–01). According to the patriarcal paradigms, both in language and in cosmology, from the Bible to Freud, woman is defined only with respect to lack, and in relation to man. She is positioned as man's mirror image.

Subjectivity and individual identity are relevant only peripherally to Cortázar's narrative purpose in the short fiction. Cortázar does not pursue the theme of individual self-actualization in these texts, nor do his mirror/window reflections function as vehicles for self-discovery. On the contrary, women in his stories are the results of the projections of male protagonists. Rather than characters, the women often remain *figures* who are positioned in the direction of the male protagonist's desiring eye. Jenijoy La Belle, in *Herself Beheld: The Literature of the Looking Glass*, examines scenes of women contemplating themselves in mirrors in Western literature. While in Cortázar's stories it is *men* who exploit women's reflections, her comments about the visual role of women in modern Western culture apply to the following analysis:

> In European culture for at least the last two centuries a female self as a social, psychological, and literary phenomenon is defined, to a considerable degree, as a visual image and structured, in part, by continued acts of mirroring. (9)

The female figures in stories such as "Manuscrito hallado en un bolsillo," "Cuello de gatito negro," and "El otro cielo" are indeed framed in the projections of their male protagonists. The women's identities are not in question but rather the protagonists' structural relationship to multiple "realities." Cortázar borrows from the gender coding of Western culture to navigate his explorations into metaphysical alternatives.

Gender difference advances the fantastic movement in these stories by contributing to the construction of difference and otherness to which Paris provides access. Women and men serve the texts structurally as manifestations of the dichotomies governing

Cortázar's plots, dichotomies that the texts call upon in order to subvert them. The stories are motivated by the protagonists' desire to access not only the women themselves but the worlds they inhabit or the alternatives to which they provide passage. Cortázar's stories demonstrate through the use of windows that not only are women "other," they are confined within the figures male protagonists consciously conjure up to fulfill their erotic desires and ontological searches. In "Manuscrito hallado en un bolsillo," window panes in Paris serve both as lenses through which the protagonist views women, and as architectural tropes of erotic interstitiality.

"Manuscrito hallado en un bolsillo" relies on window reflections as the protagonist depersonalizes and fictionalizes the women he pursues. The narrator/protagonist engages in a game of glances in the windows of the Paris subway cars. He decides that "un vidrio de ventanilla en el metro podía traerme la respuesta, el encuentro con una felicidad" (*Cc* 2, 65). He makes eye contact with a woman's reflection in the glass and anxiously tries to predict her stops and connections to other subway lines. He successfully gauges the trajectory of a woman he names Margrit/Ana, follows her out of the subway, and they meet, enjoying a brief period that resembles "un encuentro legítimo" (*Cc* 2, 72). Ultimately, however, his obsession with the game of chance obstructs the relationship. His desire for her is predicated on the risk of losing her to random transit connections that do not coincide. He convinces her to return to the underground passageways to chance a repeat encounter.

This story presents the most overt Cortazarian manipulation of reflected images by a man. Rather than the women contemplating themselves in the mirror and questioning their identity, it is the man who insists on detached images, imposing fragmentation on the women he catches in his gaze. He splits his view of a female passenger into the figure before him and the reflection in the windowpane. This dual image engenders double identities, each assigned its own name. The window reflections help sustain the protagonist's imaginary projections and the divisive structure of competing realities in his game of multiple identities only available beneath Paris.

"Manuscrito hallado en un bolsillo" underscores the insistence on doubling from early on, enumerating the protagonist's potential conquests in their pair of names: Margrit/Ana and Ofelia/Paula. The names bifurcate the "person" into familiar and transnational/literary/mythological desires. The protagonist's game of chance in the métro each time converts women into (dis)figures of his erotic imagination. His fragmented desire labels the women first with a common Spanish name, while the glassy, distorted image is assigned a more fantasized and less Hispanic linguistic identity. Ofelia evokes the Shakespearean; Margrit connotes Germanic or Scandinavian descent.[16] However, Ana and Paula blend into the Spanish of the discourse in the story without evoking otherness or estrangement.

The male protagonist's doubling projection underscores his cultural ambiguity. The split destroys the singularity of the female object of desire. Only when he ascends from the underground realm can the protagonist attempt to fuse the figures back into one. Despite leaving the métro and its reflective windows, the "reality" of street life is not sufficient for unification. "Ana/Margrit" reveals her "real" French name to be Marie-Claude. This hyphenation works against the resolution of the fictional double and perpetuates the protagonist's refracted desire.

Cortázar taps the Paris construct's erotic pursuits but steers away from the conventional images of French prostitutes. The female figures in "Manuscrito hallado en un bolsillo" are fragmented figments of the protagonist's Parisian fantasies. Paris and its subway system become a means for transforming women into multiple and transnational selves (see later section on métro). The métro's magic dissolves "allí arriba," conflating the split figures. The twin images can only return to the underworld to play at reconnecting amid the metro's fragments.[17]

ARCADES

> The arcade is a building with many entrances and exits. It has its own plane, which conquers and bridges everything. Its narrowness gives space to action and its closure echoes demands.
>
> —Geist, *Arcades: The History of a Building Type*

Seductive transitions in the short fiction rely on windows for the precarious separations between realms. The Parisian arcades, at first glance, may seem like narrative extensions of Cortázar's use of windows. However, while the windows offer entrance or escape, the covered urban passageways in "El otro cielo" build connections. They function like glass corridors that invite voyeurism, while they orient and shelter passage. Simultaneously above-ground tunnels and riverless bridges, they unite otherwise separate city buildings under a transparent "cielo falso." In "El otro cielo," the Parisian arcades architecturally launch the transitions between

Europe and Latin America, and metaphysically facilitate fluid movement in time and space.

"El otro cielo" is an example of Cortázar's fiction that proposes parallel simultaneous worlds that overlap in the text. The plot shifts between Buenos Aires in the 1940s and Paris around 1870, and relies on arcades in Paris and Buenos Aires as zones of connection. The Pasaje Güemes in Buenos Aires, modeled after the Parisian arcades, is the transitional space that offers access to the Galerie Vivienne in Paris.[18] The arcades' luminous glass roofs, mythological frescoes, and corner stairways to private chambers invite the narrator/protagonist to step out of one world and enter another. The arcades not only join the adjacent sides of city buildings, they metaphorically join Buenos Aires and Paris in Cortázar's blurred narrative boundaries. The story comes to privilege the passageways over either of the protagonist's conflicting worlds and ends when he can no longer cross into their interstitial zone.

These exotic passageways entangle the narrator in a double life. He moves between his sedate occupation as a stockbroker with a fiancé named Irma in Buenos Aires and the realm of prostitutes and criminals in the Paris arcade district. The narrator, in search of an alternative to the tedium of his *porteño* existence, is easily lured by the seductive and dangerous world of the arcades. The story inverts the traditional dichotomy between the civilized metropolitan center and the barbarous periphery. Paris here becomes the dangerous seductress, while Latin America (even its urban centers) represents routinized boredom. The caped Lautréamont/Maldoror figure (called "el sudamericano") who hovers in the arcade district underscores the theme of voyeuristic eroticism as well as the cultural ambivalence between Europe and Latin America. The narrator/protagonist pursues an affair with the prostitute Josiane who lives in the Galerie Vivienne, and whom he fantasizes about protecting from the strangler who has attacked several prostitutes. They together witness the public guillotining of the perpetrator, a climax in the intensifying threat of Josiane's world that causes the narrator/protagonist to pull away. The demands of his bourgeois *porteño* routine begin to thwart his attempts to access the arcade realm, and ultimately he retreats into its safer domestic scene.

The arcades as images of Parisian modernity occupy a fundamental place in the Latin American Paris construct. As Walter Benjamin describes, the arcades embody the collaboration of art and commerce, the decorative and the technical, glass and iron (*Baudelaire* 155–76). These images of modernity are linked to commodification in the exhibition and sale of newly manufactured things. The innovations of gas lamps and glass roofs privilege the visual experience of the passerby in these new constructions that extend the realm of the *flâneur*. Not only were these structures employed for narrow commercial shop alleys, but expanded versions of the intimate arcades were built for World's Fair exhibition halls and train stations. As passageways, they always sheltered transitory movement such as temporary exhibits, pedestrian traffic, and train connections.

Cortázar, in "El otro cielo," manipulates the arcades to further his erotic and fantastic associations with Paris. The story builds on the arcades as metonyms of European modernity to associate them with a voyeuristic eroticism.[19] The text also positions the arcades as fantastic bridges that join two distant times and spaces. "El otro cielo" uses the arcades to problematize the private and the public, the interior and the exterior, the familiar and the foreign, money and love. The arcades' architectural properties draw attention to these issues in the creation of urban spaces that are neither completely open nor entirely enclosed. The characteristics Johann Friedrich Geist enumerates in his panoramic study of arcades around the world—skylit public space on private property, systems of access, and spaces of transition—confirm their structural function in "El otro cielo."[20] The arcades are the first modern shopping centers, "[g]reat expenditures for architectural and decorative features are made to seduce the consumer, to generate the desire to consume" (Geist 52). Cortázar's story exploits the seductive consumerism of the arcades where sex is sold as the main commodity.

The story capitalizes on the stock exchange reference as the center of the arcade neighborhoods' prostitution zone, to extend the relationship between transit and finance in the story's erotic geopolitical economy. "El otro cielo" begins with the narrator's reminiscences about his adolescent visits to the Pasaje Güemes and its prostitutes. The first arcade image in the story, then, associates these architectural spaces with places where sex is for sale. The narrator even employs a metaphor of the consumption of material goods (clothing) for his first sexual encounter in the arcade: "territorio ambiguo donde ya hace tanto tiempo fui a quitarme la infancia como un traje usado" (*Cc* 1, 590). According to Benjamin, the textile and fashion industry provided the initial commercial impetus for the arcades in Paris, due to the increasing need for stock to be stored and displayed. The two references to pockets (*bolsillos*) create another link to the stock market, both linguistically and metonymically. As a diminutive form of *bolsa*, the pockets subtly introduce the financial dimensions of this exchange. His pockets hold his "miserables centavos" as well as his hands, both necessary items for his bought pleasure.

Gender difference also figures into the oppositional tensions of the story's structure. As series of multiple windows, the glass structures in "El otro cielo" suggest some of the gender issues examined in "Manuscrito hallado en un bolsillo." The feminine presence once again is split between Irma and Josiane, who represent the protagonist's conflicting desires. The two women serve to project the protagonist's needs in terms that accentuate the gendered clichés of Paris in the Latin American imaginary. Irma stands for enclosed domesticity, and Josiane, who inhabits the arcade realm, represents eroticism and danger. Their names help situate them linguistically within their respective geographical-cultural realms. The character names become sonorously associated with their linguistic context: Irma, a plain, two-syllable name in Spanish, contrasts with Josiane's soft "j", dipthong and silent but poetically recognized last syllable. Cortázar uses these phonetic distinctions to map out the protagonist's conflicted zones of desire. Names and their sounds are among the signs that distinguish between the narrative fragments associated with Buenos Aires and Paris and contribute to the spatial tensions in the story. While Buenos Aires/Irma embodies the trappings of domestic family life, Paris/Josiane is the illicit mistress. The story exploits Irma and Josiane for its fantastic ends, allowing them only figural connotations as bodies that represent their respective places of residence.

The movement and architecture in this story steer explicitly toward a sexual fulfillment that is never fully realized. In a variation on *Rayuela,* where Horacio explores city streets in pursuit of la Maga, the narrator/protagonist in "El otro cielo" wanders passively until reaching the arcade district in Buenos Aires that the story associates with Paris, prostitutes, and sexual initiation.[21] The Pasaje Güemes is the conduit that links him to his other world in Paris. The *porteño* arcade signals Europeanizing architecture and city planning that continued into the early twentieth century. The arcades become narrative vaginas that envelope the narrator/protagonist until he begins to penetrate them at will. After the story's meandering foreplay, the protagonist reaches his "término del deseo" (*Cc* 1, 603). The Galerie Vivienne is his "caverna del tesoro" (*Cc* 1,

590) whose plaster garlands continually draw him in. The narrow construction expands when Josiane invites him into her private room, usually off-limits to clients, rather than the brothel. As the arcades surround him, they spatially take over the story. Allusions to Irma and Buenos Aires temporarily fade as the Parisian arcade world encompasses the protagonist and eclipses the story's other realm.

The neighborhoods surrounding the arcades in both cities sustain the narration's ambivalent beginning that leads the protagonist into the interstice. The story begins with the suggestion of melting, enmeshing territory: "Me ocurría a veces que todo se dejaba andar, se ablandaba y cedía terreno, aceptando sin resistencia que se pudiera ir así de una cosa a otra" (*Cc* 1, 590). Blurred and yielding boundaries are characteristic of the arcades: "The contours of existing relations between buildings are not destroyed but blurred. In one sense, it becomes unclear where the outside ends and the inside begins" (Rolleston 19). The text of a major photography collection on the arcades mentions that ". . . les Passages se réjouissent de leur fluidité facile et de leur instabilité silencieuse. . . ." (Delvaille 17). The arcades offer an atemporal and aspatial quality to the travelling protagonist. They are the borders, the customhouse of the story's movement, the "in-between" space the narrative occupies.

The text manipulates these blurred boundaries in the discourse with "la bolsa" as a tricky sign that throughout the story serves to confuse Buenos Aires and Paris. Both the Pasaje Güemes and the Parisian arcades are located in the commercial stock market district of their cities, and "la bolsa" marks the hinging sign between the two frontiers. The protagonist's work routine, whether linked to Buenos Aires or Paris, places him in the very vicinity of accessing his other world. Each mention of "la bolsa" in the story plays on this ambiguity. The phrase becomes a discursive hinge that establishes the fantastic exchange between the two worlds:

> ese mundo que ha optado por un cielo más próximo, de vidrios sucios y estucos con figuras alegóricas que tienden las manos para ofrecer una guirnalda, esa Galerie Vivienne a un paso de la ignominia diurna de la rue Réaumur y de la Bolsa (yo trabajo en la Bolsa), cuánto de ese barrio ha sido mío desde siempre, desde mucho antes . . . cuando apostado en un rincón del Pasaje Güemes. . . . (*Cc* 1, 591)

"La bolsa" is the sign that confounds the narration's separations between spatial and temporal realms by perpetuating their (con)-

fusion in a privileged site of bifurcating referents. The French names and the temporal qualifiers, rather than clarifying the location, only puzzle the reader about which "bolsa" is referenced here. The narration systematically avoids the French term *la bourse*, while it converts "la bolsa" into an international, translinguistic reference through the discourse in Spanish. The present tense of the verb "trabajo" links the area to the present and to Buenos Aires, yet the "bolsa's" syntactic relation to the French street simultaneously draws it into the Parisian world. The stock market as "bolsa" in the narration superimposes the two districts in order to "exchange" cities, women, sex, language, and identities.[22] As Rifkin concludes in his discussion of the city's "zones of bargain pleasure" in French films, photography, and songs, sources Cortázar clearly draws from, the prostitute in the representation of Paris serves to highlight "the restless life of the commodity, the uncertain wanderings of desire, the perplexing distance of the margins . . . and the effects of class domination" (200–01).

The arcades of "El otro cielo" erect interstitial cultural spaces, crossways of architectural, historical, and literary worlds. While the short fiction collectively draws intertextually on Baudelaire's *Le Spleen de Paris*, Georges Bataille, and Cortázar's own intratexts such as *Rayuela*, this story especially entangles in the Parisian arcade district Lautréamont's Maldoror. The extensive Lautréamont intertext goes beyond the two epigraphs from *Les Chants de Maldoror* that introduce the story's two parts. The story hosts a cluster of cultural transplants—Cortázar, Lautréamont, the narrator/protagonist, Laurent, the strangler, and the *sudamericano*—who straddle Paris and Río de la Plata. Biographical associations abound among the authorial and fictional figures, most obviously Lautréamont's dual Uruguayan/French national identification, and his address on the rue Vivienne.

However, these biographical coincidences seem trivial compared to the intricate textual borrowing from the *Chants*. Cortázar's story includes the Maldoror reminiscences of perversity, voyeurism, and pedophilia. The strangler's prostitute victims, the voyeuristic violence of the guillotining scene at the end, the obscured light, and the cavernous spaces and garlands in the arcades' frescoes all reverberate the Maldororian intertext. The narrator/protagonist fears the reclusive, caped character known as the *sudamericano*, and recoils from him as a spectral double who reminds him of his own interstitial situation as a South American in Paris. The *sudamericano* comes to represent figurally an entire continent, the Latin American as an exotic "other" under European observation.[23] Both "El otro cielo" and *Les chants de Maldoror* feature the arcades as zones occupied by bicultural interlopers who transgress conventional aesthetic positions.[24]

The climactic guillotining scene, one of the most explicit Maldororian motifs in "El otro cielo," signals the narrator/ protagonist's retreat. The protagonist begins to find accessing the arcades more and more difficult as the demands in Buenos Aires from his mother and Irma increase, along with the *bolsa*'s chaotic activity upon the outbreak of World War II. The guillotining scene, in which Josiane's arcade cohort will watch rather than participate, steers the story away from the arcade neighborhood.[25] This spatial detachment is underscored by the South American who also attends the public display. He remains the story's persistent intertextual fragment situated at the margins of the arcade realm, always removed from the other characters. During his last visit to Josiane, soon after the guillotining, the narrator/protagonist learns that the South American, a conflation of "Laurent" the strangler and Lautréamont, has died. Without his shadowy double, the protagonist will also return to his *porteño* bourgeois routine.

The morbid image of the beheading draws on the arcades' structural disjuncture and their separateness from the street world. This voyeuristic episode also subtly draws attention to the arcades' interior shop displays and the commodification of the body. The scene exploits physical dismemberment to suggest correlations between the passages' visual commercialism and sadistic practices. Many of the arcade storefronts historically displayed wholesale merchandise for various trade industries, such as dolls, mannequins, masks, and artificial body parts:

> Têtes pour coiffeurs, perruques, postiches; matériel d'artistes, mannequin en bois articulés; poupées anciennes; masques de carnaval; mannequins pour tailleurs et grands magasins; mains coupées servant de présentoirs à bagues, tout relève du dépeçage. A ce malaise de salle de chirurgie s'ajoute une sexualité des plus troubles. (Delvaille 31)

The "troubling" sexuality incorporated into this enumeration evokes the protagonist's transgression into "other" sexual practices in the arcade realm that suggest Maldoror's sadistic gestures.[26]

The voyeuristic experience through the gates of the prison simultaneously attracts and repells the protagonist with its erotic perversity. The guillotining scene highlights the ambiguous play in "El otro cielo" between fragmentation and connection, complementing the image of the arcades. All of the structures in the story draw fragile, porous borders that join but at the same time sustain division. The Paris arcade neighborhood functions as a marginal, precarious subworld that seduces the narrator/protagonist but cannot hold him. The guillotining scene haunts the protagonist, challenging him to choose or be severed from the arcade world and the part of himself that flourishes there.

In this story of fluid boundaries and passage, the arcades triumph as the interstices of longing that lead to erotic adventure. For the protagonist of "El otro cielo," the arcades represent a clandestine and privileged zone that is simultaneously an interior and exterior. Cortázar constructs a narrative arcade out of this story that blurs the boundaries of public street life and secret privacies. The arcades in "El otro cielo" are the interstices between cities, nations, languages, literatures, and an individual's daily wanderings. The story takes the stock market, initially associated with a building that the protagonist enters and exits as an employee, and splits it into two ambiguous and blurring *bolsas*. The text never refers to them in the plural, but rather uses the singular *bolsa* to stress its monolithic stance as an international institution, thereby underscoring the neocolonial economic relationship between Latin America and developed countries. The story's prostitution serves as a metaphor for the cultural and political "purchase" of Latin America by Anglo-American and European powers. The Pasaje Güemes embodies the cultural colonialism that has penetrated the protagonist's imagination, such that his desires are dictated by the Latin American conception of Paris and physically lead him into the Parisian arcades. In these passages, the protagonist views a different sky and begins to fulfill his desire. He retreats from them, concluding back on the homely side of his alternative heaven, but leaves standing the interstitial narration whose translucent ceiling illuminates fantastic passage.

METRO

In modern Athens, the vehicles of mass transportation are called *metaphorai*. To go to work or come home, one takes a "metaphor"—a bus or a train. Stories could also take this noble name: every day, they traverse and organize places; they select and link them together; they make sentences

and itineraries out of them. They are spatial trajectories. . . .
[N]arrative structures . . . regulate changes in space. . . . [T]hese
places are linked together more or less tightly or easily by
"modalities" that specify the kind of passage leading from
the one to the other. . . . [S]tories, whether everyday or literary, serve us as means of mass transportation, as *metaphorai*.

—Michel de Certeau, *The Practice of Everyday Life*

[E]n esa estación no había los interminables pasillos de otras
veces y las escaleras llevaban rápidamente a destino, a eso
que en los medios de transporte también se llama destino.

—Cortázar, "Manuscrito hallado en un bolsillo"

Movement and travel are integral to Cortázar's fiction. Travel furthers his texts' defiance of the spatiotemporal divisions and limitations of bourgeois conventions. Movement also provides strategies
for conquering the cultural geography of distance inherent in
postcolonial identity. While Cortázar uses the travel motif extensively throughout his fiction, his stories concerning Paris rarely
treat efforts to get to or leave the French capital ("Autopista del
sur" and "El otro cielo" are among the few). The Parisian tales
seem already rooted in an urban ambiance, their discourse and
structure entrenched in a fictional urban maze. It is movement
within Paris that guides the protagonists into unexpected circumstances to question the ontological and cultural givens of contemporary urban identity. Along with its bridges, neighborhoods,
buildings, and arcades, Paris's underground transit system as a mode
of travel allows for fantastic encounters and promotes social and
philosophical change.

The métro in Cortázar is simultaneously a literal and metaphorical vehicle. In the three central stories concerning the subway system,
the metaphorical and metaphysical overtake the literal. In "El
perseguidor," "Cuello de gatito negro," and "Manuscrito hallado en
un bolsillo," the métro's function as public transportation is subordinate to its fantastic potential for challenging the constructs of contemporary cosmopolitan thought. For Johnny Carter, in "El
perseguidor," the métro collapses the divisions between time and space.
For the protagonists of "Cuello de gatito negro" and "Manuscrito
hallado en un bolsillo," the métro's intense speed, jolting movement,
and close quarters offer opportunities for fantastic erotic encounters.
The space of the subway network—Mondrianesque according to the
narrator of "Cuello"—possesses qualities that lift some of the conventional restrictions and permit extraordinary gestures and gazes.

As in the architectural motifs of windows and arcades associated with Paris, the métro in Cortázar's stories establishes interstitial spaces that position the characters between "origins" and "destinations": "situarse también en los intersticios . . . cada uno instalado en su burbuja, alineado entre paréntesis. . . ." (*Cc* 2, 66). Here the narrator of "Manuscrito hallado en un bolsillo" interprets the métro as a space that separates as well as connects. Like the arcades in "El otro cielo," the transition or passage of travel, the *en route*, expands in importance while the trips' beginning and end are rendered in disillusioned fragmentation.[27] In "Manuscrito hallado en un bolsillo" and "Cuello de gatito negro," the characters' transportation destinations are never clarified and certainly never reached. Each one transforms his subway trip into a practice for identifying and pursuing bizarre encounters with women rather than a means to a designated location: "[c]ada estación del metro era una trama diferente del futuro" ("Manuscrito" *Cc* 2, 66). Desire is substituted for destination in the Cortázarian distortion of the subway system that serves the characters' erotic and ontological itineraries.

Interstitial zones of movement characterize Cortázar's innovations in the narrative travel motif. He exploits these transitory spaces precisely to undermine conventional movement across grounded space and replace it with time travel, overlapping spatiotemporal zones and fantastic transitions. Martha Paley Francescato elucidates three functions of travel in Cortázar's fiction. Travel serves as a metaphor for the "new man" in search of alternative societies, presents erotic experience as rupture with "old" societal norms, and proposes crossroads that force characters to choose between options, all of which are charged with the cultural past. Travel propels the characters "más allá de problemas personales hacia ámbitos que tienen que ver con lo cultural, social, político y filosófico" (136–37). Cortázar repositions his characters in time and space by situating them in the passageways that have the potential to guide them into new social territories.

The windows and arcades architecturally prepared the terrain for the subway's spatiotemporal innovation:

> The glass vault is furthermore the initial stage of a systematic development of a space of transition and movement, a kind of space which originates in the arcade, continues in the railway station, and ends up in the subway tubes, where, freed from the street level and historical conditions, it attains an aerodynamically ideal cross

> section and a technologically refined form which makes
> fantastic velocities possible. (Geist 55)

Just as the windows and arcades served the stories as transitions
between alternative realms, physical transportation within Paris
allows for access beyond tangible destinations.

Movement is the vital ingredient the métro provides, introduc-
ing the interconnectedness of space and time in "El perseguidor."
The novella begins just after Johnny Carter loses his saxophone in
the métro, carried away by his own distractions and philosophical
musings. The métro is Johnny's metaphor for his expansive connections to an "other side," analogous to his experience of playing
music that propels him to another level of being outside of time,
"la música me sacaba del tiempo" (Cc 1, 229). Subway travel for
Johnny represents the elasticity of time:

> sólo en el métro me puedo dar cuenta porque viajar en el
> métro es como estar metido en un reloj. Las estaciones
> son los minutos, comprendes, es ese tiempo de ustedes,
> de ahora; pero yo sé que hay otro. . . ." (Cc 1, 233)

Bruno, the story's narrator, is Johnny's biographer, who struggles
with the musician's eccentric behavior and abstract ramblings. While
he recognizes his subject's musical brilliance, he feels inadequate
and hyperconscious of his own cultural and spiritual limitations:
"[l]o único que me inquieta es que se deje llevar por esa conducta
que yo no soy capaz de seguir (digamos que no quiero seguir)" (Cc
1, 260). The story, which is neither one of Bruno's journalistic
reviews nor part of his published biography of Johnny, records his
awareness that he is merely a satellite trying to maintain his orbit
around Johnny against his star's unpredictable course among a
variety of levels of existence (Cc 1, 250).

"El perseguidor" presents a cluster of topoi common to the
Latin American construct of Paris—the most obvious being Paris
as international bohemian artists' haven—only to explode them.
Johnny does not buy into the (African)-American aesthetic pilgrimage to Paris as a ritualized site for Western culture. Indeed, Bruno
has to remind him that "París no es un casino de provincia y todo
el mundo tiene puestos los ojos en Johnny" (Cc 1, 240). The references to the métro confirm Johnny's search for connections that
transcend place and status. The subway images he interjects through-

out the story underscore the Cortazarian reversal of the dichotomies that so often structure reworkings of Parisian bohemia. Johnny
and his métro/music hyperreality overturn the insider/outsider
polarity, as Bruno realizes when he comes to the conclusion that
"Johnny no es una víctima, no es un perseguido. . . . Johnny persigue
en vez de ser perseguido" (*Cc* 1, 250). Bruno, the Frenchman, feels
transparently unhappy and disoriented around his foreign musician
"friend." Despite "mi buena salud, mi casa, mi mujer, mi prestigio,"
Bruno is the outsider at home who does not have sufficient courage
or will to enter Johnny's world, a world that does not rely on Paris.
Bruno, like the postcolonial Latin American intellectual, is simultaneously local and foreign, expert and novice, professional and
apprentice at home and abroad.[28]

"El perseguidor" caricatures both the aesthetic and commercial
by freeing Johnny from the confines of the bourgeois preoccupations that trap Bruno. As a journalist and biographer, Bruno has to
be concerned with chronology and events, a critic's life "que sólo
puede vivir de prestado, de las novedades y las decisiones ajenas"
(*Cc* 1, 253). Johnny, on the contrary, can take drugs, play music,
and concentrate on poetic associations such as the conflation of
time and space during a subway ride.

In "Cuello de gatito negro" and "Manuscrito hallado en un
bolsillo," the subway works like a system of communicating vessels that incites fantastic encounters. In "Cuello," the protagonist
Lucho takes advantage of a crowded subway car to seduce a woman
whose gloved hand rests just below his as they grasp the metal
pole. Her hand begins to climb toward his, and surprises him, since
he usually makes the first move. The narration interjects the vague
phrase "otra cosa" to introduce the growing suspicion that this
encounter, presented as one of a series of banal urban flirtations, is
stranger than initially appears. Dina has the persistent problem of
a disobedient hand that moves of its own volition (the métro stop
they pass during their physical contact is called "Volontaires"). At
the end of the story, she turns into a cat who attacks the lover her
hand seduced. "Manuscrito hallado en un bolsillo" develops from
the protagonist's fantasies based on women's reflections in the subway cars' windowpanes. The subway's matrices guide his obsessive
pursuit of Marie-Claire in a game of chance that subjects their to-
getherness to the test of random choices. The disobedient force in
"Cuello" and the interstitial uncertainty of "Manuscrito" unlock
the métro as a zone for experimenting with unfamiliar behaviors.

The underground, with its routes, cars, maps, and names, furnishes an indispensable element to reading Paris in these stories. Like a palimpsest, the city's layers collaborate in a textual process that guides and sometimes even predetermines the characters' trajectories.[29] The subway maps the stories' interpersonal connections in language and movement that reflect elements of the Paris construct while simultaneously opening the texts to explore new routes. Both "Cuello" and "Manuscrito" incorporate subway semiotics in frequent mentions of the names of various stops and routes. Both stories, for example, include Montparnasse-Bienvenue, one of the largest métro interchanges where two significant routes intersect. This is a plurisemantic sign that functions linguistically, geographically, and culturally. The geographical and cultural reference of "Montparnasse" evokes the southern section of the Latin Quarter and the bohemian artistic neighborhood of the 1920s and 1930s, along with the classical reference to Mount Parnassus, while "Bienvenue," the French feminine form of "welcome," underscores the story's erotic beckoning. The subway's movement also encourages physical contact, and both stories manipulate the twists and turns of the ride to push the characters toward one another. The abrupt halts, the few seconds on the platform between quick jolts to the next station, create the stories' rhythm: "evitando rodillas en ese instante en que la pérdida de velocidad traba y atonta los cuerpos" (Cc 2, 68). In "Cuello," the two long paragraphs that lead into the story's extensive dialogue rely heavily on a vocabulary of mechanical and human movement: virajes, balanceo, girando, barquinazo, resbalar, retorcerse, apretarse (Cc 2, 106–09). The metallic and electric motion gradually steers the narration toward bodily contact.

A counterpart rather than an alternative to the city's above-the-street heights and between-street passageways—bridges over the Seine, rooftops, and arcades—the subway's depth plunges the characters into transgression. They rely on public transportation for implicitly "forbidden" contact with the "other." The métro becomes Cortázar's alternative site for connecting with the Baudelairian urban crowd transfered from the street to underground tunnels.

The métro offers potential access to the illogical, nonrational side of experience where creative genius, animal impulses, and random chance override the mundane conventions of human behavior and thought. However, human limitation (generally men's, in these stories) impedes most characters from successful and prolonged contact with these alternative realms. The cars' jolts and stops are metaphors for the characters' failure to sustain connections. Bruno will remain peripheral and parasitic to the inner realm of Johnny's music by holding onto his bourgeois assurances of contracts, translations, and professional contacts. Johnny, who succeeded in tapping the other side, dies. The protagonist of "Cuello" uses the métro for romantic conquest but finds that he is the victim of his own caprice. The power of Dina's hand and her feline metamorphosis make him the object rather than the subject of his erotic pursuit. "Manuscrito" holds out more than the others the possibility of erotic and emotional fulfillment via a long-term plunge into the underground network of chance encounters.

All three of these stories challenge the protagonists to travel beyond the confines of their personal and cultural preconceptions (racial, sexual, aesthetic) with the métro as a means of access. However, Parisian modernity splits the terrain into "el mundo de arriba" and "el mundo de abajo" ("Manuscrito" *Cc* 2; 67, 72) and reveals most characters' incapacity to make the connections. Just as the characters' erotic expectations of Paris in the end lead to disillusionment or disaster, so its potential to break through metaphysical boundaries and defy ontological categories also disappoints. The postcolonial search continues in the interstices, beneath, above, or between the structures that determine urban identity in an attempt to redefine those origins and destinations.

METAFICTION AS CORTAZAR'S URBAN PLANNING

> J'ai eu aujourd'hui, en rêve, trois domiciles où j'ai trouvé un égal plaisir. Pourquoi contraindre mon corps à changer de place, puisque mon âme voyage si lentement? Et à quoi bon exécuter des projets, puisque le projet est en lui-même une jouissance suffisante?
>
> —Baudelaire, *Spleen*

Paris serves Cortázar's fiction as a draft of an urban model that the stories redesign. The metafictional strategies in the Parisian stories build on the city's urban textuality and its cultural construct in Latin America with implications that are both metaphysical and political. Many of these texts link Paris to creativity through characters who work there as translators, photographers, musicians, graphic artists, or writers. Cortázar rewrites Paris's role as a prescribed initiation for expatriate artists. He first undoes the association of Paris as an idealized creative space, but very differently from the disillusionment of Güiraldes's *Raucho* or Salazar Bondy's *Pobre gente de París*. His aim is not to dissuade young idealists through tales of Parisian poverty and artistic anonymity. In fact,

the irony of these stories is that Cortázar deconstructs the creative
expectations of a stay in Paris despite his characters' artistic success. In Paris, both Johnny Carter's and Bruno's careers peak in "El
perseguidor," the *bolsa* in "El otro cielo" booms, and Roberto Michel
in "Las babas del diablo" works as a professional translator. Nevertheless, material success and artistic recognition seem peripheral
to the characters' pursuits of metaphysical expansion. Paris represents the cultural baggage of bourgeois conventions they confront
in internal conflicts that block their passage. These stories examine and question the creative process and use Paris to expose their
characters' limitations (emotional, spiritual, cultural, sexual) and
graph their efforts to overcome them.

These short stories redesign Parisian urban space in order to
expose the confrontations between European and American aesthetic modeling and between competing versions of what constitutes "reality." Cortázar's metafictional maneuvers in Paris make
room for cultural expression that unmasks the interstitial nature of
Latin American postcoloniality. Reworking the Paris construct of
intensive creative output in these stories stresses the problematics
of postcolonial bicultural identification. While expatriation often
functions as a reference point, the characters' spatial displacement
is of less concern than their inherent crosscultural hyperawareness.
The stories frequently obscure the protagonists' national or cultural identification ("Axolotl," "Manuscrito," "Cuello") beneath
the alienating marginality they experience in Paris.[30] For these
characters, Paris is an arbitrary place (Johnny in "El perseguidor"),
an inaccessible place ("Carta a una señorita en París"), a place
beyond death and distance ("Cartas de mamá"), a perpetual bridge
rather than a destination ("Manuscrito hallado en un bolsillo").
Cortázar writes into his fictional Paris hyphenated and bilingual
names (Roberto Michel, Marie-Claude), multiethnicity (Dina in
"Cuello" is called "mulata"), the persistent theme of the translator, and women as split or blurred selves to draw attention to the
composite cultural identity of postcolonial urban intellectuals.

Within the context of Cortázar's metafictional aims throughout his writing, the stories that incorporate Paris directly target the
city as a creative catalyst and producer of signs. More intricate
than a borrowing of street grids and place names, Cortázar's texts
exploit Paris as a model for modern urban experience and employ
the city as the stories' intertextual blueprint for postcolonial awareness. In an essay that introduces a photographic study of Paris,
Cortázar affirms the fluid interdependence between writing and

place. He accentuates Paris's active role in metaphors for the city such as a sponge, a deck of cards, a system of communicating vessels, or a place that invents its own vocabulary. His characters who inhabit Paris participate in the city's literary urban planning:

> Ese viajero andará por la ciudad a lo largo de días y de años sin llegar a saber en qué día o en qué año la realidad que lo envolvía cambió de signo y la ciudad, tanto tiempo andada, empezó en algún momento a andar por él, a recorrerlo como él la había recorrido. (Cortázar *París*)

As Paris is fictionalized, its characters and stories all mutually construct one another. From their titles alone, stories such as "Carta a una señorita en París," "Cartas de mamá," and "Manuscrito hallado en un bolsillo" are positioned within a series of metatextual frames that link Paris with writing. "Manuscrito," for example, not only frames the story with a metatextual title about a found document, the plot is also grafted onto the subway system as a written code of signals, zones, and maps. This subterranean code undermines the practical conventions of urban transportation as the story detours from any fixed destination in order to explore the broader range of chance meetings.

These stories are launched in a Paris that is supposed to generate creative output, according to Latin American cultural projection, but more importantly produces explorations that reinterpret "reality" and advocate alternative social structures. The characters' emerging translations, photographic enlargements, and musical recordings diminish in significance compared with expanded consciousness, species metamorphosis, and fantastic eroticism. In "El perseguidor," the success of Bruno's biography of Johnny becomes a commercial detail that only partially distracts him from grappling with Johnny's "other side," his "lado patológico" that Bruno hesitates to include (*Cc* 1, 264). Bruno has become an expatriate in his own country through the alternative world of black jazz and improvisation ("en un plano aparentemente desasido donde la música queda en absoluta libertad . . . una música que me gustaría poder llamar metafísica" [*Cc* 1, 242]), but still resists complete participation in that antilogos.

Bruno stands in the uncomfortable position of the critic/friend/ advocate/white male, a position that obfuscates the centrality of Paris in the interdependent and transnational reality of their mutual success. "[L]o difícil es girar en torno a él sin perder la distancia, como un buen satélite, un buen crítico" (Cc 1, 250). Bruno's task is to maintain the careful distance that lies somewhere between the center and the margin. The story is about the effort to establish and occupy that interstitial zone in relation to the star, rather than about producing a biography. The reader of these stories never gains access to the biography, recordings, enlarged photo, or the translations; the text values the process over the product and presents the outcome as peripheral to the ontological challenges it proposes.

In these stories, Paris and writing collaborate to accentuate an expansive creative process. The city is rarely a final destination, rather it continually opens possibilities for further exploration. Windows, arcades, and the métro are Paris's textual inscriptions that provide access and encourage movement among numerous levels of experience. Cortázar's characters write in order to catalogue the aesthetics, metaphysics, and politics of their interstitial position. Bruno apologetically states, "[l]o malo es que si sigo así voy a acabar escribiendo más sobre mí mismo que sobre Johnny" (Cc 1, 251). Saúl Sosnowski calls "El perseguidor" an entry into the critic's workshop ("Pursuers" The Final Island, 166), and notes that writing, in stories such as "El perseguidor" and "Manuscrito," "is a way of objectifying, of trying to understand something that is not logical, of pushing it onto the written page" (164–65). Cortázar's stories invite the reader into the narrator's process of integrating a desired reality.

Paris contributes to this objectifying procedure with the orderly structure of maps, subway stations, bridges, and neighborhoods. The city becomes a written mechanism of control that the stories seek to subvert. Cortázar's narrators occupy a liminal space between competing structures and engage words to write within the urban categories that Paris offers. They often use the present tense ("apenas lo escribo me da asco . . ." ["El perseguidor" Cc 1, 248], "[a]hora que lo escribo . . ." ["Manuscrito" Cc 2, 65]) to stress the continuity of interpretation over the sequential moments of the events. "Axolotl" concludes with a metafictional twist, "me consuela pensar que acaso va a escribir sobre nosotros, creyendo imaginar un cuento va a escribir todo esto sobre los axolotl" (Cc 1, 385). The repetition of "va a escribir" insists on the human need to make sense verbally of the metamorphosis. In each of these cases, writing bridges the past with the present, animals with humans, the illogical with the logical, the fantastic with the conventional.

Writing in Paris in these stories is analogous to traversing the city's bridges in attempts to connect disparate zones of reality. The architectural and metaphysical conspire to allow for the fluid movement that Cortázar's narrators struggle to recount. They find themselves in what Sara Castro-Klarén calls Cortázar's dislocated gaps and porous structures of knowledge ("Ontological Fabulation," in *The Final Island*). These are the metaphysical analogues to Parisian architectural interstices. Both the spatial and metaphysical mediate between European and American cultural and political legacies that seem mutually exclusive but meet in these fictions. The texts, in their architecture and metafiction, provide the connections for exploring (if not ultimately choosing) alternative social and cultural modes.

A number of critics impose on Cortázar's fiction a fantasy/reality polarity that overlooks the metaphysical exploration and geopolitical critique so explicit in his texts' displacements.[31] Castro-Klarén counters this facile dichotomy and confirms his goal of exposing and debunking the social and aesthetic conventions that shape modern urban life:

> The fiction that Cortázar writes is a challenge and a mockery of the empirical epistemology of nineteenth-century realism and twentieth-century everyday understanding of the world, but it is not born out of a simple egotistical desire to do something "new" or escape the "real" world into "fantasy." ("Ontological Fabulation" 144)

His writing opens a communicative space between a variety of possible imaginative realms. The arcades, *métro*, highways, and windows all represent Cortázar's metaphysical interstices. His characters often are split between two geohistorical spaces or two models for understanding the world, and yearn for passage into the most desirous and inaccessible of the two. His stories exemplify what Morelli, in *Rayuela*, suggests in a new novel form:

> rellenar con literatura, presunciones, hipótesis e invenciones los hiatos entre una y otra foto . . . tener que inventar los puentes, o coser los diferentes pedazos del tapiz. . . . (398–99)

The short stories also work toward connecting the pieces—photographs, subway stations, letters, musical notes, biographical details, reflected images—via narrative bridges that pass over the boundaries erected by conventional structures.

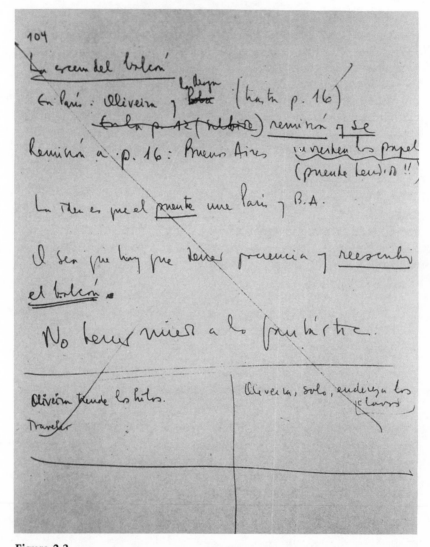

Figure 2.3
Manuscript page from *Rayuela*: "la idea es que el *puente* une París y B. A./o sea que hay que tener paciencia y *reescribir el balcón*" (*Cuaderno de bitácora* ms. 104, p. 226).

Writing is a transnational endeavor for Cortázar, a trans-gressional project that poetically joins contiguous worlds. His narrator/translators write self-consciously of their role as linguistic and cognitive bridges between realms. The metaphor of translation is a commonplace in colonial and postcolonial studies that expresses the continual adaptation required of the individual, the community, and the nation. The limitations of language(s), all too rooted in a culture's epistemology, result in a frustration for these translators who seem unable to clarify their texts. The postcolonial position only obscures their efforts to translate due to nearly inescapable political tropes, economic and aesthetic dependence, and cultural conventions in which Paris is entangled.

"Las babas del diablo" presents a series of translations, from Michel's linguistic translation of a Chilean academic text into French to the visual transference of the enlarged photograph. The narrator, however, problematizes most critically a third level of translation, his verbal rendition of the story itself: "[d]e repente me pregunto por qué tengo que contar esto . . ." (*Cc* 1, 214). His indecision regarding narrative point of view results in an experiment that interrogates the very nature of narrative, communication, and interpretation. In his vacillation between various frames and perspectives, the narrator relinquishes authority over the text to the camera lens. The story privileges the desiring eye that has more power than the word in Paris. The multiple perspectives, from Michel's fifth-floor window, his typewriter, the square at the tip of the island in the very heart of the city, and through his lens, all envision an urban scene of exploitation that language seems powerless to capture. Only through the enlarged *visual* scene does Michel finally apprehend the seduction's intention, and reinserts the man in the car into his interpretation. Like the elusive clients of whoring predators, words in these stories resist enclosure in strict paradigms and, like the postcolonial subject, seek refuge in the interstice.

The architecture of these stories provides metaphors for Cortázar's theories about writing, metaphysics, and postcolonialism. All of these narrators function like translators. They are mediators, between languages and worlds, who write from and of the interstice. Their process is housed in the passageways, windows, arcades, and underground routes that Paris furnishes. Cortázar's fantastic *rendezvous*, spatial and temporal blurring, and eccentric transcendence that rely on Paris are not disconnected from his sociopolitical message. His reworking of the Paris construct reshapes gender and the sociology of artistic creation in metatextual territories. Transnationalism in Paris is neither idealized nor demonized, but rather recontextualized in narrow zones where cultures, languages, and metaphysical perspectives collide and

protagonists confront otherness. Paris in these stories is an interstitial zone of inscription in which the global economy, sexuality
and eroticism, language experimentation, and the engineering of
modernity mark Latin America with the violence of European urban
constructs. Cortázar's texts erect narrative passageways that not
only shelter curious *flâneurs* but launch tenacious investigations
into the metaphysics and politics of postcoloniality.

Chapter Three

The Immovable Feast

———————— ❖ ————————

Paris and Politics in Manuel Scorza's La danza inmóvil

Latin American postcolonial writing contributes to the pervasive debate between urban and rural cultures contesting over definitions of new national identities. The city becomes a symbol of cosmopolitan modernity and foreign artificiality, while rural settings often represent a lack of sophistication more than compensated by "authentic" independence and local vigor. The civilization/ barbarism debate articulated by Sarmiento in the mid-nineteenth century still reverberates in twentieth-century writing. Regional novelists strive to outline an aesthetic project situated in a Latin American landscape rendered independent of European colonial modeling. As regional writers search for an autochthonous voice, their writing inevitably exoticizes and exaggerates local settings. These rural spaces emerge from a tense relationship with urban centers, either at home or abroad. Since the 1920s and 1930s in Latin America, the regional novel has served as a forum for negotiations over cultural identity waged between the country and the city.[1] Untamed nature in these texts functions as both a cultural ideal and a commodity in which local landscape and regional social struggles confront cosmopolitan aesthetics.

Manuel Scorza's oeuvre provides the most dynamic example of a Latin American "regional" writer in dialectical relationship with urban cosmopolitanism. That a book on the role of Paris in Latin American writing dedicates a chapter to Scorza would surprise most of his readers. He is best known as a neoindigenist whose writing adheres to the social convictions of the earlier indigenist literary movement while reflecting some influences of the "boom"'s cosmopolitan aesthetics. His regionalist orientation has not kept Scorza from being perhaps the most translated Peruvian writer. His prolonged European residencies and his Marxist ideology afforded him an array of publishing opportunities beyond the scope of most regionally committed writers.[2] Ironically, despite an aesthetic that critiques multinational exploitation and neocolonialism in contemporary Latin America, Scorza's novels have an even greater transnational distribution than most urban writers. His last novel, *La danza inmóvil* (1983), positions Paris as the nodal point in a series of intersecting cultural and political practices. The novel deconstructs Paris's role in erotic fantasy, revolutionary organization, and literary marketing. This shift away from the topics of his earlier work exposes that in the interval between his novelistic project of the 1970s and his last novel, he came to redefine the "local" as a cultural category much too restrictive in an increasingly global literary market and political economy.

Scorza develops his own Peruvian regional novel in the 1970s that perpetuates the urban/rural tensions so embedded in Latin American cultural politics and writing. His novels dramatize local collective causes that fail to produce lasting social change. The consciousness-raising his fiction proposes reveals an urban bourgeois sensibility trying to grasp a local *mestizo* worldview. He ultimately broadens his narrative horizons to include cosmopolitan political debates and the challenge of continuing European cultural hegemony. Despite his regionalist orientation, Scorza's fiction exposes his own conflicted social identification and reveals the local and the international as interconnected realms. His last novel, *La danza inmóvil*, exposes the blurred boundaries between regional social struggle, international political organizing, and transnational cultural marketing.

Scorza's novelistic production provides an example of fiction as a promoter of social activism, fiction as a potential catalyst for change, and fiction as a self-reflexive political commentary. Difficult to categorize but often labelled "neoindigenist," Scorza's novels encompass the jungle and mountain areas of the Andean region and portray the vast inequities in land ownership and political control between these disadvantaged areas and the more developed Peruvian coast. His five-part narrative "ballad," *La guerra silenciosa*,[3] recounts the peasant organizing in the Cerro de Pasco region in the late 1950s and early 1960s in reaction to the arrival and gradual control over the region of the North American Cerro de

Pasco Corporation. Using the local as a synecdoche for affirming a continental "New World" cultural identity, Scorza's fiction takes on Peru's complex regionalism as a microcosm of class and ethnic conflict and calls for a surge in Marxist activism.

His goal in the first five novels is to raise consciousness about the *serrano* peasants in order to validate their efforts at labor union organizing and to affirm rights to the land. The saga of the community's fight for land rights and the enumeration of injustices suffered at the hands of local officials and transnational corporate employees makes a greater *plea* for action than it outlines a *plan* of action: "La narrativa de Scorza aparece más como una invitación al cambio que como una propuesta de cambio" (Forgues, *Estrategia* 136). Each novel ends in a failed uprising and a bloody massacre. The challenges of postcolonial resistance and action thus compose the ideological preoccupation of these novels. The fifth novel of the series, *La tumba del relámpago*, concludes with a critical perspective on the divisions in the Peruvian Left that have weakened leadership possibilities in local struggles. Scorza clearly links the regional Cerro de Pasco situation to the national context. He begins to broaden his focus as he concludes the five-novel cycle with the acknowledgment that local political battles are being fought on an increasingly global terrain. Subsequently, in *La danza inmóvil*, he exploits the collaboration of the local and the global in textual confrontations that push beyond the boundaries of his earlier work.

Critics have judged harshly Scorza's five-volume saga for a rhetorical position that is feigned or false in the narrative. Carlos Alonso, in his study of the Latin American regional novel, states that regional writing means "becoming an anthropologist to one's own culture" and that the discourse reveals "overwhelming and dizzying familiarity" (5). Scorza's participation in the Cerro de Pasco struggles, however, was a political decision that he made as an outsider with respect to that community. In the prologue to the first volume, *Redoble por Rancas*, Scorza refers to himself as a "witness" and a "chronicler," yet still maintains that he is writing a novel. His positionality remains problematic, and reveals

> las contradicciones de un escritor desvinculado del proletariado y desolidarizado de la pequeña burguesía en los valores de la cual no quería reconocerse, aun cuando formara parte de ella. (Forgues, *Estrategia* 146)

His narrative recipe includes humor, hyperbole, irony, dreams, and fantasy. So-called "eyewitness" reporting exploits superreality to subvert the dominant political order. Despite the politicization of his fantastic poetics, Mabel Moraña and other critics find his vision of the indigenous world artificial and reductionist:

> [l]a estatura mítica que se les confiere desrealiza el significado final de las acciones y las provee de un sentido poético alegorizante. . . . se revelan sucesivamente como espejismos o vanos intentos de acceder a alguna forma de incidencia sobre la realidad. (Moraña 183–85)

According to critics like Moraña, his project results in exoticizing the peasant communities by highlighting their supernatural beliefs and powers. Never a veritable member of the community, Scorza's commitment to the community's struggles is considered an outsider's adopted idealism.

However, what many critics consider Scorza's "distance," inauthenticating humor and dismissive irony actually comprise conscious strategies for the renegotiation and revival of indigenist literary expression. From *La guerra silenciosa*'s first volume, *Redoble por Rancas*, Scorza reveals the emergence of an already hybrid novelistic form that strives to renovate traditional indigenist aesthetics in light of new narrative experiments in Latin America. Conditioned by the *nueva novela* of the 1960s, Scorza's work fuses social realism and mythical fantasy, political critique and ironic humor, *crónica* and fiction.[4] Tomás Escajadillo discusses Scorza in the context of *neoindigenismo* in his recent book, *La narrativa indigenista peruana*, and helps bridge the critical gap between *La guerra silenciosa* and *La danza inmóvil*. Escajadillo mentions four characteristics that distinguish neoindigenist writing from "orthodox" or "traditional" indigenism: the use of magic realism to reveal the Andean mythic universe, intensified lyricism in the narrative prose, the integration of the indigenist "theme" into national issues, and an increasingly complex arsenal of literary techniques (55–78).[5] While *La danza inmóvil* presents an autocritique of the indigenist mode, Scorza's earlier work already demonstrates "una posible intención de trabajar 'al margen del movimiento'" that initiates a "tradición 'contestataria' de la novela indigenista" (Escajadillo 92).

Scorza's *La danza inmóvil*, published just prior to the author's death in 1983, offers a self-reflexive commentary on the author's own experiences and cultural identification. Here Scorza expands

Figure 3.1
Manuel Scorza in Paris in the early 1980s.

his local landscape and cast of characters as he opens his fiction to the contemporary international realm of Leftist organizing that he situates in Paris. *La danza inmóvil* is a metafictional novel that investigates literary production as critically as his earlier novels confronted local political and economic structures. In a challenging aesthetic shift, Scorza offers a transnational autocritique of the Third-World novelist in the international economy.

La danza inmóvil incorporates the many conflicts of an internationally travelled and translated writer who has been committed to local struggles at home but who now lives and publishes abroad. While *La guerra silenciosa*'s aesthetic project linked local social realism to magical realism, *La danza inmóvil* encompasses post–"boom" international cosmopolitanism for a harsh critique of the literary market and commodity culture. This is a self-reflexive document that confronts the doubts and contradictions of his earlier writing. In this last novel, Scorza juxtaposes an Andean peasant revolution with an urban, international world centered in Paris. As the plot vacillates between Peruvian and Parisian settings, the characters waver as well in their affections and commitments to revolutionary activism and international culture represented by Paris. The intra- and intertextual complexity of *La danza inmóvil* straddles Paris and the Peruvian jungle, questioning the transnational production of politics and culture. Scorza examines Leftist activism, regional writing, and international literary marketing along with his own position in cultural and political projects. His evaluation finds all of these processes inextricably interconnected and all of their endeavors ideologically compromised.

La danza inmóvil is Scorza's first "urban" novel, "una reflexión sobre el arte y la nación" (Forgues, *Palabra* 88). He intermingles a critique of both neoindigenist and urban cosmopolitan literary conventions in a hybrid genre that links local, sociopolitical struggle with international sentimentality. The novel employs Paris as the complex stage for the play of political, erotic, aesthetic, and textual rivalries. Scorza draws on Paris's legendary promise of sexual adventure for expatriate men and of firsthand contact with European high culture to expose the city as a fossilized touristic museum for failed romantic and erotic fantasy. While these aspects of the novel portray the traditional disillusionment with the City of Light (Salazar Bondy, Güiraldes), the novel's real innovation derives from its cultural politics. The plot includes the story of its own production, in a metanarrative that ironically criticizes the transnational production of a large corpus of contemporary Latin American fiction.

Scorza reveals Paris's role in a commercial network of publishing centers that appropriates Latin American narrative. He sharpens his critique of Paris's (and Europe's) publishing hegemony by according the city the role of an international gathering place for revolutionary activists. In *La danza inmóvil*, Paris becomes a double-edged sword for the writer/activist who strives to take advantage of its position in both the literary market and Pan-Latin American revolutionary struggle.

STRUCTURAL TENSION IN *LA DANZA INMÓVIL*

The novel has a contrapuntal structure with three stories that alternate among the chapters, and Paris provides the setting or the imaginary reference for all of these strands. The Paris publishing world is the first of the three, introduced in the novel's opening scene. The business negotiation at the famous literary brasserie La Coupole between a Peruvian novelist and a Parisian publisher continues in fragments throughout the novel, and provides the frame for the other tales.[6] The story of the Latin American novelist's search for recognition in Paris alternates with chapters recounting the revolutionary guerrilla Nicolás's escape through the Amazon, and the third, a love story, between the Peruvian writer Santiago and Marie Claire. Both subplots overlap with and depend on the frame. In the romance, for example, Santiago turns out to be a revolutionary as well as a writer, and Marie Claire is the woman who caught his eye during lunch earlier that afternoon at La Coupole. The scene at La Coupole leads into the revelation of the writer's revolutionary novel in the intercalated chapters. At the same time, the boredom, hypocrisy, and humiliating alienation of the lunch scene cause the writer's romantic imagination to "write" himself into a new story, the romance with Marie Claire.

The initial scene continues throughout the novel as a recurrent frame to offer a scathingly bitter but humorous critique of the international literary marketing of Latin American contemporary fiction. A Peruvian novelist in Paris, desperate to publish, enters La Coupole. Among Japanese tourists, American politicians, and Eastern European Nobel-winning scientists, he endures lunch with the editor of Universal Publishers and the Mexican director of their "New World" collection. The novel he hopes to sell them is about a captured Peruvian guerrilla fighter in the Amazon who relives significant episodes of his life before undergoing torture. When the series director disparagingly associates the Peruvian's novel with the earthy regional narrative of the 1920s, the unpublished guest retorts in defense, "En mi libro, hay personajes que narran la historia desde París" (Scorza, *Danza* 17). The mention of Paris reconnects his work with the urban, international current of Latin American writing and distances it from local nationalistic settings. The novel's self-reflexivity positions the autobiographical character as a conflicted member of a transnational cultural economy that targets the commoditization of Latin American fiction.

Desire, or the romantic pursuit of an ideal, governs all three of the novel's interwoven plots. The sensual and erotic episodes of Nicolás's and Santiago's tales, in their respective pursuits of freedom and of their Parisian lovers, run parallel to the writer's pursuit of publishing. The sensuality and suspense of Nicolás's escape through the Amazon and Santiago's affair with Marie Claire frequently shadow and overtake the frame scene, which temporarily disappears in the novel. Yet the common reference point for erotic desire in all three subplots is Paris, its cafés, cultural establishments, and beautiful women. The names of restaurants, bars, and cafés, an enumeration beginning in the first chapter, immediately associate erotic desire with institutionalized signs (usually French) for sensual pleasure: Las Delicias, Le Rendez Vous, L'Etoile d'Or. La Coupole is the crowned setting, the Parisian domed height that brings the writer to the threshold of publishing success and erotic adventure. There a contract may be negotiated, and there the most beautiful woman will greet him. Santiago and Marie Claire experience (in the writer's fantasy) vestiges of Paris as the only place where one can experience "el encanto de lo inesperado," the "danza inmóvil" where a painting in the Louvre momentarily comes alive (168). Almost within his reach, Paris once again seems to promise the satisfaction of all desires, but that promise is deceptive. The irony of *La danza inmóvil*'s frame lies in its skillfully maintained critical distance. Santiago's publishing saga manages repeatedly to lure the characters and the reader into the city's romanticized traps while at the same time revealing the hypocritical mechanisms at work in the Latin American cultural construct of Paris.

The two subplots, one Andean and one Parisian, come to an end, fatefully circumscribed within the initial frame. Finally, Nicolás's flashback catches up with him, and he is captured and tied to the tree where he will be devoured by ants. Santiago decides, within his fantasy, to abandon the revolutionary struggle in order to stay with Marie Claire. But his illusions are destroyed when he discovers her at an orgy of Parisian artists in the sculpture studio of an old Peruvian friend.

The final chapters of the novel follow these dramatic *dénouements* and return to the luncheon scene at La Coupole. Here Scorza's integration of dreams and fantasy plays an important role in concluding the metafiction, as the character's fantasies subvert the capitalistic marketing of his novel.[7] Two alternative conclusions link the love affair that ocurred only in the writer's imagination, what Scorza calls "un sueño soñado" (Forgues, *Palabra* 88), with the "real" scenario of publishing negotiations in Paris. In both versions, Marie Claire approaches their table, in one version as the publisher's daughter, in the other as his press agent. Both personae want to meet Santiago, first because she has read his books, and then because she recognizes him and recalls their imagined affair. He will not pardon her for the pain of "la pasión inmemorial que me había consumido mientras ella cruzaba por entre las mesas, por entre todas las mesas de todos los restaurantes del mundo" (236). In both cases, the writer resists her recognition, denying that he is the Santiago of either story with which she associates him. He abruptly leaves the restaurant, refusing to attach his identity to either fiction. He is wounded by his own imagined tale and disdains the Parisian publishing world that provoked it.

The narrator of *La danza inmóvil* criticizes the Paris that is considered an aesthetic ideal according to certain class and cultural conventions in Latin America. However, he resigns himself to the reality of Paris's power to manipulate and influence significant elements in the formation of the literary canon. In fact, he embraces the very power factors he disdains in the pursuit of a publishing contract for his novel in Paris. Scorza publishes *his* novel in Barcelona, entangled in the same entrepreneurial cultural mechanisms that his novel's story exposes. The novel ironically illustrates Paris's ubiquitous presence as an iconographic representative of European culture in the Latin American cultural conception of aesthetic standards adopted by some urban elites. It is not French *literature* that this novel designates, but Paris as the *axis mundi* for all high culture. For Scorza, the Louvre, the Bibliotèque Nationale, European classical music, wine labels, French cuisine, and architecture all circulate as signs of high culture. Paris is the meeting place for revolutionaries, Leftist intellectuals, and expatriate artists, as well as the repository for art's canonical forms.

The versions of Paris and the Amazon outlined in *La danza inmóvil* superimpose a mythic concentration of meanings and references onto the concrete, geographical realities and contributions of a culture. Scorza grounds his "settings" in the historical past, what he calls the "histórico real," as well as in the superreal, or "mitológico":

> un nivel histórico real, que ha sido ratificado siempre por quienes han ido al lugar, con personajes reales que están vivos; y hay también un nivel mitológico, fantástico, que exige sin embargo una aclaración: no utilizo el Mito como un escape de la realidad, sino como una aclaración de la realidad. (Forgues, *Palabra* 81)

For Scorza, both the Andean and the European settings function mythically on several levels. Paris harbors romantic fantasy and nostalgic reminiscing as well as the business realities of international publishing. The Amazonian scenes, with their suspenseful episodes of escaping prisoners and revolutionary organizing, function as illustrations of an exotic, touristy travelog.

PARIS IN THE LITERATURE OF LATIN AMERICAN LEFTIST ACTIVISM

Scorza does not overlook direct political critique within his metafictional meditation on global cultural currents. In fact, he uses Paris in *La danza inmóvil* not only to attack European cultural hegemony and the "Third-World" intellectuals that perpetuate it, but also to examine the state of the political Left in Latin America. As Robert Siegle states in *The Politics of Reflexivity*,

> Reflexivity suggests that narrative derives its authority not from the "reality" it imitates, but from the cultural conventions that define both narrative and the construct we call "reality." (225)[8]

Scorza uses fiction as a semiotic training ground for his proposal of revolutionary poetics and politics. He attacks the conventions that motivate cultural production along with those that foment ideological posturing. *La danza inmóvil* asserts the interconnectedness of the political and the literary through its self-conscious and self-critical structure.

Scorza continues the debates and conversations that conclude *La tumba del relámpago* on transnational ground in *La danza inmóvil*. The last novel of *La guerra silenciosa* chronicles the tension in Peruvian party politics and labor unions, and thereby expands the focus from the local *serrano* struggles onto a more urban and national domain. The novel ends with a pessimistic critique of the Latin American Left's imported ideology, which is blamed for the peasants' failures. "La desgracia de nuestras luchas es que no coinciden con nuestras ideologías; la rabia, el coraje son de aquí, y las ideas son de allá" (*Tumba* 235). The political scientist Jorge Castañeda similarly chastises Latin American intellectuals for their importation of ideologies.[9] While Castañeda recognizes the contribution of intellectuals ("They have bridged the multiple chasms opening wide between the rest of the world and Latin American political and economic elites" [180]), Scorza voices concern for the authenticity of political ideals and notes the often strained application of foreign notions to Andean social struggles. Scorza's candid critique of the Left coincides with his doubts about his own efficacy in the movement. The novel calls for an urgent reorientation and internationalization of the Left from its local, national, and continental dimensions.

The evaluation and reshaping of armed Leftist activism from *La tumba del relámpago* to its projection onto a transnational arena in *La danza inmóvil* reflect the shifts in the Latin American Left in the 1970s and 1980s. While the Cuban Revolution motivated international unity among Leftist groups and parties in Latin America in the 1960s and the early 1970s, changes in political focus diluted this idealistic cohesion. The emphasis in the 1960s on fighting poverty and denouncing dependency shifted in the later 1970s, particularly in response to the dictatorships of the Southern Cone, toward a resistance to authoritarian rule that stressed democracy and human rights. Cuba's initially indirect mythic influence (see Castañeda 186–87) turned strategically instrumental in the late 1970s with the island's decisive support of Central American revolutionary activity. Scorza also anticipates the global focus of cultural criticism in the 1990s, such as García Canclini's recent book on consumer culture that calls for "formas supranacionales y poslocales de administrar los conflictos" (*Consumidores y ciudadanos* 194).

The doubts, personal conflicts, and crises of conscience among the characters in *La danza inmóvil* reflect the political climate of the Left in the 1980s in the move away from party politics toward grassroots movements.[10] The conflicts that tear at Nicolás and

Santiago demonstrate that Leftist identification was undergoing
another major reconceptualization. The novel demystifies Paris's role
as a harbor for high culture and avant-garde art. In its place, the city
occupies the role of transnational coordination of armed rebellion.
The characters' vacillating commitments to their causes purportedly
are motivated by their Parisan romances. The displaced revolution
waged on transnational ground lacks the immediacy, idealism, and
active engagement of the Left's local and regional operations. The
lingering seductive power of an anachronistically eroticized Paris
triumphs over the politicized Paris whose allegiances are elsewhere.

Alongside the compromised role of cultural producer, Paris
serves *La danza inmóvil* as a gathering place for international revolutionary activists. This role for Paris accomplishes more than a
geopolitical transition in Scorza's work from the regional spaces of
La guerra silenciosa into a global arena. It also recontextualizes the
Latin American Paris construct as a strategic site for transnational
Leftist organizing. This renewed role, one that Cortázar exploits in
Libro de Manuel, and that Alfredo Bryce Echenique also examines
in *La vida exagerada de Martín Romaña* (see chapter 4), ironically
undercuts Paris's cultural hegemony for characters who use the
city to plan international subversive maneuvers for effecting change
in Latin America. The brief comparative discussion to follow on *La
danza inmóvil* and *Libro de Manuel* exemplifies the correlation
between politics and eroticism in these versions of the Latin
American Paris construct.

Cortázar's *Libro de Manuel* (1973) serves as Scorza's central
intertext for his last novel and as his principal source for the Paris
construct in Latin American culture. Paris serves *La danza inmóvil*
as its political and erotic referent for all of its narrative threads
through the city's function, as in *Libro de Manuel,* as an international revolutionary meeting place. Scorza's intertextual revision en-
capsulates the unresolved issues of human rights, access to resources,
neocolonialism, and political subversion in Latin America. Both of
these novels stand in marked relief to the regional tensions that
escalated just after their publication. Scorza did not predict the expansion of Sendero Luminoso in the 1980s in Peru, just as Cortázar
did not prophesy the terrifying military regimes that would take
over in the 1970s in the Southern Cone. Nevertheless, both writers
foresaw the need for an increasingly radicalized aesthetic that could
confront political problems through both content and form.

In their language and structure, both novels employ a centrifu-
gal movement that dispels the Europeanizing metropolitanism of

the Latin American Paris construct. *La danza inmóvil*'s resonance of *Libro de Manuel* draws from five significant elements: Parisian cultural institutions, codified language, French female characters, political indecision, and metafictionality. Each of these realms offers Paris a pivotal role in the plot and structure of the two novels. Both Scorza and Cortázar spurn the high-culture image of Paris, its social prestige and artistic allure with their "desbarajuste de la sacralización de París" (Reichardt 210). These novels replace the notion of Paris as a hegemonic cultural center with a Paris that functions as an arbitrary site for a random and temporary cluster of marginal characters who eventually disperse.

La danza inmóvil reconfigures the conventional narrative map of Paris, its street scenes, strolling *flâneurs,* and riverside vistas, and turns the city into an international hub for Latin American subversive organizing. Scorza converts the city into a crossroads for smuggled cash, falsified passports, and hidden *compañeros.* Neighborhoods and subway stops in Scorza's novel map out "los compañeros dispersos en la clandestinidad de París" (125). One chapter reunites fellow revolutionaries from Bolivia, Peru, and Cuba through furtive exchanges about briefcases full of cash, airport itineraries, and secret meetings. Similarly, in Cortázar's *Libro de Manuel,* even making love in Paris serves to "establecer un territorio fugitivo de contacto" (*LM* 151). Paris becomes a metaphorical airport or train station where characters hurriedly meet, hide, and then flee again.

These two novels deflate Paris as a paragon of high culture through the manipulation of spatially and culturally charged reference points that are all drawn from the Paris construct. While Cortázar presents Paris's seamy subculture of prostitutes and striptease bars in *Libro de Manuel,*[11] Scorza attacks the city's hegemonic cultural institutions. Both novels decenter the plot away from the Latin Quarter—bohemian Paris's literary cliché—to situate important scenes in alternative neighborhoods. *Libro de Manuel* disperses the action to the Marais, the Place Clichy, Pigalle, and cafés along the city's working-class periphery. When one of the characters arrives in Paris for the first time and asks if he is in the center of the city, another replies, "Aquí no hay lo que se llama un centro, o el centro está un poco en todas partes" (*LM* 156).

La danza inmóvil grafts its plot onto a touristic cultural itinerary, making stops at sites such as La Coupole, the Jardin du Luxembourg, the Ile St. Louis, and the Louvre. As the novel "empties" Paris of its symbolic vigor, it strips its cultural icons and renders them hollow rituals. García Canclini includes the Louvre in his discussion of hegemonic artistic institutions, symbols of "traditions" and "territories" that modern culture challenges. The Louvre, like other high-culture domains, has become "un programa iconográfico que dramatiza ritualmente el triunfo de la civilización francesa, la consagra como heredera de los valores de la humanidad" (*Culturas híbridas* 45). *La danza inmóvil* is less concerned to critique French cultural institutions than to expose the Latin American (and generally international) valorization of them. Scorza counters that semiotization of France for external consumption with a novel about itinerant artists and revolutionaries who "producen fuera de sus países y descontextualizan los objetos" (García Canclini, *Culturas híbridas* 48).

Both *Libro de Manuel* and *La danza inmóvil* radicalize language as they propose strategies for building a new social and political order. Their language games challenge petrified thinking in attacks on the restrictive linguistic and social codes that postcolonialism and neocolonialism impose. Lonstein's neologistic rambling in *Libro de Manuel* undermines commonly accepted modes of communication. Scorza employs analogous language play in *La danza inmóvil* to describe Santiago and Marie Claire's passion:

> Subibijábamos al sueño. Dormidespertábamos. Y nueva-
> mente moriviviamos, odioamábamos, sueñidespertábamos,
> desaparexistíamos. Y nuevamente depeasoñipaci-
> fidespertábamos, descaradamente felices. (66–67)

This passage underscores the connection between conventionally contradictory realms of experience, a connection that the entire novel strives to reassert. Santiago's dilemma consists of seemingly wrenching choices, between love and revolution, poetry and politics, and words and action. His erotic romance with Marie Claire (whom he first speaks to in the Jardin du Luxembourg when he sees her reading Marx) serves to heighten his sense of conflict and also to reveal the false imposition and inherent narcissism of those categories.

These two novels also satirize the practice of certain genres of writing through language play. The collage and continual translation of European and Anglo-American journalism in *Libro de Manuel* subvert the appropriation of information and the imposition of versions of those reported events as they are recontextualized in the novel and the scrapbook. *La danza inmóvil* pays homage to

Libro de Manuel and its journalistic collage in a brief scene in which Marie Claire manipulates newspaper headlines to create "mis propias noticias":

> Marie Claire había redactado su periódico, pegado los textos sobre una hoja de diario verdadero, compuesto los titulares con esas letras de imprenta que utilizan los artistas gráficos en sus trabajos. (89–90)

The material substance of this example demonstrates the physicality of language that manifests in cultural objects. Ultimately it refers to fiction like *Libro de Manuel* and *La danza inmóvil* that directly exhibit their textual building blocks.

Scorza's novel more extensively parodies the wilderness adventure novel and the action film (Westerns), with cinematographic flashbacks and cuts, in the intercalated chapters of the Amazonian novel. Here Scorza critiques the exoticization of the "natural" American landscape and its commodification for export. The narration in these sections is as sensual and bodily as in the erotic scenes in Paris, and again serves to link the local and the cosmopolitan through language. The novel attacks the expectations of literature that, as Djelal Kadir critiques, "belongs to 'exotic' regions and other-world cultures through which cosmopolitan readers expect to be taken on tour" (Kadir xi). The text intermingles *dolor* and *deseo*, hunger and thirst, physical torture and physical pleasure in both the Amazonian and Parisian scenes to cross over the expected regional boundaries.

Names, as connotative markers and signs of identity, become particularly crucial to deciphering these novels' transnational worlds. Just as Cortázar's short fiction often relies on women's names to mark shifting territory (Josiane in "El otro cielo," for example), *Libro de Manuel* and *La danza inmóvil* depend on the names of the protagonists' lovers to unravel the politics of the Paris construct. Francine, in *Libro de Manuel*, and Francesca, in *La danza inmóvil*, function as synecdochal figures, not only of France but of the phenomenon of the Latin American Parisian gaze. As variants of "France," these names serve the novels as linguistic, gendered embodiments of sexual motifs related to Paris. Rather than characters, these names introduce depersonalized signs that point to a commodification of both women and Paris. The names take on the function of consumer tags that advertise the conflation of the city and the body and associate bourgeois cosmopolitanism with sexual consumerism. Andrés refers to Francine as the "francesita libresca y cartesiana" (145); she works in a bookstore in the Marais, one of Paris's oldest historic districts, whose proprietor is Madame Franck. Along with Francesca, *La danza inmóvil*'s Marie Claire and Colette form a cluster of cultural icons that the novel ironically strips of personhood or "characterization" in the hollow reductionism of their connotative context. Beyond their linguistic roots, these French names tap cultural realms (the writer Colette, the magazine *Marie Claire*) that evoke and contribute to the image and politics of Paris for Latin American urban identity. These names and their characters' fictional roles feature commercial endeavors—prostitution, bookselling, and popular press magazines—that link them to Paris as merchandise the city offers for sale.

The metafictionality of *La danza inmóvil* (the fragmentation and pastiche, a novel within the novel, multiple narrators and "authors") recalls the collage aesthetic of *Libro de Manuel*.[12] The parallel stories Scorza fragments and intersperses suggest a book (or books) in the making. The structure sustains ambiguity about which story or book (if not all of them collectively) is posing as the "fictional" manuscript entitled *La danza inmóvil*, by the deferral and distrust of all of the plot's threads. While Scorza's earlier work does experiment with narrative voices and metafictionality, his last novel presents a much more radical revision of novelistic practice. Both texts consider books highly suspect, "esos fósiles necesitados de una implacable gerontología" (*LM* 25). These novels propose alternative, revolutionary books that show their seams (the cut-and-paste of *Libro de Manuel*, the abrupt intercalations and overt contract negotiations in *La danza inmóvil*) and thereby divulge the process of their own emergence as cultural objects.

The protagonists' indecision and self-interrogation over their political stance feed the fragmentary, vacillating structure of the two novels. Andrés's cinematographic dream in *Libro de Manuel* awakens his awareness about his political purpose, but not without a nagging uncertainty: "soy un hombre que tiene una misión que cumplir, pero mientras lo estoy sabiendo y sobre todo sintiendo, sé también que no tengo la menor idea de cuál es esa misión" (110). The compiler "el que te dije" also questions the underlying motives of their project and the political effectiveness of writing. Both Santiago and Nicolás in *La danza inmóvil* cling to their amorous experiences in Paris. Santiago falls into the trap of love versus revolution when he is seduced by Paris.

[M]e recordaban la lucha que pronto afrontarían mis compañeros. 'Afrontarían,' pensé, en vez de 'afrontaremos', y angustiado dije en voz alta: 'afrontaremos', pero en mis palabras sentí el desasosiego de quienes, para disimular el temor que les producen los parajes solitarios, se hablan a sí mismos. (161)

Nicolás's memories of Francesca are apparently more vital to his survival than the revolutionary cause. Toward the end of the novel he and Nicolás meet in Paris, a metafictional encounter between "fictional" and "real" characters that results in dramatic didacticism as Santiago confesses to Nicolás his doubts about his future as a revolutionary. In a café on the rue Voltaire, drinking *Beaujolais*, Nicolás is not successful in persuading Santiago to remain faithful to the cause.

These novels expose the inadequacies of a verbal revolution in severe critiques of wordy philosophizing. Santiago in *La danza inmóvil* and Andrés and "el que te dije" in *Libro de Manuel* struggle with the choice between words and action.[13] The paradox of revolutionary literature is precisely that it produces more words than change. Scorza confronts this contradiction throughout his last novel in order to demonstrate how fiction (and all cultural production) perpetuates class divisions and hegemonic cultural politics. As García Canclini suggests, "los *gestos* de ruptura de los artistas, que no logran convertirse en *actos* (intervenciones eficaces en procesos sociales), se vuelven *ritos*" (*Culturas híbridas* 44). Staging Santiago's inner conflicts in Paris starkly reveals his less-than-repressed bohemian fantasy, his vacillating political commitment to revolutionary change for Latin America, and his desperate aspiration for success in the global, cultural marketplace.

The intertext of *Libro de Manuel* in *La danza inmóvil* underscores Scorza's reevaluation of art and literature. Art for Scorza and Cortázar does not occupy an isolated and protective realm for private consumption; rather, it expresses the intersection of journalism, criticism, history, political commentary, publicity, education, and tourism. Both novels demand to be read such that the various metafictional threads leave questions and gaps, in order to establish dynamic interactions among story levels as well as with their social contexts and with the reader. "Analizar el arte ya no es analizar sólo obras, sino las condiciones textuales y extratextuales, estéticas y sociales, en que la interacción entre miembros del campo engendra y renueva el sentido" (García Canclini, *Culturas híbridas*

143). While Cortázar's *Libro de Manuel* calls for extreme subversion in language play and political action, Scorza's *La danza inmóvil* takes Latin American Leftists to task in a self-critical stance that also implicates him as a novelist and an intellectual in Europe.

PARIS AND CULTURAL PRODUCTION
IN *LA DANZA INMÓVIL*

Scorza's last novel documents through fiction the changes in Paris's image and role as the text considers its own creation, production, legitimation, and distribution. While previous communities of writers proffered an image of the city as the capital of literary inspiration, *La danza inmóvil* designates Paris as a strategic territory for commercial recognition. The local Andean scenes of revolutionary struggle at the core of Scorza's earlier novels are subordinate in *La danza inmóvil* to narrative experiments that incorporate and problematize the hegemony of Paris and European capitals on Latin American cultural production. *La danza inmóvil* demystifies Paris by exposing the city's control over literary production. Scorza punctuates his narrative discourse with intertextual signs of Paris's transitional and multifaceted role in Latin American culture.

Scorza's novel fictionally documents the shift in Paris's image and role from a bohemian fantasy to a center for cultural legitimation and commercial success. As one of the required first steps toward international recognition, Paris has become an essential determiner of the canon or "list" of works accepted and included in the hegemony of cultural institutionalism.[14] Particularly since the international "boom" in Latin American narrative since the 1960s, Paris and a handful of other European capitals have contracted, published, translated, marketed, and distributed Latin American fiction. At the plot level as well as within its structure and discourse, *La danza inmóvil* criticizes the control that Paris has exerted on aesthetic sensibilities and marketing strategies.

The "boom" marketing of Latin American fiction in the 1960s and 1970s functions as an economic backdrop to Scorza's novel. Hernán Vidal associates the "boom" with the apogee of consumerism in which Latin American narrative is transformed into "mercancía de distribución y consumo masivos, sometido a sistemas de propaganda, promoción y comercialización similares a los del cine, la televisión, la ropa de moda y los aparatos de uso casero" (*Literatura* 67). The history of the "boom" reveals a complex transnational network that includes Paris, Barcelona, and a few Latin American publishing capitals as co-producers of a new international market.[15] With this transnational commercialization of Latin American culture, many Leftist critics in the 1970s warned against estrangement from local concerns amidst the North American and European literary and marketing currents. Vidal also criticizes the contradictions between the supposed Leftist ideology of many "boom" writers and the capitalist system that assured their success. These writers "intentan una crítica autosindicada como revolucionaria contra los efectos de la dependencia que les dieran prominencia histórica" (Vidal, *Literatura* 67).

Although *La danza inmóvil* would seem to scorn this literary market phenomenon along with critics like Vidal, Scorza's attitude is ambivalent. That Scorza published this last novel in Barcelona only adds to the irony of his self-critique. Despite the obvious first-world appropriation of Latin American culture as an exotic "other," Scorza recognized this newly emerging and expanding readership as the "primer territorio verdaderamente libre de América." Alluding to the writers of his generation, he affirms,

> hemos creado una instancia pública, superior al poder de información de una prensa minada por la burguesía; porque nosotros, los escritores, todos juntos, tenemos millones de lectores, una especie de gran plaza pública donde [se] discute. (Campra 178)

For Scorza, literature that acquires the dimensions of the popular public square entails added ideological responsibility. In the late 1950s, Scorza started his own publishing endeavor called Populibros that produced inexpensive massive editions of novels that were sold at literary street fairs. Scorza's project dovetailed with the international "boom" as a countermarketing effort that provided accessible editions for local readers.[16]

La danza inmóvil exemplifies the "boom's" popular and international consequences and Scorza's scrutiny of cultural production trends in which he actively, if ambivalently, participates. Clearly, an important corpus of Latin American narrative still looks to Paris for recognition in both the intercontinental and inter-American canon. Notable Peruvian critic and publisher Abelardo Oquendo calls a stay in Paris "the intellectual's obligatory military service."[17] A contemporary Uruguayan critic and an anthologist in Paris, in 1990, calls French the "vehicular language" and Paris the bridge to enable writers to begin publishing, and then to continue publishing in other languages within Europe.[18] According to many Latin American intellectuals, contact with Europe, and preferably Paris, is acknowledged, recommended, and sometimes even required for literary success.

Connections with the European publishing industry are not only essential for publishing internationally but also for establishing the writer's reputation at home. David Lagmanovich divided Argentine writers into two distinct territories: Buenos Aires and "el interior" (the provinces). In his critique of the control of the capital and of international publishing, he states that the writers from the provinces cannot become "autores argentinos" until they have published in Europe.[19] Paris as literary capital legitimates Latin American literature, assigning it new value through the city's intellectual and cultural institutions. Paris helps create Latin American narrative as a commodity, marketing and distributing it as an appropriated European good whose value is attributed and whose canon is in large part determined via transnational interactions. The texts that participate in this appropriation yield to European cultural hegemony that controls their distribution.[20]

La danza inmóvil reveals the conflictual bargaining, the negotiation of Latin American identity, within a Europeanizing cultural market. The novel includes the story of its own emergence as a cultural commodity, incorporating the legal negotiations, media campaigns, and literary public relations as ironic metaproductional twists. Scorza's incorporation of Paris in its canon forming and publishing role in *La danza inmóvil* constitutes an elaborate example of the thematic and discursive results of this crosscultural production of literature.[21]

This novel is Scorza's critique of the "boom," and even more specifically, his critique of *literatos* "que han convertido a París en un eje central y motivador de su labor artística y observan a América desde La Coupole, desde le Jardin des Plantes. . . ." (Gutierrez 38). In the same way in which he attacks those he considers false intellectuals, Scorza criticizes the Paris that perpetuates a deceptive trap. *La danza inmóvil* empties Paris of its idealized cultural contents:

> . . . salgo a la calle: vacía; recorro el Boulevard: vacío; paso las tardes en la Biblioteca Nacional: vacía; me embriago en L'Etoile d'Or: vacía . . . bebo vino en la Taverne de Henri IV: vacía . . . cruzo semanas vacías y por el día vacío tambaleándome deambulo hacia la noche vacía de París vacío. (215)

Ultimately, Paris abandons the characters. The all-enveloping world they projected results in a cold, touristic place where they spend only fleeting moments. In *La danza inmóvil*, the characters are triumphant neither in politics nor in passion. Santiago plans to abandon the cause, and the novel ends without any clear conclusion. The city of seduction cannot save Nicolás from his torture, nor can it answer Santiago's various confused quests. It is Paris that leads him to trade in his revolutionary ideals for romantic fantasies, which are in turn abruptly dispelled by the city's literary bureaucracy.

Paris never delivers what the characters presume it promises. Scorza attacks on emotional and political grounds what García Canclini analyzes from the perspective of consumerism and communications:

> Además de la ciudad histórica, la de los monumentos y los barrios que atestiguan el espesor de los siglos, y la ciudad industrial, desplegada desde los años cuarenta, existe la *ciudad globalizada*, que se conecta con las redes mundiales de la economía, las finanzas y las comunicaciones. (*Consumidores y ciudadanos* 69)

The novel strips the city of symbolic vigor. What is left are wandering remnants of deflated illusions. Juxtaposition with the Amazon and revelation of Paris's disillusioning underside expose the literary capital as an institutionally controlling network.

THE GLOBAL IN THE LOCAL

Scorza's *La danza inmóvil* demonstrates the political dimensions of contemporary debates over high culture and mass culture, urban and regional writing, and postcolonial identity. His last novel not only explores stylistic and structural innovations but also demands scrutiny of the international publishing industry and of the idea and practice of revolution for Latin America. For Scorza, politics, business, and culture are inextricably linked processes. Writing engages the novelist in a global endeavor, a project that produces culture as a commodity while it examines the political nature of verbal expression and reconfigures the dynamics of transnational interactions. Cultural commodification corrupts aesthetics, degrades emotions, and empties the icons of national or regional identification of their meaning. On the other hand, it also boosts distribution, promotes translations, and encourages the trafficking of new objects that redefine the politics of the local and the global.

In the transnational and crosscultural process of *La danza inmóvil*, the lines between the European and Latin American worlds often blur. Beyond the inclusion of Paris as theme and structure, the discourse registers the story's various worlds in linguistic and semiotic interpenetration. Signs that generally pertain to one world begin to appear in the other. Streets, names, foods, indigenous versus European references, and lexicon intermix, serving as shifters or points of crosscultural contact. While *La danza inmóvil* initially appears to designate clearly separated realms—the guerrilla's escape in the Amazon and the writer in Paris—eventually the characters in the Amazon reminisce about previous romantic escapades in Paris, and Santiago's identity as a doubting revolutionary fuses with that of the writer in Paris.

Rivers often serve as pivotal signs in the discourse's rich texture, effective and subtle shifters since they belong in both the Parisian and the Amazonian zones of the novel. Toward the end of the novel, one chapter ends with Santiago leaning on the railing of one of the bridges over the Seine, considering suicide; "miró otra vez las aguas sucias del Sena. . . ." (220). The next chapter begins as Nicolás "siente amor por el río, acaricia el lomo de aguas pardas, el poderoso flanco del río por donde su balsa desciende victoriosa" (221). A street in Paris, the rue du Comandant Gibau, bifurcates in its simultaneous references to the military (echoing military titles familiar among the Peruvian rebels) and to French history. Marie Claire is another split sign as her name simultaneously indicates both a character in the Paris scenes and the title of the French magazine that the soldiers talk about in the Amazon. Rather than distinct, polarized cultural and discursive territories, the signs throughout the narrative reflect the fluid overlapping boundaries of transnational cultural production.

Extensive episodes enmesh the language and objects of the novel's competing territories. Franklin Gutierrez calls this Scorza's multidirectional language. He finds in particular a central contrast between the military sections, with their brusque and imperative tone, and the soft, sensual poetic tone of the love story. Other contrasts throughout the novel juxtapose Marxist philosophy and high-culture aestheticism, or cosmopolitan romance and jungle survival. In the chapter entitled "Francesca entre los lagartos," for example, Nicolás reminisces about Francesca, his lover in Paris, while in the midst of his escape through the Amazon. The short chapter is decorated with the flora and fauna of the Amazon: names of trees (*tangana, shapaja*) and birds, foods (*mate, yuca*), descriptions of the jungle's heat and its victim's thirst. Sensual memories of Francesca are laced throughout this suspenseful scene that finds the hero on the brink of death. He grasps for the memory of an evening with Francesca in Paris, drinking Sancerre, listening to Mozart, undressing her:

> El trató de no ver la blusa demasiado entreabierta, el comienzo de los senos, las aguas empedradas de lagartos blancos hasta seis metros miden estas bestias, cientos de lagartos rayan el agua. . . . (170)

The discourse synchronizes, in the same sentence, Parisian romance with Amazonian peril. Nicolás tries to resist Francesca's seduction, considering

> lo importante que, según Lenin, es sustituir el parlamentarismo verbal y corrupto de la burguesía por organismos inventados por la Comuna, donde la libertad de opinión y de discusión no degenere en engaño, pero el aliento de Francesca le quemó la nuca de la burguesía, el cuello del parlamentarismo venal y corrupto, la piel tibia de los organismos inventados por la Comuna, la catarata negra de los cabellos de Lenin y supo que no podría seguir viviendo sin lanzarse a ese precipicio. (171–72)

The signs of sensual stimuli emerge from all of the novel's textual realms: erotic desire, political struggle, and cultural production and identification. The precipice is simultaneously the space on the verge of amorous seduction, between life and death in the jungle, and eventually the deciding bridge between personal and political commitment. The publishing lunch at La Coupole, degrading and humiliating for the writer, provides the frame within which various textual levels contend for space to be imagined, written, and published. The passions of individual liberty and collective causes battle it out, competing for chapters, outdoing one another in sensual imagery, danger, and suspense. Neither of them wins, for neither political causes nor individual romance can stage a victory over the European literary capital's commercialization of words.

La danza inmóvil subtly includes an evaluation of his earlier novelistic project through the articulation between political activism and cultural production. In approaching Scorza's novelistic production as a whole, his last novel, rather than contradicting his earlier fiction, responds to his current situation as an artistic creator and activist. If *La guerra silenciosa* is a call to action, then *La danza inmóvil* is an invitation to educated intellectual leadership to take stock of its position, acknowledge its regional biases, and come to terms with inevitable compromises. Scorza's last novel exposes failure on the part of individuals and of local, regional, and international political practice. The novel turns these limitations into a critique of itself as a text, as fragmented and compromised as its parts.

Scorza's last novel reveals his dissatisfaction with literary genres as well as with modes of political activism. His work confirms the need for renovating the forms and discourses of both. As Frederick Buell describes in *National Culture and the New Global System*,

> . . .we have been inventing new pasts to serve our altered needs, new narratives (including narratives of the failure of narrative) to tell ourselves the story of how we got to a present different from what was previously expected. . . . (7)

Scorza's novelistic projects attempt to invent new solutions in apocalyptic and magical worlds. With his last novel, he constructs a metafictional universe that superimposes the persistence of Paris in Latin American cultural consciousness over the transnationalization of previously local struggles. The novel's contradictory alternative endings, what Brian McHale would include in the category of "self-erasing narratives,"[22] inscribe the failure of cultural and political battles on common ground. For according to Scorza, these battles *must* be envisioned as intertwined processes, since the cultural and the political constantly impinge on one another. *La danza inmóvil* presents his argument against the artificial fragmentation of discourse and story, against any imposed disjunction between art and social reality. His last novel responds to what Castañeda describes as a common perception of the past in Latin America, "largely shaped by this confluence of working class, collective nostalgia, and intellectual reconstruction of events and people by participants wistfully regretting a time they helped create" (42). *La danza inmóvil* pierces that nostalgia to call attention to a new urgency on the level of both representation and action.

La danza inmóvil attempts to reposition the privileged place of the urban evident in the "boom" novel, what Vidal calls that generation's "polarization" and "desbalance espacial" (*Literatura* 87). Scorza states that he works toward dismantling the bourgeois, urban novel in order to resist the brutal limitations of the city and its control of cultural production:

> Yo pienso que la novela urbana es la muerte de la novela, porque en la novela urbana la urbe va a concentrarse luego en reglamentaciones tan estrictas que ya no dejan lugar a nada. (Escajadillo, "Scorza" 61)

La danza inmóvil is Scorza's last response to the urban novel. To break out of what he views as the genre's strictly regimented space, he provides an extreme example of his own hybrid, self-reflexive form. Scorza incorporates myth, dreams, and imaginative fantasies into his urban discursive space to have his characters dance on a plurality of ontological levels. The novel continually stages clashes in which oppositional categories invade one another's territory. Rather than maintaining the distance between politics and poetry, revolution and love, the global and the local, Scorza questions and breaks the rules that conventionally determine how political and erotic desire are to be inscribed.

Scorza's *La danza inmóvil* is part of a cultural phenomenon that crosses the convenient boundaries of institutions, nations, languages, and traditions, questioning their very production. Hugo Neira characterizes Scorza's texts as "cultural interfaces" between two distant cultures, one that inspires and the other that produces. Scorza "se sitúa entre dos escenarios culturales, el europeo y el latinoamericano, uno que difunde y el otro que inspira, para concluir ocupando un espacio de frontera entre ambos, una interface cultural, una forma lujosa de la marginalidad" (106). This cultural production is a collaborative process and involves an expansive cast of places and players. The strategic and contagious interpenetration of European and Latin American media and publishing that launched the "boom" continues to coordinate a large sector of Latin American narrative production since then. Scorza's metaproductional strategies both document and ironically criticize culture's transnational mechanisms.

La danza inmóvil obliterates any vestiges of the bohemian, romantic writer now replaced by a new sociological reality in the literary market. Rama describes the "professional writer" who manages to write fiction as his or her principal employment, who "deja atrás la bohemia y la musa, se hace productor" ("El Boom" 295). Scorza's *La danza inmóvil* degrades bohemian Paris, turning the once-romanticized setting into a business center for literary negotiations or a strategic site for subversive political activity. The commoditization of Latin American narrative, whether one disdains it, resists it or ridicules it, is so real that it is even fictionalized. The metaproductionality in this novel unmasks the difficult identity of a protagonist who struggles to be a writer, reflecting his desperate reach for a now-tarnished Parisian ring. Nicolás, Santiago, and Scorza himself are transformed into variable cogs in the transnational process of literary production. The fictional characters' dependence on Paris (and Scorza's on Barcelona) becomes a politically and culturally compromising yet inevitable step in their dance toward artistic expression and professional definition. Erotic desire and political commitment are now negotiations, as is the canon with all of its propositions and alternatives. Inscribed in *La danza inmóvil* are negotiating desires: the desire to write and publish, to fight and love, to be recognized abroad yet maintain an engagement with local struggles. In his last novel, Scorza confronts art with politics to demonstrate the disjunction between current transnational culture and a European hegemonic past. Paris's provocative idealizations pervade all of Scorza's fictional domains until the city itself is rendered an enduring fiction. Paris is shown to reign over the Latin American cultural imagination, despite cynical revolutionaries and ironic novelists. In *La danza inmóvil*, the city owes its success to its fabrication.

CHAPTER FOUR

On the Border

————————— ❖ —————————

Cultural and Linguistic Trespassing in Alfredo Bryce Echenique's
La vida exagerada de Martín Romaña *and*
El hombre que hablaba de Octavia de Cádiz

Alfredo Bryce Echenique chooses Paris to stage postcolonial confrontations. His texts often displace Latin American characters in
Europe, where they contend with misunderstandings and disorientation. In the French capital, the periphery challenges the center in
raging battles over cultural signification. His characters' communicative difficulties reveal much more than comic touristic blunders
or the anxiety of foreign alienation. The semiotic complexity in
Bryce Echenique's writing attests to his hyperawareness of Latin
America's postcolonial condition. Much of his writing from the
1980s particularly registers the pressure of European political, social, and literary manifestations on Latin American conceptions of
culture. His discursive strategies in these novels intensify the
crosscultural estrangement of travelers who continually must rene-
gotiate their identities through language. Paris becomes the metropolitan setting that conditions their experiments with an array of
political, professional, erotic, and social class identifications.

Bryce Echenique's novelistic diptych *La vida exagerada de
Martín Romaña* (*MR* 1981) and *El hombre que hablaba de Octavia
de Cádiz* (*OC* 1985) explores the crosscultural dynamic of Latin
American intellectuals in pursuit of European experiences. Paris
structures all of the protagonist's expectations as his geographical
hub as well as his literary point of contact. The story begins with

Martín Romaña's trip from Lima to live and study in Paris, and continues as he travels between Paris and a number of European cities. His narration, a combined travelog and personal diary, records his blurred cultural boundaries and confused class identification. Martín writes to reaffirm and reestablish his confounded identity in strange surroundings. These novels chart movement among culturally distinct worlds that the narrator distinguishes through linguistic experimentation and intercultural jokes. *MR* is marked by Martín's personalized language that stretches the grammatical boundaries of Spanish to account for new realms of meaning and experience. *OC* expands on this cultural and linguistic mapping to ridicule social class consciousness and its relativity.

This fictional project is one of many narratives about Latin Americans in Paris that emerges from the legend of Paris's prestige to demystify "real" experience with European life. While many of Bryce Echenique's narratives include episodes in Paris, *MR* and *OC* expose the image of Paris constructed in Latin America and challenge this construct on literary, linguistic, and political terrain. An introduction to a Barcelona edition of *MR* calls the novel "un implacable ajuste de cuentas entre su autor y la abnorme ciudad— maravillosa para el visitante y monstruosa para el habitante...." (Fernando Sánchez Dragó ii). Julio Ramón Ribeyro calls the novel a Paris guidebook that demolishes the Paris myth for young Latin Americans "que siguen pensando en la Ciudad-Luz como en el emporio del arte, la fiesta, y la revolución" ("Habemus genio" in Ferreira and Márquez 191). While in *MR* Martín chronicles his process of assimilating the Parisian shock of nonrecognition, in *OC* he struggles with his marginalized status as "un extraño en el paraíso europeo" and shows how "la sociedad europea califica a un extranjero tercermundista" (Sánchez León in Ferreira and Márquez 201). The novels reveal the protagonist's acute reactions, not only to his new surroundings but also to his previous assumptions about his own cultural identity. Martín exploits the psychological and cultural implications of the traveler's disillusionment upon reaching a desired destination. In his autobiographical opus, Martín uses writing to sort through outmoded literary and sociopolitical content associated with Paris in Latin American urban identity.

MR tells the story of Latin American university students in Paris in the late 1960s, with climactic episodes during the May 1968 "revolution." Martín's Peruvian girlfriend, Inés, joins him in Paris and they marry. The couple participates in a Marxist revolutionary group with other Latin American students, and Martín, the aspiring writer, is elected to write a "novela de sindicatos pesqueros" that takes place in Chimbote, a Peruvian fishing village. Their marriage disintegrates, along with Martín's mental health and his commitment to revolutionary causes. *OC* continues the story of Martín's professional and emotional life in Europe. After he and Inés are divorced, he works as a lecturer at the University of Paris. Octavia is one of his students, and she becomes the interlocutor of his writing. He pursues an affair with her despite the obstacles of age, social class, and nationality. As the sequel's title indicates, their liaison is reduced to Martín's solitary longing. Eventually he leaves academic life for a career in writing travel guides, and returns to Peru.

In both *MR* and *OC*, Martín's notions about Paris motivate all of his European pursuits. He explores bohemian creative circles, Leftist activism, "foreign" marginality, sexual experimentation, and social hierarchy, all shaped by the Paris of his cultural and literary anticipations. Bryce Echenique offers a fictionalized version of the city's vigorous cultural magnetism and political symbolism for young Latin American intellectuals. There Martín faces the racist and classist categories of Latin America's postcolonial relationship with Europe and struggles to refashion his cultural identity within a transnational context.

BRYCE ECHENIQUE'S PARIS CONSTRUCT

Paris has a vast repertoire in the Latin American imagination, according to Bryce Echenique. The following passage from his *Crónicas personales* offers an autobiographical sketch that ennumerates the array of roles Paris plays in *MR* and *OC*:

> París-gran ilusión. París-hermana mía. París-hermosísima ciudad. París-ciudad en la que descubrimos hasta qué punto somos extranjeros. Yo, peruano, tú, mexicano, él, venezolano. París-ciudad complicada y, sin embargo, hay esos días, París, en que se te ama tanto porque gracias a ti aprendimos del mundo, de nosotros mismos, de nuestros países, de la amistad, de nuestro empuje en la soledad, del coraje ante la peor adversidad, del orgullo infantil, de las reglas del juego que jamás aceptarías, puesto que cuanto mejor las aprendías menos capaz te sentías de quedarte para siempre en ellas. París-ciudad que te enseñó a escribir, pero porque tú deseabas escribir. París-ciudad en la que

conociste a los primeros amigos escritores latinoamericanos, e ingleses y franceses, e italianos, y qué sé
yo, con los que trabaste amistad, puesto que habías
abandonado Lima, tu ciudad natal, sin haber escrito una
línea. Y entonces vinieron los años jóvenes, de mujeres
amadas y horas larguísimas de trabajo y amigos que
pasaban por casa y te decían: "Sigue adelante, escribe,
trata de publicar ese cuento." París-ciudad en la que
descubriste los partidos políticos del progreso y del
cambio. . . . París-ciudad en la que aprendiste a comprender
que mucha de aquella gente atravesaba una febril
primavera porque estaba en París, para luego retornar a
Latinoamérica a engordar o perder el pelo en alguna
burocracia militar o simplemente de derecha. París-
profundo mirador para el desencanto, pero uno es terco e
insiste en encantamientos. París-torre de marfil dentro de
la cual se lloraba la muerte del Che con el mismo tipo de
llanto con el que se lloraba la carta en que se leía la
traición de un amigo, o la muerte del tercer pariente que
fallece desde que vivo en París. Iba pasando el tiempo.
(*Crónicas* 143–44)

This bitterly ironic, appreciative yet vindictive chat between the
author and Paris resembles the conversational tone of Bryce
Echenique's fiction. Paris is attributed a personified heroic or antihe-
roic presence and serves as a filter for Latin American experience
abroad. The passage renders Paris, the second-person but silent participant in the dialogue, a persistent force that the first-person must
come to terms with aesthetically and politically. The narrative so-
liloquy, directed both at Paris and at the Latin American sources of
that version of Paris, parallels the personal diary trope in *MR* and
OC. Bryce Echenique inserts Paris into his characters' intimate,
familial nostalgia as well as their sociopolitical awareness.

The two novels intertextualize the Latin American protagonist's
Parisian experience. Like Cortázar's stories and Scorza's *La danza
inmóvil*, Bryce Echenique pushes beyond the static setting and its
stock of allusions and references to actually *cite* extra-American
material as a textual corpus of history and signs. The narration
incorporates and invents signs from both European and Latin
American cultural sources that structure the story. Paris becomes
a Latin American cultural construction that synecdocally represents all of Europe.

Bryce Echenique integrates clusters of French cultural miscel-
lanea familiar to Latin Americans into his version of the Paris

construct. Parisian streets, French films, popular nostalgic singers like Edith Piaf, Yves Montand, and Maurice Chevalier, tourist brochures, and documentaries offer source material for the Paris that is "read" and received in Peru. Martín describes a collaborative effort between Hollywood, French public relations, the tourist industry, and Latin American reception:

> Y desde la eterna primavera parisina, que la Metro Goldwyn Mayer se encargó también de eternizar, el general De Gaulle, cual sonriente arcangelote, bendecía este mundo *made in France* que llegaba hasta nosotros en paquetitos enviados a las Alianzas Francesas, conteniendo películas, diapositivas, profesores bien pintones, y alguna que otra alusión a la libertad de todos los pueblos ... [yo] conocía tan bien París a través de los documentales sobre Notre-Dame, Tour Eiffel, l'Opéra (me obligaba a pronunciar así), Maurice Chevalier, Le Louvre, etc., vistos boquiabierto y por toneladas durante mi adolescencia de limeño cinemero.... (*MR* 156–57)

Martín must adjust his expectations of this marketed, utopian "package" of Paris he was fed in Lima to his "lived" experiences there. He struggles against his own expectations as well as those imposed by entire segments of his culture that look to established "European" standards.

These novels' use of Parisian material creates a collage of literary allusions, institutional mechanisms, erotic expectations, political aspirations, and professional roles. Martín's cumbersome cultural baggage intertextualizes Vallejo, Darío, Proust, and Hemingway. Literary references combine with music, film, street life, travel, history, and social class in a vast display that considers any cultural material textual ammunition. His sources are not only French; Latin America, North America, and Spain contribute to Bryce's Paris construct, demonstrating the transnational production of cultural attitudes and norms. Rather than an exported French product or an invented Latin American image, Bryce's Paris is the result of intercultural communication. Various territorial sources converge in these novels, spilling their contents onto one another to disorient, reassemble, and redefine their message.

The literary elements of Martín Romaña's European construct especially draw on Proust and Hemingway. Each of these literary figures, both their lives and their texts, serves the novels as a subtext, what Michael Riffaterre defines as "narrative units of

significance that account for readers' ability to find their way un-
erringly in fiction . . . [a subtext] works like a memory built into
the narrative" (54–55). *MR* and *OC* incorporate literary subtexts as
frames of referentiality for Paris. Their recurrence and repetition
provide "hermeneutic guideposts" through the novels and continually remind the reader of Paris's literary construction.

Bryce Echenique has been considered the Peruvian Proust since
the publication of his first novel, *Un mundo para Julius*, in 1970.
He enjoys the association himself, and states that when his work
began to be published he looked forward to returning to Peru to
inform his mother that "finalmente Proust existía para la familia,"
only to return to find a new servant at the door who told him, "la
señora no está, señor Proust" ("Confesiones sobre el arte de vivir
y escribir novelas," in Ferreira and Márquez 34). Critical studies as
well as interviews with the writer have recognized Proust's
influence.[1] The Proust subtext, particularly in *MR*, grows out of
the traveler's anticipation. Martín approaches Paris with the expectations of the city's cultural meanings in Latin America, just as
Proust's narrator dreams of Balbec and Venice, but when he finally
encounters these long-awaited places he is sadly disillusioned. Paris
is that romantic dream that Martín hopes will result for him "tal
como lo soñamos cuando nos soñamos juntos en París, en Lima. . . ."
(87). However, upon arriving, Martín finds that Notre Dame
"irradiaba más en Lima" (24). Martín and Inés accompany his mother
to Illiers, Proust's childhood country home and the basis for his
novelistic Combray, to fulfill her literary pilgrimage. Martín refers
to the "muchachitas en flor" (176), a reference to Proust's *A l'ombre
des jeunes filles en fleurs*, when a friend boasts about his flirtations
with a fifteen-year-old girl.

The Proustian subtext is not only thematic but also discursive.
Beyond overt allusions, these novels borrow from Proust stylistically
and structurally. Antonio Cornejo Polar notes, "la sombra de Proust
aparece una y otra vez y sirve para definir la índole del relato."[2]
Bryce Echenique has his narrator employ many of the discursive
strategies exploited in *A la recherche du temps perdu*. Martín especially makes use of "analepses" and "prolepses," or temporal jumps
backward or forward in the narration's chronology (Genette, *Figures
III* 90–114).[3] These novels' autobiographical stance, metafictional
projection, obsessive cyclic memories, and psychoanalytic parody all
transmit a reworking of Proustian form and content. For Bryce
Echenique, as well as for Martín, these evocations are bound up in
Paris and the literary sources of its construct in Latin America.

The Hemingway subtext permeates the novels' Spanish and French terrain as Martín romanticizes Hemingway's fascination with Spain (*The Sun Also Rises, For Whom the Bell Tolls*), and his stay in Paris (*A Moveable Feast*). He searches for the "hemingwayana" (*MR* 70) dimensions in his own experience. The protagonist uses these intertexts to try to reconcile a combination of his anticipated versions of places, based on his own reading and imagination, with his own current circumstances. Spain does not measure up to Hemingway's bravato, nor is Paris the feast supposedly prepared for North American writers in the 1920s.

> Claro, el pelotudo de Hemingway se lo trae a uno de las narices a París con fracesitas tipo *éramos tan pobres y tan felices*, gringo cojudo, cómo no se te ocurre poner una nota a pie de página destinada a los latinoamericanos, a los peruanos en todo caso, una cosa es ser pobres en París con dólares y otra cosa es serlo con soles peruanos . . . qué pobres ni qué felices ni qué ocho cuartos. . . . (*MR* 137)

Martín injects his own colloquial Spanish into his cultural text of Europe. Eventually, after enduring European life a bit longer, he begins to translate it back into a Latin American or specifically Peruvian version.[4]

> Releía como siempre la poesía de Vallejo y empezaba a pensar que era una revisión, para uso de latinoamericanos, del *París era una fiesta*, de Hemingway. (*OC* 209)

Martín's Parisian context, both in *MR* and *OC*, relies on literary readings and renderings that are frequently at odds with his own experiences. Martín attempts to realign his Parisian construct with his own language and cultural texts from home. Martín's discourse linguistically yields to and reembraces his Latin American cultural identity. His diary paves the way for the return to Peru that concludes each of the novels.

According to Martín, "una vida en Europa suponía una buena dosis de bohemia" (42). The bohemian subtext of *MR* and *OC* requires poverty (à la Vallejo) but promises erotic adventure. The two novels form a contemporary, international version of Murger's *Scènes de la vie de bohème*, whose self-proclaimed "artists" enjoy the sensuality of erotic encounters, food, and music in the midst of their grim financial circumstances. Martín and his other non-French companions expect to find the Paris of "easy women." The women among the boarders in one of Martín's first residences do not conform to this stereotype, and Martín tells a friend that "este techo no parece estar en París: está plagado de vírgenes" (MR 108). When Martín and Inés write home with the news of their marriage, an uncle associates their announcement with Paris's loose morals: "sin duda [Martín] había embarazado a Inés, ya ustedes saben lo que es París" (MR 130).

Martín's subsequent liaison with Octavia also depends on Parisian social expectations. Octavia, as a French aristocrat, is inaccessible, and this relationship provides a satiric antidote to bohemian lowlife. After bohemia's broken promises of erotic escapades, and a failed marriage with his Peruvian adolescent sweetheart, Martín's frustrated pursuit of Octavia prolongs his Parisian agony. If he cannot live out Paris's literary and artistic scenarios, then he will try to tap into its social class hierarchies (see later section on OC).

Established French institutions make up another central component in the Paris construct of MR and OC. Characters' encounters with universities, cultural organizations, transportation systems, landlords, and concierges orient their Parisian experiences. These encounters constitute the principal ingredients of Bryce's unsettling humor and mark an anxious interfacing between cultures. Bryce uses institutions as frames for social satire. The French university system structures Martín's life in Paris from the beginning as a student in MR and then as a lecturer in OC. In his extensive mocking of French academic life, he critiques everything from the university cafeterias to its parking lots and plumbing. He analyzes campus neighborhoods among his many mappings of class and social status in Paris. Martín teases in OC that the students' cars are more valuable than the professors' at the Nanterre campus of the Université de Paris.

MR and OC take on the domestic institutions of Paris hotels, top-floor servants' rooms, concierges, and landladies. Both novels ridicule the traditions and prejudices that are entailed in any Parisian housing transaction. The hotelero in MR, for example, decides that Martín must have a serious tropical disease since he showers so regularly. He dubs the intransigent landlady in the Latin Quarter "Madame Labru(ja)." In Martín's next Left Bank apartment, the landlady accepts him as a tenant, but despite his friends' personal recommendation, she refuses to give him a lease. As a young, poor foreigner, he finds himself at the mercy of the social institutions to which, he continually laments, Hemingway seemed immune.

Martín hopes the ninth-floor "techo" that he shares with an assortment of international laborers will give him a real connection to the proletariat. However, his modest quarters, which Martín calls "un rincón cerca del cielo," more obviously evoke the textualized motif of the struggling artist's Parisian garret. Martín's writer's block grows most acute when he tries to produce the social–realist novel on Peruvian fishermen, a project in which he has no faith. The narration evokes social and aesthetic assumptions through these domestic spaces, only to strip them ironically of their romantic glamour.

MR and *OC* also satirize the ideal of achieving fame or professional notoriety in Paris and thereby undermine the city's role as a literary capital. This recurrent theme of the Latin American Paris construct has been evident in examples from writers such as Sarmiento, the *modernistas*, and Scorza. However, just as Bryce Echenique reduces French institutions to caricatures, he also deflates and problematizes the foreign expectation of Parisian artistic recognition. Miguel Angel Asturias, César Vallejo, Julio Ramón Ribeyro, and even Alfredo Bryce Echenique himself appear intermittently in the novel. Their international recognition provides a model for Martín. He strives to identify with the Peruvians in particular who have traversed Paris, and he encounters Bryce Echenique and Ribeyro in such codified literary spaces as the Latin Quarter's Aux Deux Magots café. Martín's preposterous literary rivalries emerge from the model of the literary capital associated with Paris since the Belle Epoque.

Martín's own lack of literary recognition leads him to scorn the international cultural assumption that a residency in Paris promises artistic productivity and success. His *cuaderno* includes pathetic scenes of Latin Americans striving to be noticed by the French. For example, in *MR*, Martín's Peruvian physician at a French clinic is to be honored with a ceremony. The loyal patient offers to bring along some fellow foreign students to increase the audience. Although the doctor admits that the ceremony, whose twelve attendees are subjected to a recording of the Peruvian national anthem on a scratched 78, was inconsequential, Martín is convinced that now his doctor can return to Peru with an open door to opportunity. "Nadie te va a cholear ni a ponerte trabas para que abras consultorio donde quieras. . . . Tú eres un médico peruano que ha triunfado en Francia" (*MR* 46–47).

Bryce Echenique offers an ironic critique of the recurrent theme of Leftist political activism in Paris, already observed in Scorza's *La danza inmóvil* and Cortázar's *Libro de Manuel*, which reflects the bohemian subtext as well as Latin America's postcolonial situation. These novels satirize the political subtext of Paris as keenly as they critique the city's literary and cultural "models." He presents a sharp caricature of artificial political posturing that leads to collective disillusionment. The May 1968 street demonstrations that occupy much of *MR* evoke Paris's images of libertarian struggles, from the French Revolution to the Paris Commune. However, in *MR* and *OC*, the characters' participation is misguided or half-hearted. The legacy of bohemian images associated with Paris implies a marginalized and melancholic social presence. Martín's self-referential descriptions admit to his cohort's deliberate fabrication of contemporary bohemian images in economic adversity and social marginality:

> cara de ropa vieja ya marcada por el determinismo
> geográfico que significan un rincón junto al cielo parisino,
> años de restaurant universitario, una escuelita ínfame para
> ganarse el pan, más varios años en cuclillas en los waters
> de hueco en el suelo que me tocaban uno tras otro. (*MR*
> 201–02)

The narrator's ironic stance converts the foreigner's class status into a stereotypical facade that parodies the nineteenth-century literary construct.

Bryce Echenique joins the social and the political in his depiction of Paris throughout this diptych. He places the May 1968 student movement at the center of *MR* to expand the image of Paris often restricted to a site for establishing artistic and social standards. The political organizing that *MR* satirizes changes the rules of the literary bohemian subtext that Martín strives to live out. Third-World bohemia in 1960's Paris demands engaging in political struggle, a commitment that Martín is never prepared to make. Bryce Echenique also uses Paris in *MR* for a reexamination of young Latin American Leftists at a particular historical moment. Martín's pursuit of Octavia in *OC* seemingly contradicts his initial Parisian social class preoccupations; however, his observations of a neurotic European aristocracy confirm the city's role as a space for the display of social hierarchies. Martín's appraisal of Paris takes aim at his own political limitations and Latin America's social fixations to provide a critique of a cultural generation's Parisian projections.

MR: THE NARRATOR'S PERSONALIZED LINGUISTIC DEFENSE

Language and writing are Martín's survival strategies in his confrontations with the codified world of Paris. His prior reading, pre-travel imagining, and initial perceptions upon arrival offer him contradictory records of Paris's semiotic order. Since he is unwilling to let go of his Latin American-based preconceptions of Paris, Martín increasingly personalizes his language to defend himself against the bombardment of cultural differences. He continually integrates the divergent sources of Paris's textuality in creative language manipulations. He embraces writing as a cure or rehabilitation for fatigued decipherers of transnational signs.[5] Martín narratively subjectivizes his world with translations, hybrids, and word inventions to counter the cultural transpositions he endures. His is a counter-discourse in response to postcolonial disorientation.[6] He redefines Paris and the rest of his foreign surroundings with Peruvian colloquialisms, regional Americanisms, and even Limenian expressions, presenting the otherness of Europe in personalized and intimate language.

Several theories of postcolonial literary expression help account for the eclectic linguistic variance in Bryce Echenique's Spanish, particularly masterful in *MR*. Because of postcolonial theory's focus on place as the site of cultural and social production, it highlights the symptoms of displacement that the language of *MR* so keenly displays. Much more elaborate than a conventional "setting," Paris in these two novels becomes a dynamic semiotic crossroads where various languages intersect and meaning is transformed. Bryce Echenique's novels integrate Paris as an extensive discursive field that operates in various cultural arenas. Martín chooses language and narration as his defensive weapon, and his upper-middle class, Limenian Spanish enters the French capital with the express purpose of contesting European hegemony in a linguistic arena.

W. D. Ashcroft argues that the intersection of languages is *the* distinguishing feature of postcolonial literature (71). None of the fiction incorporating Latin American ideas of Paris takes this to the playful and caustic extremes of *MR*. The first part of Martín's autobiographical project broaches the distance between Latin American and European notions of class, culture, and aesthetics with Paris as the index for divergent codes. Martín as narrator performs feats of language variance in the exploitation of what Ashcroft calls "devices of otherness," from inventing neologisms to transcribing colloquial orality.[7] The narration in *MR* generates an array of deviant language that reinscribes Paris within a newly awakened postcolonial consciousness.

Bryce Echenique practices a playful bilingualism in *MR* and *OC*, the most obvious indicator of postcolonial counterdiscourse. The narration communicates in a lexically splintered discourse in Spanish into which several other "national" languages and specialized vocabularies intrude.[8] *MR* includes lexicon from other languages (such as English, Italian, and French), as well as from codified systems (such as Marxist and Freudian jargon). Martín's Spanish is transformed by an interplay of primarily French and Peruvian content. In his intertextual bilingualism, Bryce Echenique mixes angry references to Hemingway's *A Moveable Feast* with Proustian social climbing and American colloquial insults.

MR especially exploits the cultural polarity and ambivalence between Paris and Lima, purposefully blurring their differences. In Martín's narration, signs cross and overlap not only language boundaries but cultural modes, idiomatic humor, and semantic codes. In Paris, *putamadre* becomes a verb ("Putamadreé como loco..." [*MR* 21]); in Lima, Marcel Proust becomes a new noun (" ... en un loco marcelprousteo..." [*MR* 18]). The references to French culture are more than mere allusions; they are made Spanish, translated and gramatically woven into the narration. Beyond the thematic and semantic, the language in these novels experiments with sounds and syntax, poetically wrenching words and references from their expected geographical and discursive contexts. Martín's narration establishes what Bakhtin calls new "word-linkages" that challenge the "habitual matrices" of language use (169). The narrator appropriates this new world of signs, embedding them into his language, although not without a tension that signals their otherness.

Bryce Echenique traps his narrator/protagonist in a hybrid world of signs. The narrator adopts French terms and expressions, transposing them into his own hybridized Spanish. Thus the French lexeme *clochard* (homeless vagrant) is transformed into a new Spanish verb, *clochardizarse* ("un latinoamericano jamás se clochardiza" [*MR* 51]), meaning "to become a *clochard*." The trash collection crisis during the strikes in May 1968 was starting to "alcanzar alturas eiffelianas" (*MR* 247). The narration weaves in cultural references and marks their difference with translation and syntactical transposition. These examples of language variance in *MR* make novelistic discourse the "index of cultural difference which affirms the distance of cultures at the very moment in which it proposes to bring them together" (Ashcroft 71). One illuminating study of the European language as "other" in West African novels calls this translating process "relexification,"

> an imaginative, world-creating attempt at forging a new literary-aesthetic medium or "third code" out of the alien, dominant (European) lexicon. It is also an attempt at appropriating the Other's language in order to make it one's own and bend its otherness or fixity to artistic and ideological exigencies. (Zabus 350)

Although in Bryce Echenique's Spanish he borrows from within European romance languages, he still treats French as "other." Appropriated within Spanish, these translated or relexified expressions signal the otherness of French culture for the Peruvian narrator. Homi Bhabha likewise considers translation a postcolonial poetics that "(be)sets the boundary between the colony and the metropolis" (213). Martín forces his Spanish to represent the shifting and overlapping realms of meaning and expression that he faces in Paris.[9]

Martín also manipulates signs from other specialized languages and integrates them into his Spanish. His participation in the Marxist student group generates a number of internationally hybrid terms. Martín makes the French *groupuscule*, the noun referring to a student political activist group, into an adjective to describe the "slogans grupusculares" of his companions (*MR* 211). The "guerrilleros parisinos" (*MR* 310), who are certainly "gochistas," "siempre me andan derecheando, capitalisteando, mediotinteando" (*MR* 317). Relying on language as his only defense, Martín disdainfully calls his Marxist companions "camaradowskis" (*MR* 116). Martín transposes psychoanalytic terminology as well. Plagued by his wife's sudden preoccupation with Freud, Martín creates several syntactic versions of "Edipo": the verb "edipear" and the adjective "edipísimo" (*MR* 194, 195). He borrows foreign linguistic material from its expected cultural context and assimilates it into his Spanish.

As Martín increasingly subjectivizes his European experiences in his narration, his Spanish not only incorporates neologisms and translations but also applies Americanisms to European situations. At his most intimate linguistic personalization, Martín expresses his Parisian life in metaphorical Peruvian phrasings. He describes parties in Paris as a "huaynito tristísimo," making reference to the Peruvian popular song form associated with *mestizo* culture (*MR* 95). A North American friend's hotel room in the Latin Quarter becomes a "pocilga andina" (*MR* 289). In Lima, he used to measure things in the terms and even the language of supposed European (especially Parisian) standards, and now he comes to assess his Parisian experiences in Peruvian language. The France–Peru axis becomes his principal semiotic gauge.

He judges trains, for example, by this scale of signs. Martín, his mother, and his wife Inés travel to the Côte d'Azur on

> el tren más elegante de Francia, o sea el más elegante que había tomado en mi vida, porque trenes de lujo sólo había tomado en el Perú, y sólo cuando mi padre pagaba el billete, además, pero es sabido que el mejor tren del Perú equivale más o menos al peor de Francia. . . . (*MR* 200)

On another trip, this time in Spain, when the train advances very slowly, Martín vents his frustration "maldiciendo el maquinista porque este tren parece peruano o es que el tipo conoce mi ansiedad y no quiere que llegue nunca" (*MR* 318).

Martín's regionalized, colloquial language helps him retain his Peruvian, even more specifically Limenian, identity. Regional expressions such as "vaina," and indigenisms such as "estar chocho," "cholo," and "le importa un comino" abound throughout the novel. This is Martín's method of retaining his Peruvian identity in the throes of cultural bombardment. His conversational tone, even though he is often speaking French or English in Paris, or Italian in Perugia, maintains the expressions and cadences of Peruvian Spanish. The Peruvian punctuations and exclamations such as "uyuyuy" and the repeated "Ah ya" of the attentive listener appear in his transcribed conversation with his neighbor Nadine, although she is French. In this way, he reports more thoroughly on his own emotional perceptions than on precisely what was said. He uses his personalized, frequently hybrid, and resistantly Peruvian language defensively, for example, with the expression "de ñangué."

> Eran, como solía decir mi padre, de ñangué, palabra ésta
> que he buscado desde la Real Academia hasta los
> peruanismos, sin suerte para ustedes, porque a mí me
> basta con recordar el gesto de mi viejo diciéndola y lo
> entiendo todo. (*MR* 98–99)

He insists on using a specialized lexicon, and he refuses to inter-
pret or define it for his readers.[10] Frustrated and fatigued by the
semiotic confrontation in his life and in his writing, Martín maintains his grip on his linguistic home ground, even if it may exclude
his audience.

The Paris–Peru polarity comes to define Martín himself. A
fluctuating blend of these two worlds draws from a series of cultural conceptions and contexts. *MR* and *OC* use language for ironic
effect to contort the cliché of the Latin American writer in a Parisian garret. Martín's attempted roles, as middle-class husband,
political activist, or university lecturer, remain circumscribed within
the confines of his postcolonial, multilingual, and transnational
psychonarrative register. Martín's self-definition seems unable to
dodge either Peruvian or Parisian content. During the May 1968
activity, Martín only wishes he could look more "revolutionary."
He hopes the movement will be contagious, that it will change his
"aspecto mediotíntico por una buena cara de póster." He studies all
of the components of the particular Parisian look he is after. He
reminds himself,

> soñabas de tener cara de slogan, caminada de blue jean,
> barba y pelambre, mirada de activista, pinta de poster . . .
> soñando que te parecías al Che Guevara cuando
> barricadeabas, y a Jean-Paul Sartre cuando escribías. (236)

Martín searches for the costume and the mask that will ensure
him entrance into the text of his choice. His problems spring from
his shifting textual choices and the conflicting array of figures with
whom he wants to identify.

Bryce Echenique's discourse exhibits what Deleuze and Guattari
explore in Kafka, the personal deterritorialization of a national
language, his *own* language, in which he becomes a nomad, an
immigrant, a gypsy (*Kafka* 35). At the end of the novel, in a psy-
chiatric hospital in Barcelona, Martín introduces himself to his
fellow patients, "Vivo en París, porque leí mucho a Hemingway

para ser escritor, y soy peruano" (*MR* 440). Martín's identity straddles several worlds and engulfs him in competing literary and linguistic zones. His situation models "la quiebra y mezcla de las colecciones que organizaban los sistemas culturales, la desterritorialización de los procesos simbólicos" of modern urban culture that García Canclini highlights in his discussion of hybridity (264). Paris infiltrates his readings, travels, Spanish, politics, and cultural identity in a self-inflicted intertextual bombardment. With these novels, Bryce Echenique launches a counterdiscursive response to Parisian cultural onslaught in Latin America. In search of an identity, Martín's writing stages confrontations with a range of lexical sources, syntactic categories and socioinguistic mappings. His narration of crosslinguistic skirmishes encodes the issues of postcolonial identity with inventive humor and sociopolitical irony.

OC: THE FICTION OF SOCIAL CLASS

Place and identity work together in *MR* and *OC* as Martín struggles to ascertain where he belongs. In *MR*, Martín relies on non-European, "foreign" alliances for his identity. In *OC*, Martín's world expands beyond the closed community of expatriates, and as he makes contact with more Europeans, he has to contend with the complex hierarchies of their social structure. The issue of social class becomes particularly acute in his second volume. He tries to negotiate his own identity in relation to the social situation around him. He is still a Latin American in Europe, but now he is divorced, has earned a university degree, and teaches literature in Paris. Martín has to adjust to the shifting terms of his marginality.

Martín carries with him from Peru certain *topoi* about Europe that determine his class consciousness. Among these thematic associations is the bohemian as aesthete who contests dominant or "high" culture. The bohemian subtext of *MR* and *OC* means surviving poverty and social marginalization, but all for the ennobling cause of social revolution (*MR*) and artistic achievement. As a foreign student with limited resources during the first years of his residence abroad, Martín has little problem enacting the bohemian role he associates with living in Paris.

Martín selects living quarters in Paris based on preconceptions of social class image. His array of domestic situations becomes an allegory for his experimentation in Paris with social marginalization. He first occupies a room in a "hotel sin baño," since he considers it too bourgeois to have a room with a private bath. This inexpensive housing solution helps define Martín as a potential international revolutionary, "un extranjero marginal e intelectual" (*MR* 271). When he is evicted from the hotel for taking too many showers, he hesitates to take an apartment, concerned that his image will change once he has the convenience of his own bathroom. He does rent a studio for a short time, but he distributes numerous copies of his key to other "revolutionary" friends so they can make use of his "socialized" private bathroom. Next he rents the ninth-floor walk-up servant's room, during a period that coincides with his participation in the Marxist group. However, despite his efforts, he cannot force Paris to rewrite and redetermine his class status. When Martín and Inés eventually marry and settle in an apartment in the Latin Quarter, they often avoid the elevator and opt for the nine flights of stairs in their continuing attempt to resist a bourgeois lifestyle.

In *OC*, Bryce Echenique extends this geography of social space. Throughout the second part of his story, each new acquaintance presents a challenge in comprehending and integrating himself into what he judges a strangely archaic but enduring organization of social class. Martín especially is plagued by the dilemma of having been too bourgeois for Inés, yet not aristocratic enough for Octavia. His bohemian marginality backfires when his social lineage is questioned from both sides of the Atlantic. He becomes enraged at the suggestion that he cannot "entrar por la puerta principal de su casa" and meet Octavia's parents. Octavia argues that, to her family, Martín has numerous strikes against him: he is older, divorced, Latin American, a writer, and a professor; in sum, he is dangerous to the family's class status. Martín counters defensively,

> Inés me abandonó porque yo era algo así como tú en Francia: un oligarca, una mierda, un oligarca podrido. . . . No me vengan con que los latinoamericanos de París somos todos guerrilleros, o escritores revolucionarios, más el buen salvaje que es un indio de mierda. . . . Se trata de que me he pasado media infancia y adolescencia dando plata para las misiones del Africa en el colegio más caro del imperialismo yanqui. . . . O sea que no soy un árabe de mierda ni un negro que barre el metro de París. Y además, cuando quise serlo, por amor a mi ex esposa, a los árabes y a los negros, no me dejaron serlo. . . . (*OC* 128)

Appropriate class identification continually eludes Martín. His comic exaggeration traps him in the class crevices of his relationships. Love and romance, for him once erotic and emotional, pit him against the tensions of both American and European class identity. Martín's narration renders the social scale absurd, satirizing both cultures' racial and socioeconomic rigidities. He strives to collapse the absolutism of social class, a stubborn obstacle in his quest for self-identification.

Martín maps neighborhoods in *OC* to identify Europe's divisive social classifications. Since he associates the Latin Quarter with bohemia, he notes a contradiction between his landlords, the Forestiers, and their neighborhood. They live a conventional bourgeois family life, surrounded by what Martín considers countercultural elements—"cómo podían vivir en esa zona del barrio Latino, entre hippies, punks, gochistas, clochards y cafés poblados por una fauna cosmopolita que era todo lo opuesto a lo que ellos representaban" (*OC* 26). Martín's confusion is heightened by his preexisting notions about the Latin Quarter as being representative of life in Paris in general: "vivir burguesamente es todo lo contrario de la forma en que en el mundo entero la gente cree que se vive en París" (*OC* 27). Once again, his assumptions about European life conflict with his on-the-spot observations.

The Latin Quarter also functions in *OC* as the polar opposite of Octavia's neighborhood. Octavia secretly visits Martín from four o'clock to eight o'clock daily to avoid arousing her parents' suspicions. In her foray from the Right Bank into the Latin Quarter, she crosses social class lines. She becomes a foreign presence, an emissary from a world that shares little more than the same city as Martín. When Martín crosses the Seine to approach Octavia's house, he is arrested by the police and warned against continuing to see her (*OC* 200).

The Place de la Contraescarpe in the Latin Quarter is the capital of Parisian bohemia for Martín. The narration persistently depicts his neighborhood with a touristic multicultural tone. The novel includes a repeated scene there at an Asian restaurant called La Sopa China. There Octavia has "vino con tapita de plástico" for the first time in her life; "[e]s más, no sabía que existía semejante barbaridad proletaria" (*OC* 159). They frequently follow their meager, romantic meals at this local restaurant with a visit to the Rancho Guaraní, another "ethnic" establishment in the neighborhood with live Latin American music.[11] Octavia expresses her enthusiasm over the exotic "otherness" of this section of the Latin

Quarter by proclaiming her loyalty to "Che Güevará" and shouting "Vive l'Amérique Latine!" (*OC* 160). Octavia consciously collaborates in class renegotiations by lending Martín social capital. When Martín is feeling vulnerable as a foreign tenant without a lease, Octavia suggests that she arrive in her ex-boyfriend's "coche de lujo." She parks conspicuously in front of his building to attract the landlady's and the concierge's attention. As in all of the transactions and encounters between Octavia and Martín, neighborhood and class associations work together to define the characters and their motives.

Octavia also introduces Martín to European aristocracy. The novel playfully alludes to the classical origins of her name as the wife of Mark Anthony during the height of the Roman Empire.[12] Martín meets Octavia's Italian and Portuguese ex-boyfriends, her Belgian cousin Prince Leopold, and eventually her noble Milanese husband.[13] Martín tries to comprehend the internal hierarchies of these "cabezas coronadas," "los que pertenecen a una familia con cierto tipo de título" (*OC* 174). His own conceptualization of European social life did not include this category. Confused, he badgers Octavia for clarification. He constantly compares his own name, lineage, and family history to these illustrious old European families, those of "apellidos muy largos."

An accumulation of last names, or an "apellido largo," becomes one extreme of another Brycean polarity in these novels. On one end of this polarity are artists and writers, particularly if they are from Latin America. In one scene, Martín visits Octavia and her husband in Milan. Martín describes a party they give in his honor as "rota en dos enormes pedazos irreconciliablemente enfrentados" of "artistas" on one side and the "amigos de apellido largo" on the other. Octavia's husband is a count who becomes depressed if he is not serving as a patron to a marginalized artist "conseguido a la flor y nata del fracaso" (*OC* 326). He adopts Martín in an absurdly inverted relationship of dependency in order to give his own life meaning. Martín initially agrees to this arrangement to be closer to Octavia, implicating himself in a fictionalized reproduction of European Renaissance literary history. Martín's own marginal status offers him a way out. Octavia and her husband remain inscribed in their own fictions of social class, trying to perfect the roles assigned to them by an elaborate fantasy.

Throughout *MR* and *OC*, Martín tries to insert himself into the social identification his lovers demand. He is continually confounded by the rigid requirements, always beyond his control, which determine his class status according to Inés and then Octavia. He remains transitory and marginal, even with respect to other displaced or expatriate Latin Americans. After attempting a contrived position in the young revolutionary group in *MR*, he later finds himself ironically cast in an anachronistic scenario of royal patronage. Martín's paradox illlustrates the contorsions of social class embedded in the Paris construct for Latin American intellectuals. Martín's repeated failure to integrate, accepted neither by Third-World bohemia nor European aristocracy, is a symptom of inhabiting the postcolonial periphery.

THE METAFICTION OF IDENTITY

Bryce Echenique displays a range of metafictional artifice in his novelistic diptych. The autobiographical stance of *MR* and *OC* poses Martín in his "sillón Voltaire," filling first his blue and then his red journals. The diptych even bears the subtitle, "Cuaderno de navegación en un sillón Voltaire," referring directly to the very process and setting of the story's writing. The fictionalized *journal intime* introduces both controls and liberties on language. Language, for Bryce Echenique,

> no es simplemente una herramienta de comunicación o un espejo de la realidad; más bien es el agente creador de una realidad hiperbólica y satírica donde sus personajes no pueden desligarse de aquella voz que la expresa. (Ferreira 135)

Martín remains a prisoner of his own language. His European settings invade his discourse, and his fictions overrun his life. He only partially escapes by disobeying the rules that delineate between fiction and "reality." As narrator, he ignores his own narrative boundaries by allowing other characters to coauthor his story.

Martín breaks the autobiographical frame with numerous mentions of Bryce Echenique and Ribeyro. He evokes his intimacy with the Latin American literary scene in Paris by including encounters at cafés with these published figures whose international recognition he strives to acquire. These tongue-in-cheek allusions blur the roles of character and "author," suggesting Martín's "reality" within Ribeyro's and Bryce's circles. Martín complains about what Bryce says about him to others in Europe and states that he must struggle to undo the damage of Bryce's misrepresentations. Martín laments that he and Bryce were on the same trip to Brussels, "desgraciadamente, porque de él saldrán luego tantas bromas pesadas, tantas pérfidas historias, tantas versiones de esta historia que deforman completamenta la mía" (*OC* 91). Although he and his "author" seem to work at cross purposes in terms of their respective narrative "versions," occasionally Martín admits that Alfredo has the story straight: "Confieso: no miente el pérfido Bryce Echenique cuando jura y rejura que cada día estoy más para novela. . . ." (*OC* 81). Suddenly, the colloquial idiom "estar para novela" gains a literal meaning, reaffirming Martín's fictionality in the midst of his own narrative. Bryce's character has inscribed his author in a duplicitous relationship of admiration and rivalry amidst teasing references that undermine authorial control.

Martín yields his authority even more, however, when he empowers Octavia to write her own identity. *OC* chronicles the story of Martín losing control of his fictions. He is in pursuit of a woman under a false identity that he further fictionalizes. She conceals from Martín certain pieces of her life and falsifies her identity. Martín reads into her obscurity an invented anecdotal history. Octavia functions as an illusive figure who never occupies the full space the narrative seems to offer her. She is constrained by Martín's conflicting demands on her, as well as by her family's class imperatives. Martín counters her deceptive development with a relentless insistence on his own private version of her.

Octavia's name becomes the central hermeneutic device of *OC*'s metafictional scheme. The narrator delays telling the reader Octavia's "real" name (Octavia Marie Amélie de la Bonté-Même [*OC* 173]), only to reveal at the end of the novel that her name was never actually Octavia at all. Martín's subjective world once again translates into his own naming system:

> Adoraba a Octavia y me encantaba el hecho de poderla llamar siempre Octavia de Cádiz. *Ella era Octavia de Cádiz para mí. Mi* suerte, *mi* mente, *mi* cuerpo, *mi* pasado, todo lo que yo era me hacía estar plenamente convencido de que mis sentimientos correspondían exactamente a cada partícula de la realidad. (*OC* 103, emphasis added)

Martín may call Octavia whatever he pleases, because as a writer he "authorizes" reality. His restricted access to much of Octavia's existence furthers the fantasy of her identity. He declares Octavia immortal (*OC* 122), and he eventually questions whether she exists at all: "Octavia de Cádiz no era real, era una ideal, fue una quimera" (*OC* 364). He invents or redesigns reality to the extreme of believing it himself and no longer distinguishing between his life and his fictions.

Martín's exaggerated version not only rewrites other characters' identities but also revises his own. He and Octavia affectionately adopt names from Hemingway's characters in an intimate intertextualization of that fiction. Octavia even more frequently calls Martín "Maximus," usually repeated three times, underscoring the hyperbole at the core of both *MR* and *OC*. Martín eventually adopts the pen name Maximus Solre, basing the invented surname on Octavia's cousin's property in Belgium. He grows so accustomed to it that by the end of *OC*, "Martín Romaña era aquel imbécil que siglos atrás había vivido en París" (*OC* 360). His "real" name is converted into a fiction that his recent pseudonym supersedes.

At the end of *OC*, Martín discovers that Octavia's name is actually Petronila. In his epilogue, he concludes that he "había vivido toda una vida de soledad en excelente compañía," and begins to face "la verdad verdadera" (*OC* 374). Rather than accusing her of semiotic betrayal, he realizes that together they fashioned her falsehood. To regain some semblance of control, he persists in his own naming categories. Even after death, another threshold the novel crosses, he declares to Leopoldo who accompanies him to heaven, that "seguiré llamándola Octavia toda la . . . toda la . . . Leopoldo, ayúdame por favor con el vocabulario del cielo" (*OC* 375). He is determined to access the proper language with which to account for his surroundings, continually conscious that wherever he is, he writes as an outsider.

Bryce Echenique works at erasing the borders between fiction and "reality" in *MR* and *OC*. Martín's language demarcates and patrols the regions of his story, to the extent that "la única frontera real es aquella que separa al 'yo' del mundo que lo rodea" (García Bryce 17). Martín attempts to define himself within cultural difference and class rigidity. His identity as a writer emerges out of the *tropezones* of his Peruvian self-consciousness in European territory. His metanarrative becomes the customhouse of his individual and collective border crossings.

Just as Martín crosses narrative boundaries in his journal writing, he crosses national boundaries in his travels between France and other parts of Europe. Although his linguistic boundaries are fluid, serving to defy the limitations of his situation, he unsuccessfully searches for fixed structures in national borders. Martín is convinced that his marital problems with Inés will be resolved in Spain: "Lograrían arreglarlo todo en España, *bastaría con cruzar la frontera*, el amor conyugal renacería, y en estrecha colaboración con la Madrepatria" (*MR* 407, emphasis added). He expects that crossing the Spanish–French border will cure everything from his skin rashes to his depressions. These borders betray him, however, dashing his expectations.

Bryce Echenique's characters expect borders to help them demarcate territories that are blurred by postcolonial disorientation. However, the process of differentiation often presents them with illusory markers. In *OC*, Martín makes the border between France and Belgium a metaphor for Octavia's ephemeral identity. In a crucial episode in *OC*, just north of the Belgian–French border, Octavia disappears. Martín searches for her with a lantern in the dense fog. Finally he thinks he has located her, but the hazy silhouette he mistakes for Octavia turns out to be a signpost with the name of the border town, Aulnoye. Back in the car, Martín finds a note from Octavia, "un papelito que lo explicaba todo pero que no aclaraba nada" (*OC* 122). The note instructs him to look for her at the Aulnoye train station. Therefore, the road sign confirms Martín's first clue toward their reunion. He congratulates himself on his intuitive direction: "yo tenía toda la razón, yo sabía que ese letrero . . . por algo quería correr hacia ese letrero" (*OC* 122).[14] Martín's efforts to decipher the signs in this episode underscore the obscurity of borders and boundaries in his world. Signs that are supposed to direct him result in nothing more than signs. He is faced with the ultimate postcolonial dilemma of signs that for him have no recognizable referents. Borders promise to clarify and delineate, but they only disorient Martín with their ambiguity.

Bryce Echenique situates himself along with his characters on these precarious borders. In *OC*, Martín mentions that Bryce Echenique always pondered over the term *métèque* (in Spanish, *meteco*), the crude insult so frequently encountered in Paris by foreigners. This classical Greek term referred to new residents of a polis who did not have the status of citizens. In French slang, it sends an unwelcoming message to Mediterranean or North African immigrants. According to Martín, Bryce Echenique made vain attempts to find *meteco* in a dictionary. Finally,

> ... se pasaba horas instalado en la frontera franco-española,
> gritándole meteco inmundo a cada automovil con placa
> francesa que entraba en España, basándose para ello en el
> acuerdo de doble nacionalidad que tenemos los peruanos
> con la madre patria, y en una aplicación muy estricta del
> principio de la relatividad. (*OC* 49)

In this episode, Martín locates Bryce Echenique in what Homi
Bhabha calls an "unhomely moment," a "rite of extra-territorial
and cross-cultural initiation . . . [that] relates the traumatic ambiva-
lences of a personal, psychic history to the wider disjunctions of
political existence" (9–11). The incident problematizes civil status,
institutional affiliation, national identity, and language competency
in the borderland of a postcolonial situation. Bryce Echenique's
counterdiscourse in *MR* and *OC* reasserts the postcolonial subject
from the margins to the center. Paradoxically, for all of their marginality as Latin Americans in Europe, Martín and his fictionalized
version of Bryce Echenique are also very cosmopolitan Peruvians.
The Latin American intellectuals in Paris in these novels continually find themselves caught in conflicting self-definitions within
transnational institutional mechanisms, due to their insistence on
renegotiating the periphery's relationship with the metropolis.
Novelistic language issues the fictional passports that document
alien passage and accounts for the "unhomely" defamiliarization of
postcolonial contestation. The fictionalized border patrolling of
license plates, identity cards, work permits, and race and class
associations in these two novels assigns intimate, psychological
content to bureaucratic functions through Martín's narrative of self-
reorientation.

On the borders between cultures and languages, Bryce Echenique
problematizes the struggles for identity in Latin American writing.
His fictional language is a subjective, semiotic experimentation
that skips over the borders of any one national language. His
crosscultural linguistic humor both maintains distance and encourages proximity as he sits on the border to ponder pejorative slang.
He joins his characters in teasing and pitying the Latin American
writer in Paris who is never clear about which borders—linguistic,
political, aesthetic—circumscribe his creativity. He and his characters are stuck on the border of postcolonial cultural (be)longing,
and they confront that uncertainty with the intimate play of invented language and pretend identities.

Martín's story takes place in territories of transgression. He bends the rules of language, oversteps the boundaries of class, and confounds the separation between "reality" and fiction. This diptych is the result of his exaggerated effort to "belong" in Paris. His Paris is a textualized and politicized place that he concocts out of a clash between a history of literary reminiscences and the immediacy of a postcolonial identity crisis. His narration uses Paris as a battleground for aesthetic resistance, where he combats class and cultural limits in an attempt to write a borderless frontier.

CHAPTER FIVE

Paris under Her Skin

---------- ❖ ----------

Luisa Futoransky's Urban Inscriptions of Exile

Cher dos puntos y la ortografía de pesadumbre de estar
exiliada hasta para dos miserables líneas en tu idioma

—*De Pe a Pa*

Paris occupies a privileged position in Luisa Futoransky's fiction. She composes her stories around international itineraries with historical, religious, and literary landmarks in which Paris figures always as a desire and often as a destination. The Latin American construct of Paris emerges in these novels from Argentine childhood memories; from quoted fragments of other texts; and from direct citations from the city's walls, newspapers, and social conventions. Futoransky's work positions Paris as a cultural and geographical hub but refutes its promise of "cultural" prestige and sensual pleasure. Conditioned by the city's underlying structure of meanings and references for Latin America, her characters get lost between the Paris they predict and the Paris they must decipher.

Postcoloniality and gender conspire in Futoransky's fiction. Her novels challenge common Parisian themes in Latin American writing by revealing their gender bias and revising women's passive roles. She most critically rewrites the role of Paris in stories of sexual experimentation, traditionally presumed a male domain. Her female protagonist must reconfigure the roles assigned to her in an anachronistic script written by and for men in order to write openly about women's search for sexual fulfillment. The gender issues of the protagonist's displacement in Paris intersect with her explicit

115

interrogation of postcolonial and authoritarian situations all over the globe. The city is positioned as a ubiquitous geopolitical referent that reflects transnational gender politics.[1]

All of Futoransky's fiction focuses on displacement. She has been living outside of Argentina since the late 1960s, and in Paris since 1981. She states in an interview, "yo soy una persona que trabaja mucho con el exilio, porque hay mucho exilio detrás de mí."[2] Exile for her does not begin with her flight from Argentina during the "Guerra Sucia," but with the pogroms in East Europe in the early part of this century. As the daughter of East European Jews who immigrated to Argentina, then as a Latin American resident in Asia, and currently as a Latin American living in Paris, she has experienced exile within a variety of geocultural situations. Whether as an Argentine Jew or exiled artist, she calls herself a perpetual "outcast."

Futoransky's novels continually expose the particularity of place through ethnographic observation. She interprets an array of cultural practices—from ancient sacred rites to contemporary international tourism and petty office politics—to analyze modern urban nomadism with an ironic social relativity. Her novels, *Son cuentos chinos* and *De Pe a Pa: De Pekín a París*, grapple with the psychological, linguistic, and cultural challenges of an intercultural world. The novels' geographical and sociological commentaries trace the gender implications of transnational urban semiotics. The texts map fictional explorations of postcolonial cultural identity from the protagonist's itinerary of successive displacements.

Futoransky's metafictional experimentation supports the prevailing theme of exile in her narrative. Her writing concocts a network of intertextual disjunctions that resists grounding her in any specific tradition. The diffusion of these citations and allusions intersects in Paris, where Futoransky's narrators deposit their displaced fragments. She undermines the Latin American construct of Paris, in particular, its image of high social status and prestige, in arbitrary fictional convergences. Biruté Ciplijauskaité's characterization of experimental women's fiction in *La novela femenina contemporanea* contributes to an understanding of Futoransky's autobiographical metafiction and to her revision of the Paris construct. The critic identifies three central purposes in women's rebellious writing: a revindication of the erotic and the sexual, a rejection of linguistic and social structures, and the use of lyrical expression for protest or affirmation. All of Futoransky's novels exploit narrative techniques to contest sexual repression, sociopolitical tyranny, and conventional expectations of women's discourse.[3]

Son cuentos chinos employs the intimate journal form, a novelistic stance that fictionalizes the autobiography while at the same time allows for authorial intervention. In *De Pe a Pa*, the narration vacillates between a narrator in the third person and the protagonist in the first person. Futoransky oversteps the boundaries of autobiographical fiction to allow the author to interact with her characters. The narrative discourse in both novels incorporates poetry, prayer, journalism, travel writing, ancient and contemporary fragments in the protagonist's intertextual process of self-discovery. These novels become fictional urban scrapbooks in which the narrator/protagonist cites the sacred and the profane, documents international tourism, fantasizes about sex, and denounces social and political repression. *Son cuentos chinos* and *De Pe a Pa* question the construct of the image of Paris while they ponder the craft of fiction.

Futoransky's anecdotal Paris rests on a textual storehouse of episodes onto which she graphs language, street maps, icons, visual cues, and culturally coded behaviors. The protagonist's relationship with her own language is ambivalent, as this chapter's epigraph affirms. Her Argentine Spanish in Asia and Europe pits language familiarity against the strangeness of new surroundings. In Futoransky's work, Spanish copes with concepts, objects, and customs it usually does not have to accommodate. She becomes frustrated when her beloved *castellano* does not have the flexibility to decipher or explain her surroundings. Even her titles, borrowed from colloquial expressions, attempt to link her own language to the situation into which she has thrown herself. Futoransky challenges the various signs systems her characters encounter. Her fiction underscores the inadequacy of any national language (and even its regional or dialectical variants) to represent transnational experience.

Luisa Futoransky's first novel, *Son cuentos chinos*, treats urban transnationalism through the Argentine protagonist's encounter with China. The novel takes the form of a personal diary written by Laura Kaplansky, an exiled radio journalist and aspiring poet who lives and works in Peking. The novel's development depends less on actions and events than on a collage of quotes, intimate prose and free-verse fragments that tell the story of Laura's emotional, intellectual, and spiritual life. Most of the scenes focus on her intimate encounters with two African diplomat lovers and the bureaucratic frustrations of working in China. The narration's series of crosscultural impressions hover around three geographical centers. Buenos Aires represents Laura's childhood, Peking establishes her current surroundings, and Paris serves as her reference point for nearly all of Western culture and determines many of her metaphors for sexuality and gender.

Laura Kaplansky's transnational tale continues in *De Pe a Pa: De Pekín a París*, when Laura turns down a university teaching position in China to live and write in Paris. There the precarious existence she describes in *Son cuentos chinos* persists. Laura's life in Paris includes meetings with other Latin American expatriates, psychoanalysis, searching for housing and employment, and visiting French cultural and historic monuments. Her literary aspirations cast her into one of the most familiar roles for expatriates in Paris. She suffers the stereotypical poverty, illness, disillusionment, and demoralization, with plenty of allusions to Hemingway, Fitzgerald, Vallejo, and Cortázar. The novel ends with a parody of European canonized forms in the outline of an Italian opera called "Cuarentena de la dama." The operatic tragedy is a painful rash that Laura develops, and the novel ends as she is released from the hospital.

DECODING IN PEKING

Although *Son cuentos chinos* does not take place in Paris, it prepares the way, both anecdotally and intertextually, for the Paris of its sequel. *Son cuentos chinos* integrates the Latin American conception of Paris into its transnational network. The novel uses that projection to offer glimpses of the decoding process that the character will face in *De Pe a Pa*. The progression from one novel to the next is more than episodic sequencing. The city strategically binds Futoransky's fiction by serving as a geographical and an intertextual source. From these novels' distinctive autobiographical perspectives, Paris remains the common locus of recognition from Latin America, Asia, and even from within Europe.

The themes of exile and solitude are intertwined in Laura's journal, where she records both her emotional instability and geographical transience. In Peking, letters arrive opened, a companion dies, and Laura regularly faces separations. The single, middle-aged protagonist who previously worked in Tokyo reminisces about her childhood in Buenos Aires, juxtaposing those reminiscences with Zen Buddhist stories in China. She refers to Paris as an international axis that facilitates the travel and telephone links that are otherwise obstructed in Asia. Repeatedly confused and exasperated by the administrative controls, censorship, and loneliness of Peking, she decides to leave for "otra vez parís, madrid, tel aviv, atenas, roma o nueva york" (164).[4] Laura continually imagines Paris in *Son cuentos chinos* in her project of transnational urban connectedness and intimate self-realization.

Paris figures prominently in *Son cuentos chinos*'s mapping of Laura's spatial relationships of familiarity and estrangement, despite its geographical and cultural distance from China. While Buenos Aires is her most familiar association, and Peking provides her current but very foreign surroundings, Paris remains the territory only familiarized through reading and projection. Laura has fantasized about Paris since she was an adolescent poet in Buenos Aires. She evokes the city repeatedly, although she has yet to visit France. Quantitatively, the fourteen mentions of Paris almost rival the number of Chinese terms and place names the narrator defines. It represents the only non-Latin American place that the Latin American character evokes to inject familiarity into the strangeness of her current environment. Paris functions as her thread of continuity and identification in the confusion of foreign experiences.

The narrator/protagonist automatically associates Paris with any cosmopolitan encounter. In one short passage, she refers to a Latin American *asadito*, a French party, the tarot, the I Ching, and Mikonos, Greece (27). Some Parisian anecdote or reference almost always appears in her enumerated associations: "koumbá también pasará, como el taxista iraquí de jerusalem, el cuentista jujeño en parís, el tenor sueco en buenos aires . . ." (45). Laura compares her residence in China, the Hotel Peking, to the Parisian brasseries Le Coupole or Le Select (75). Despite these exclusive references, Peking does not offer her a glamorous international lifestyle, but rather reveals an anguished examination of her contradictory worlds. Peking is the foreign zone that Laura processes through her varying familiarity with other zones. Paris resides in Laura's imaginative familiarity as she gropes to explain her international world. Laura relies on Paris to make coherent China's unusual and often obscured reality. The French capital is expected to measure her experiences, to provide the "known" standard by which she can evaluate everything else.

The narrator associates Paris with sensual pleasure. Laura evokes the city during the exercise of a simulated "homework" assignment, "composición de tema libre . . . pensemos entonces en situaciones de placer":

> en París, por Saint-Michel darán un par de películas de Saura y de Fellini, la gente irá comiendo crêpes y sandwiches griegos por la calle, beberán kir en las terrazas y kir royal en "La Closerie des Lilas", caminarán del Beaubourg a Les Halles y el Pariscope se regará de vino y se untará de quesos y todos irán de silla en silla. . . . (119)

She situates her pleasurable setting in the Latin Quarter, her imagined locus for the consumption of foreign films, wine, cheese, crepes, and cheap sandwiches. *Pariscope* (the weekly guide to artistic events), food, films, neighborhoods and bars all combine in Laura's collective notions of culture and pleasure. This ambulatory enumeration reveals Paris's seductive allure for Laura. She visits a fantasy from afar that offers her vicarious sensual gratification. Directly following these images of Paris, Laura visualizes her lover, Djagó, kissing "toda mi vasta superficie," and then imagines a long-awaited phone call from her Argentine lover, Juan Daniel (119).

Futoransky reworks a male-imagined Paris into an intertext of desire and sexual longing for women. In an interview, she evoked the Argentine commonplace that babies come from Paris, and underscored the ideas of "la creación y la sexualidad detrás de la palabra París." The Paris construct traditionally limits sensual desire to men's pursuit of young French women, often prostitutes. In Futoransky's fiction, however, a woman narrator directly rejects this reduction of women to sexual objects of expatriate male pursuit. Laura uses Paris to expand her own erotic potential. The city becomes the *site* for sensual pleasure, rather than a storehouse of possible, anonymous sexual partners. Futoransky's first novel maps the protagonist's geopolitical trajectory and sensual longing as a complex response to both the Argentine military dictatorship and her status as an exile. Laura inserts Paris in her politics of gender to combat state and sexual repression. As a zone on which to project her romantic fantasies, her revisionist Paris will license women's sexual empowerment and social liberties. As Mary Beth Tierney-Tello discusses in *Allegories of Transgression and Transformation: Experimental Fiction By Women Writing under Dictatorship*, authoritarian regimes produce an

official discourse [that] indeed gives a singular and highly
traditional "reading" or interpretation to the sex/gender
system, attempting to make its function appear natural
and beyond question . . . the authoritarian regime tries to
limit the populace's own libidinal reproductions. (6)

Experimental fiction written in exile attacks the regime in power
at the same time it pierces long-standing social constructs like
Paris for Latin America. The process of gendering comes under
assault in *Son cuentos chinos* from the narrator-protagonist's
transnational perspective.

Futoransky contests gender politics both at home and abroad.
Her protagonist, Laura, clearly pursues an erotic agenda, as a form of
resistance to state-sponsored terrorism in Argentina as well as a
response to sexual repression in China and sexist exclusion of women
in Latin America's imagined Paris. Laura examines transnational
contexts to explain, justify, or liberate herself from the state's—any
state's—repressive policies. Intimacy and pleasure, as interior arenas,
represent much more elusive domains for the state to penetrate. A
long, chantlike passage toward the end of the novel enumerates a
variety of official restrictions on daily life from an array of countries,
ending each example with a responsive "pobre gente":

> que pueden coger sólo dos veces por semana porque más
> el partido dice que es malo para la salud, pobre gente
> en israel no se puede comer chancho, pobre gente
>
> ni prender la luz los sábados ni ir en bici ni nadar, pero
> coger sí, pobre gente
>
> el wotjila dice que hay que hacer hijos, deng dice que no
> hay que hacer hijos, pobre gente. (159–60)

State sanctions that control reproduction infringe on sacred doctrine and personal erotic freedom.

Futoransky's protagonist, Laura, seeks sexual fulfillment as a
triumphant personal and political gesture against state repression
and invites other Third-World women to reappropriate their own
sexuality from the control of public official discourse. Doris
Sommer's historical argument in *Foundational Fictions* for Latin
America's "passionate patriotism" (33) in nineteenth-century narrative offers an intriguing backdrop for the conflictive relationship

between desire and national identity in the context of exile. Sommer convincingly establishes the allegorical parallels between hetero-sexual union in the novel and nation formation. She draws on Foucault's examination in *The History of Sexuality* of sexual bod-ies as politicized zones of governmental control. Futoransky's work adds to Foucault's analysis of the control that fictions, and fictional scripts for places like Paris, exert on gender identities. In the case of exile from dictatorial regimes, the libidinal drive has more to do with self-affirmation, particularly for women, than collective (na-tion) (re)building. While Latin America's phallogocentric nation-building project a century and a half ago included populating the New World, seeding the fertile (woman) ground, Futoransky's femi-nist mission calls upon women to transgress their alienating gen-der categorization, an implicit form of exile, as well as official dogma and the exile of expatriation, by embracing their sexuality and eroticism.

Laura calls upon sexual icons in temples, spiritual scriptures, and Parisian fantasies to restore sensuality to her own life and to China. On a visit to a Lamaist temple, Laura accesses the room with the tantric images only open to visitors with special authorization:

> que más claro imposible como estaban de trenzadas las dos imágenes ente las cuales me detengo/ . . . una dentro de la otra con mil brazos y piernas y ojos en un orgasmo perpetuo concebido en el sueño abisal de *ser* en el otro. (173)

The Chinese tour guide intrudes on Laura's interpretation and in-sists that the images are twins and have nothing to do with sex. Laura's voyeuristic reaction represents much more than a touristic fascination with the exotic to be recorded in a travel diary. She seeks out these images and inscribes them, along with her own sexual encounters, to contest the state's restrictions on viewing, experiencing, and even interpreting sensual pleasure.

Along with the novel's revision of conventional roles for Paris—the international cultural center and the focus of sensual desire—in *Son cuentos chinos* the city also functions as one of the narrator's tools in her effort to understand her surroundings. Paris becomes another quoted, cited authority, like the fragments Laura includes from her other readings. Systems of language seem more accessible to her, thus she chooses to rely on writing and representational symbols. In an effort to elucidate the foreignness of her world, she declares optimistically, "[c]ada vez me convenzo más de que existe una relación clara y abierta entre las cosas, las gentes y sus nombres" (73). In the process of uncovering that relationship, she has a number of setbacks. Sometimes she is convinced that the keys are hidden only from her. In her discouraged state, she hesitates to "abrir puerta destino y comprobar positivamente que nos hemos correspondido un cacho en el paréntesis" (164). Hers is a world of words. The Chinese lexeme *meio*, meaning "se terminó, no está, no hay" is so prevalent in daily transactions that "[e]l *meio*, *meio* viene a ser la muralla china, pero de palabras" (47). She feels herself encircled by the great wall of semiotic mystery and misinterpretation.

To decipher the codes of the diverse cultural systems she encounters, Laura gathers about her all of the discursive forms and textual fragments that might help sort out her current confusion. She carefully observes language, behavior, dress, family life, and transportation in China. She includes quotes from Buddhist, Confuscian, Zen, and Yiddish sources, all commented on in a colloquial and very Argentine Spanish. Her prose condenses conversations, letters, meals, and telephone calls with a display of international characters. The vocabulary of incomprehension abounds in Laura's writing: "me confundo" (18), "[n]unca lo dilucidé" (94), "no entiendo" (165). She finds herself at a loss in efforts to communicate: "no le puedo, no me puede explicar nada" (166). She searches for strategies that will organize the assault of information. In one chapter, she defines five practical Chinese terms that all begin with "m": "regla mnemotécnica para manejarse y con la que se maneja China" (47). China, then, is territory that one must *manage*, but that most probably will be impossible to master.

The controls for operating this world of new symbologies seem to be beyond her grasp. "Tanto en China como en Japón se aprenden códigos invisibles que no responden a ninguna de nuestras lógicas" (43). Words and gestures have different meanings, and Laura tries to comprehend their logic, to little or no avail. "[D]urazno = longevidad; para nosotros piel dulce, piel adolescente que ya no más" (18). She would like not only to memorize the new meanings, but also to understand their underlying cultural symbolism. On one of many bus tours she participates in as an international professional, Laura visits the mountain, Tai-shan. "Los emperadores *tenían* que subir al Tai-shan y nosotros también ... Ya desde el vamos la montaña es otra cosa distinta que 'nuestra' idea de montaña" (126). Her cultural and even practical conceptions for daily interactions face firm opposition in a new context. Laura finds that her "ideas" of common things (peaches, mountains) and of how simply to organize daily life are constantly challenged.

Laura lives in China, but she finds it incomprehensible. She has never lived in Paris, yet she expects to understand it. This paradoxical relationship between proximity and comprehension is an important dynamic tension in Futoransky's fiction. Paris is positioned in *Son cuentos chinos* as being geographically remote but culturally accessible for a Latin American intellectual. The protagonist's Argentine past does not provide a recognizable and familiar world with which to measure new and foreign ones, but rather remains circumscribed in distant family intimacy. The Argentina evoked in the novel never communicates present understandings, but rather voices a closed and an isolated fragment of Laura's life. Paris emerges from afar in this novel through its conceptualization within Latin American urban culture. The numerous references to Paris subtly create a backdrop that sustains the rest of the narrative. It provides the dislocated bridge for the narrator/protagonist between her *porteño* Spanish and her Chinese surroundings. The narration hinges on the most distant space to explain and account for the protagonist's intimate past and her overwhelmingly foreign present.

DE PE A PA: STRANGER IN A FAMILIAR LAND

The sequel to *Son cuentos chinos* recounts Laura's initial adjustment to Paris and her process of reconciling the Paris she projected with her daily life there. While in *Son cuentos chinos* the reader follows Laura's personal interpretation of her experiences as she writes them from her hotel room in Peking, in *De Pe a Pa* the reader accompanies her through Paris. The narration follows Laura's Parisian trajectories, hunting for apartments in its *arrondissements*, traveling by subway, and stopping in its cafés. Futoransky's narrative continues to excerpt from other written texts, and her intertextual project is even more intricate in this novel. She incorporates episodic citations from the story of Paris inscribed in Latin American conceptions of urban culture, and she also quotes the contemporary city itself. While *Son cuentos chinos* presents Laura's personal and spiritual readings, this novel offers graffiti, public signs, and personal advertisements from popular magazines. The novel quotes Paris directly, considering its physical space and printed sources as viable textual material. From collage to palimpsest,

Futoransky uncovers Paris's social, verbal, and material messages from the doubly marginalized perspective of a woman in exile.

De Pe a Pa manipulates the subtext of the Latin American intellectual who wants to "succeed" in Europe. While Scorza dismantles the touristic, bourgeois itinerary of the Latin American *viaje a Europa* from a Leftist vantage point, Futoransky seeks to denounce the presumed familiarity with Paris that backfires on an exiled, Third-World, middle-aged woman. While "success" should involve publishing and artistic recognition, the plot mostly concerns Laura's struggle for survival in Paris. Laura used to project the Paris of international literary activity as a student back in Buenos Aires,

> . . . . los primeros articulitos, poemas en un periodicucho estudiantil, los firmó así: *Ruth París*. *Ruth*, obviamente en un intento de asumir la kaplanskidad . . . y *París* para abrazar, incluyéndose geográficamente, la cosmogonía de lo mítico literario, ya que en su adolescencia, salvo para Borges cuyo hilo conductor pasaba por la Pérfida Albión, para el resto de los comunes escribidores, literatos y embadurnadores, la respiración toda pasaba por París y tanto es así que hasta a los nenes se los hacía venir de su contorno. (14)

Her adolescent pen name roots her to the two cultural traditions her imagination straddles: Jewish and Parisian. The former is grounded in her own family background, along with Jewish historical and religious texts, while the latter directly assigns Paris as her vicarious identity.

The city and the body in *De Pe a Pa* are zones of inscription for Latin America's social and gender codifications of Paris. When Laura finally decides to experience contact with Paris beyond her "readings," she wonders:

> llegando ¿para quedarme? ¿en tránsito? a esta Ciudad Luz, intimidadora por el rumor de todas las parises-fantasmas que habíamos vivido dentro antes de tocarla—fugazmente, porque no se deja—en carne y hueso. . . . (18)

She does reach Paris and manages to "touch" it in the flesh, although the result is that Paris touches *her* in the flesh. The novel makes explicit the interconnectedness of intimacy and urban space that the conventional "story" of Latin American desire for Paris only suggests. Futoransky boldly moves beyond the rudimentary metaphor of Paris as woman and the urban realm as illicit sexual opportunity. The novel renders the body and the city—its buildings, streets, monuments—material status destined to be inscribed and then deciphered.

To reach this semiotic revelation, *De Pe a Pa* first dismantles Paris as a cultural capital through Laura's search for "culture." Her desire to connect with artistic projects, publishing, and the supposed international scene of intellectuals in Paris leads her to desperate fantasies and disappointments. In "Vida de artista" (chapter V), Laura decides to adopt the Café Cluny, in the heart of the Latin Quarter, as her meeting place. She thinks she recognizes a Chilean writer involved with a Madrid literary magazine. However, it is not the Chilean at all, but rather an Iranian who was in a French class with her several months earlier. At her apartment later that day, she hopes for mail from a publisher, or for a letter granting her an interview with Radio France. She falls asleep reading Hemingway's *A Moveable Feast*, which she chooses because "él y sus amigos escribían bastante en el Café Cluny" (61). She tries to follow the paths of Hemingway, Latin American exiles, and young foreigners in Paris, but carrying out their instructions does not yield the anticipated results.

De Pe a Pa disproves the guarantees of cultural integration and artistic success for expatriates that the Latin American construct of Paris has maintained.[5] Laura's desperate attempts to pursue literary recognition are based on the Paris she believed in from afar. As in Proust and in Bryce Echenique, the anticipated place rarely materializes like the illusions promise. Nevertheless, daily experience in the place does not eliminate the persistent ghosts. Laura, like Martín Romaña, takes on the often excruciating task of simultaneously living with the current Paris and the textual Paris.

The novel undermines common *topoi* of the Paris construct, not only to reveal their damaging emotional cost and their fallacious Eurocentrism. Futoransky uses those failures as pretexts to her semiotic examination of urban inscription. As Laura's illusions about Paris break down, she often pursues less conventional sources for guidance, despite commonsense reasoning. Once, for example, she hears about a faith miracle announced by a medium. The instructions require a visit to touch a certain grave in the Père Lachaise cemetery three times a day. The next day, "sin saber por qué" (83),

Laura wanders in Père Lachaise with her friend María.[6] She visits churches with similar detachment: "sin otra lógica que la urgencia de sus estímulos sístole-diástole . . . parte de las motivaciones ajenas" (104). Although she disparages French culture, she succumbs to Paris's textual intrigue. The ghosts of Père Lachaise send messages through their tombstones and, like the city's churches and monuments, inscribe sites that compell Laura. The novel deflates Paris's illusions for Latin Americans and reduces the city to its material textuality. Ultimately, it also reduces its protagonist to her body, its desires and pleasures a surface to be written.

A footnote from the narrator at the end of the novel informs the reader that Laura, as a character, was created to explain "qué es ser poeta suelto por el mundo, con sus particulares agravantes; mujer mayor, pobre, judía, argentina y sola" (123–24). This autobiographical revelation at the end of the second part of Laura's story restates the issues of marginality and loneliness, still unresolved, inherent in exile. Her precarious, liminal status as an outsider in Asia gives her the necessary distance to be a reader of Paris and also positions her as a potential victim of its inscription. Once in Paris, she notices that the metro is populated with young Latin American musicians (23) and African cleaning crews. The flashy travel plans and diplomatic phone calls that depended on Paris for connection from Asia seem remote in her daily struggle to survive. She takes note of the multicultural clientele at the Cluny café, and it occurs to her that its "aire de bar 'se admiten inmigrantes' " (60) is what makes her feel comfortable in the Latin Quarter brasseries. Her community is now one of Latin American exiles and other marginalied cultural workers struggling to squeeze out of Paris the basic needs of food and shelter while they also nourish hopes of artistic recognition.

In *De Pe a Pa*, Laura's sense of marginalization relates to her process of cultural translation and explication. As she identifies with the wider community of particularly Latin American expatriates, she is not alone in her semiotic adjustment. During the cited interview, Futoransky spoke of the "búsqueda de mimetización" of an initial wave of foreigners in a new place: "Hay toda una clase que siempre quiere parecerse a los propietarios de la tierra." Despite her mostly solitary experiences, she recognizes her participation in a subcommunity that puts forth enormous effort to comprehend French culture in order to gain acceptance. The following passage comments on the ritual structure of French meals that newcomers feel pressured to imitate:

[n]ativos y metecos; a falta de querernos, comemos y
bebemos. Nuestros rituales, como los de todos los
convertidos recientes, son bien rígidos. Aperitivo, entrada,
plato con verdura y salsas, ensalada de lechuga al final
cuyas hojas deben haberse secado en la maquinita ad-hoc;
quesos (como mínimo tres: duro, semiblando y blando,
servidos en tabla de madera; manteca y pan aparte, por
favor) y vinos. Jamás queso con vino blanco, que es pecado
mortal. (69)

She uses the insulting "métèque" to categorize herself with other
foreigners. They all try not only to read correctly but also to adopt
and accurately enact the gestures around them. The narrator's
community's obsession with the highly codified rules of French
gastronomy is just one example of their effort to comply with the
behavioral norms around them. However, all Latin Americans reveal their *meteco* status upon speaking French:

> siempre siempre lo suficientemente extranjero como para
> que un mínimo gesto del nativo le haga a uno saber que
> jamás, por más esfuerzos realizados en la empresa, dejará
> de pasársele la enagua, volvemos a nuestro castellano
> básico. (69)

Laura's marginality follows her throughout the novel, regardless of her improved spoken French or mastery over wine and cheese
combinations. The narrator even introduces Laura's first French
lover as a significant conquest:

> ... la primera vez que en su larguísimo primer invierno
> parisino la invitaba un francés francés sin gota alguna de
> sudaquerío natal. (80)

A date with a "real" Frenchman for Laura is more meaningful to
her as a sign of cultural acceptance than as the sort of sexual
conquest that previous Latin American narratives about Paris exalt. Nevertheless, she decides that she will never overcome the
difficulties of the vast and complex sign systems in her Parisian
context:

> ¿Cuándo, cuándo mi alma podré darme cuenta aquí de
> Quién es Quién por la manera de plegar el periódico en

el metro o pronunciar o suprimir las eses? Sin hablar de
los sobrentendidos populares de la lengua, sé que soy y
seré extranjera a perpetuidad, sin remedio no sólo por mi
pronunciación deplorablemente *tipé* sino por lo blindado
de los códigos a los que ni siquiera con cuatro generaciones
de nacidos en las mismísimas arenas de Lutecia accedería
ni por asomo. (106)

Marked by her accent, rash, age, nationality, and religion, she is
particularly doomed to be an outsider among foreign codes. Parisian residences often advertise "portes blindées," a security feature
of supposedly impenetrable armored doors. Laura considers herself
irrevocably barred from the generational, cultural, and textual
semiotics of Paris, whose codes remain "blindados." As the previous passage exemplifies, the overwhelming challenge does not come
from the need to communicate in French, but rather from the need
to communicate in Paris.

Laura is a gifted observer, an anthropological poet who notices
the visual, phonetic, commercial, international, and local signs
around her. She presumes a certain competence in distinguishing
subtle characteristics and in gleaning essential cultural information through this variety of sources. As wide ranging as her sources
are, however, they are not exhaustive. She may have learned to
choose the right bottle of wine to bring to a dinner party, but
distinguishing passengers on the metro just by how they fold their
newspapers still stumps her.

PARIS'S URBAN INSCRIPTIONS

In China, a bombardment of terms, practices, and values exploded
around Laura daily, and she turned to her writing for an intimate
synthesis that might make sense of them. Now Paris bombards her
in an unexpected assault that demands adjustments in her deciphering tactics. Futoransky's intertextuality in her second novel
not only quotes, as in *Son cuentos chinos*, French, Argentine, Ju-
daic, and occult sources but also cites the city. *De Pe a Pa* implicates Paris beyond setting and fantasy as a scriptural source whose
newspapers, graffiti, cafés, streets, subways, and architecture all
provide readings. Michel de Certeau's description of the blinding
practice of "reading" cities points out the urban reconstruction of
Futoransky's novels:

> Bodies follow the thicks and thins of an urban "text"
> they write without being able to read it. These practitio-
> ners make use of spaces that cannot be seen; their knowl-
> edge of them is as blind as that of lovers in each other's
> arms. The paths that correspond in this intertwining,
> unrecognized poems in which each body is an element
> signed by many others, elude eligibility. It is as though
> the practices organizing a bustling city were character-
> ized by their blindness. The networks of these moving,
> intersecting writings compose a manifold story . . . shaped
> out of fragments of trajectories and alterations of spaces.
> (93)

Futoransky's narrative strategy corresponds to de Certeau's kalei-
doscopic urban fragments, particularly in *De Pe a Pa,* whose
intertextuality exploits the city itself. Laura often finds Paris as
baffling to comprehend as she did Peking. Talmudic citations, rab-
binical wisdom, and Argentine memories temper the blow of Paris's
bombardment of signs. The narration presents a contemporary *reading* of the city via an added layer of visual and printed Paris. Walls,
subway routes, commercial signs, and newspapers offer messages
just as quotable as spiritual and literary sources.

The novel, for example, retells or quotes anecdotes from current media, such as the news brief that follows from the Leftist
French newspaper, *Libération*:

> Un hombre de 52 años se suicidó en su propio congelador
> el miércoles pasado en Kaltenhouse, periferia de
> Estrasburgo. El hombre fue encontrado sentado ante una
> botella de gas abierta en modo tal que murió por asfixia
> y congelación, *Libération*, 8/9/83. (106–07)

These fragments of popular culture and current media compose
Futoransky's intertextual Paris. Their juxtaposition with the sacred
and literary citations level high and low culture, literate and oral
sources, and written and verbal signs. The narrator builds onto the
conventional Paris construct a new layer of citations. These visual
messages from the Paris of print media, advertising, and commerce
are quotes from the city's current text. They demand that the reader
participate in the deciphering process, along with Laura.

Futoransky's cut-and-paste narrative style coincides with a
number of critics' appraisals of art and literature produced under

dictatorship. Nelly Richard characterizes Chilean neovanguard art and literature during this period as "arte refractario" that refers to unbending rebellion against hegemonic discourse. As a form of resistance to the military regime's controls on meaning and expression, these writers and artists manipulate the fragment in

> precarias economías del trozo y de la traza... [para producir una] dislocación del horizonte referencial que el pasado y la tradición habían trazado como línea de continuidad histórica. (14, 17)

Beatriz Sarlo also considers the fragment as a "strategy" in Argentine novelistic discourse during the dictatorship. The fragment is used as a means of accounting for history in a period of secrets, censure, disappearances, and death. Fiction "worked on the fragments of available experience" to expose the traces of history through ellipses, gaps, and intertexts ("Strategies," quoted in *Fear at the Edge* 241). Futoransky makes her protagonist wade through the Parisian baggage she brought with her, as well as through Paris's contemporary textual morass. In Laura's cultural and scriptural exile, her own carefully searched for and personally chosen texts collide with all of the citations of the city's textual history and contemporaneity.

Futoransky's incorporation of journalistic and commercial citations manipulates the visual image of the page in a spatial intertextuality that produces effective immediacy. As in Cortázar's *Libro de Manuel*, where the reader of the metafictional novel simultaneously reads the scrapbook included on its pages, in *De Pe a Pa* the reader views the city's messages along with Laura. Cortázar's and Futoransky's narrators perform the role of compilers or editors who cull through the printed present. While Futoransky's novel does not have the political urgency of *Libro de Manuel*, the dates, current references, and capricious miscellany in *De Pe a Pa* have a similar metafictional effect. Saúl Sosnowski's discussion of the collage aesthetic, or what he calls "la poesía," of *Libro de Manuel*, also applies to Futoransky's fiction:

> Y digo poesía (sin comillas) y en su acepción no genérica porque el punto de partida de esta obra liquida la jerarquización de motivos y modos poéticos. La realidad narrada se torna poética en su inmediatez. (Sosnowski 110–11)

Just as in *Libro de Manuel* the narrator is a reader of the scrapbook, in *Son cuentos chinos* and *De Pe a Pa* the narrator/protagonist is a reader who chronicles her textual path through places.[7]

In this nod of recognition toward Cortázar and his extensive Parisian fiction, Futoransky employs his collage technique but with different political aims. She steers away from his 1970's revolutionary ideology to introduce in *De Pe a Pa* a gendered critique of urban material structures. The narrator intermingles popular media with historical monuments and alternative spirituality in a textual reconstruction of Paris that threatens to invade the innermost reaches of Laura's self. From the public to the private, from exterior walls to interior soul-searching, the protagonist finds herself surrounded by Paris's inscriptions.

Visual signs then, along with linguistic adjustments in French, are equally vital in illiciting Laura's responses to her daily Parisian world. The narration must resort to verbal expression, however, to translate these visual signs. The narrator describes and copies the graffiti Laura views: "Boire + Bouffer les français ne connaissent que ça. Graffitti, Metro Avron. 25.12.81" (69). Historic plaques on buildings must be "read" to the reader. The narrator introduces Laura's reflections on plaques in the old streets of the Marais:

> París está salpicada de placas por muertos martirizados, fusilados, deportados. A veces, a más del nombre y la fecha, el tipo de agonía sufrida y una pequeña bandera tricolor, existe un florerito para recuerdos ocasionales. También en esto, seguramente, un día Latinoamérica importará el sistema. (46)

Laura summarizes the French formula for these plaques, including an inventory of their symbols and information. She identifies a system of signs, repeated and institutionalized in Paris, and expects them to be appropriated by Latin American consumerism.

Néstor García Canclini discusses the function of monuments, public art, and historical plaques that modern development assigns to specific places and rigorously classifies. This process of naming and locating for the urban public

> sostiene la organización sistemática de los *espacios* sociales en que deben ser consumidos. . . . Sin embargo, la vida urbana transgrede a cada momento este orden. En el movimiento de la ciudad los intereses mercantiles se

> cruzan con los históricos, los estéticos y los comuni-
> cacionales. Las luchas semánticas por neutralizarse,
> perturbar el mensaje de los otros o cambiar su significado,
> y subordinar a los demás a la propia lógica, son puestas
> en escena de los conflictos entre las fuerzas sociales: entre
> el mercado, la historia, el Estado, la publicidad, y la lucha
> popular por sobrevivir. (*Culturas híbridas* 280)

The narrator repeatedly surrounds Laura with diverse forms of cultural expression whose integration into her urban "text" redesigns the relationship between the center and the periphery. The novel allows graffiti, representing marginal popular culture, and historic plaques, representing institutionalized national culture, to coexist in an "extensión transclasista del fenómeno de desterritorialización" (García Canclini, *Culturas híbridas* 291). Both of these phenomena, foundational historical markers or recuperative graffiti, are examples of territorial urban expression that *De Pe a Pa* deterritorializes.[8] Laura's exiled eye captures Paris in the throes of heteroglossic discontinuity, where the city announces its social functions (tourism, national identity, immigration) in segments. Deleuze and Guattari define deterritorialization as a process that is intricately related to exile, language, and writing (see their *Kafka: Toward a Minor Literature*). Their concept characterizes Laura's transnational movement and pursuit of transitory meaning. According to their definition, deterritorialization requires one

> to participate in movement, to stake out the path of es-
> cape in all its positivity, to cross a threshold, to reach a
> continuum of intensities that are valuable only in them-
> selves, to find a world of pure intensities where all forms
> come undone, as do all the significations, signifiers, and
> signifieds, to the benefit of an unformed matter of
> deterritorialized flux, of nonsignifying signs. (13)

Meaning's relativity and whim reveal the disorientation of exile and the defamiliarization of urban space along with the homelessness of the writing process. In the novel's metafictional program, urban space and textual space suffer analogous fragmentation to underscore modern urban deterritorialization.[9]

Other visual references contribute to the novel's assortment of extralinguistic codes. The character exploits this realm to counter her overload of linguistic clues. Laura pays attention to visual details

like tatoos, tarot cards, and graffiti in Paris, just as she tried to
understand the Chinese use of ambulances for laundry delivery
while flimsy stretchers were employed to transport patients to
hospitals (*Son cuentos chinos*). The rash she develops at the end
of the novel functions as the final visual cue. Laura is marked by
her Paris experience, covered with a red, peeling, itching rash. It
is her stress, depression, and nerves that produce this extreme
physical reaction. As Judith Butler notes in *Gender Trouble*, "the
contours of the body [are] clearly marked as the taken-for-granted
ground or surface upon which gender significations are inscribed,
a mere facticity devoid of value, prior to significance" (129). Like
sexually transmitted diseases or rape, Laura's rash is a violation
of intimacy. The external, anthropological clues she remarks on
throughout the novel evade her, and the deciphering process turns
further and further inward. The signs of her world close in on her.
This last visual and physical manifestation is the fading palimpsest of Paris.

Following the confusion of China, Laura expects to understand
more deeply and manage with less effort the daily Parisian sign
world. Nevertheless, she often finds gaps in her comprehension.

> ... estoy en París porque seguido las radios libres me
> desayunan con *ne me quitte pas*, como para que yo no
> pierda el hilo del discurso, pero me repita en carne propia
> que París es gris, tan gris que es el único lugar del mundo
> donde un pintor se puede llamar Gris. . . . (20)

Laura tries not to lose the line of patter or the gist of an utter-
ance or a gesture. The French "ne me quitte pas," "don't leave
me," is also colloquial telephone discourse for "don't hang up." In
her partial or faulty understanding, she clings to every word. She
hopes to make all of the correct and appropriate semantic and
syntactic connections. However, she continually falls between the
semiotic cracks.

> ¿sabré alguna vez quiénes son los franceses; pude imaginar
> acaso a cuánto llegarían los argentinos? ¡qué sé en verdad
> de los chinos, los japoneses, los italianos, los indonesios,
> los israelíes que tanto les deambulé sus tierras!, pero,
> primero y principal: ¿sé acaso quién soy o estoy siendo yo
> por primera añadidura? (18)

She begins to doubt her own gift of anthropological observation and the validity of her own experiences in different cultural and linguistic contexts. She feels overpowered by the conflicting and confusing sign systems she confronts: "se pierden—inapresables trágame tierra—las llaves de decodificación personal de las imágenes y sólo resta la frágil, confusa, indefensión de todos los días" (47). In her defenseless struggle, she tries to grasp any systematic formula, linguistic or otherwise, that might give back or reconstruct the lost keys. Paris not only disappoints Laura, as it disappoints and betrays the characters in Salazar Bondy's *Pobre gente de París* and Güiraldes's *Raucho*, but it also confuses her. She is misled by the trendy projects, the quaint cafés, and the codified socializing that her previous "readings" promised so invitingly. She begs for Paris's everyday language and signals to reorient her.

DISCURSIVE DEFENSES

The discursive techniques in these novels—citations, changing narrative voices, formal shifts between prose and poetry, nonfictional conventions—expose the fictionality of the novels as well as of Paris. Futoransky's metafictional experimentation engages in intertextual exploration beyond the bounds of fiction to draw attention to the fragmentary construction of Paris in Latin America. The titles themselves cross generic boundaries, since they are expressions borrowed from colloquial conversation to serve the texts' semiotic purposes. "Son cuentos chinos" ("that's a pack of lies") points out the novel's fictional status, but also makes "chinos" a real referent for the story. "De Pe a Pa" ("from a to z") also works on two levels. The expression itself underlines the vast collection of textual strategies employed in the novel, while at the same time assigning Peking and Paris abbreviated signs. Starting with the novels' titles, Futoransky's experiments with modes of signification accentuate the foreignness of contemporary urban space and the betrayal of Paris's feigned familiarity in Latin America.

The narration in Spanish, both Laura's and the narrator's, is the principal defense mechanism the novel employs in the face of semiotic confusion. If journal writing offers refuge in *Son cuentos chinos*, in *De Pe a Pa* the Spanish language itself, as a system, provides reassurance. The discourse emphasizes the sounds, rules, and gestures of Argentine Spanish, creating a protective linguistic familiarity around the character. A poem fragment in *Son cuentos chinos* addresses the psychological continuity of Spanish for Laura:

> me desencontré tanto
> y sin embargo aquí me tengo
> aferrada a este natural, amado castellano
> canturreando, balbuceando, chapurreando en lenguas
> romances y de las otras
> me vaciaré de todo
> para recordarlo todo. (25–6)

Attached to her language, she retreats to it like home to allow her memory the verbal familiarity that a new system constrains.

Unlike the intimate *yo* of *Son cuentos chinos*, Futoransky's second novel maintains greater distance between the character and the discourse. The narration in *De Pe a Pa* begins in the third person, but occasionally shifts into the first person. The first person intervenes to counter the novel's more conventional narrative mode. Journallike snatches sporadically interrupt the third-person narration. A few footnotes hint at a relationship between the author, narrator, and character, suggesting a collaboration between them that defies the separation of textual realms. The following footnote is by *both* Laura and the author:

> *N. de Laura.* Jean Rhys retribuyó el apasionado entusiasmo de la autora, dedicándole en *Vasto Mar de los Sargazos* esta frase, harto significativa: "Anything might have happened to you, Louise, anything at all, and I wouldn't be surprised" (Cualquier cosa pudo haberte pasado, Luisa, cualquier cosa, y no me hubiera sorprendido.) A mí, tampoco. Merci, Jean. (*N. de la A. del*). (23)

In this note, during a section narrated in the third person, Laura speaks up to recognize the author's existence. The author, in turn, "hears of" a reference to herself in a Jean Rhys novel, via her own character.[10] This metafictional twist counters the third-person narrative stance and bridges the distance between character and discourse. At the same time that it implicates Jean Rhys and *her* intertextual Paris, this note identifies an *intra*textual complicity between Laura and the author. Both are trying to decipher the Paris they have decided to confront and transform.

De Pe a Pa includes dictionary definitions in Spanish scattered throughout the novel that supply the text with linguistic signposts in the novel's (and the character's) first language. Defined common nouns in Spanish—*casa, gallo, hospital, espejo*—offer reassurance as though the disorientation of the deciphering process demanded this guidance. These definitions quote yet another source, evoking an unidentified authority on language and its cultural significance. This scientific, impersonal intertext contrasts with Laura's emotional experience in Paris as well as with her subjective "reading" of the city as a text. These dictionary fragments interrupt the story and the discourse. Along with the journal entries, poems, and other extra-*récit* segments, they function as road signs or linguistic-cultural reminders alongside the plot and the rest of the narration.

Futoransky foregrounds language in order to accord it the duplicitous role of both facilitator and inhibitor of comprehension. Brian McHale calls the intrusion of self-conscious linguistic catalogues in postmodernist fiction "lexical exhibitionism." The introduction of arcane or foreign words, or isolated sounds or letters in the discourse, serves "to throw up obstacles to the reconstruction process, making it more difficult and thus more conspicuous, more perceptible" (151). However, the narrator in *De Pe a Pa* appears to rely on catalogued language as an interpretive tool. These definitions perform the double duty of providing clarity while at the same time distancing the discourse from the story. In McHale's terms, as terms disengaged from syntax, they drive a wedge between words and their worlds (153).[11]

Eight nouns appear in their full catalogued analysis (etymological, phonetic, and cultural). They offer oases of semantic meaning in the novel's journey through foreign and culturally mixed sign systems. The definitions also serve to enumerate the multiplicity of meanings that an "ordinary" noun conveys. The fragments include less common definitions, such as "poor house" for *hospital*: "[e]stablecimiento donde se recogen pobres y peregrinos por tiempo limitado" (115). The less familiar term and definition *fiambre* (68) highlights cultural concerns about food. Thus, the lexical terms serve as headings for the linguistic, cultural, and plot information they introduce, while they simultaneously draw attention to the novel as a metatextual and metalinguistic process.

The play on *gallo* and *gallina* (chapter IX) expands both definitions to examine a transcultural array of meanings. The two nouns serve as a semantic pair for the chapter's enumeration of textual contexts. *Gallo*, for example, pertains to Chinese astrology

("El gallo también es uno de los doce animales del horóscopo chino"
[93]), to French symbology ("Pero el gallo asimismo es el símbolo
de Francia y, por tanto, de los franceses" [93]), and to colloquial
expressions in Spanish ("en menos que canta un gallo" [96]). These
common nouns problematize the novel's fictionality and discursive
control while advancing its crosscultural semiotic exploits. Fiction
usually does not admit these linguistic digressions, definitions, and
technicalities. In this transgression of fiction, words, instead of
telling the story, *become* the story.

    These dictionary entries elude the narrative voice that most of
the novel manipulates. The impersonal direct citation of the
definitions skillfully intervenes in the novel's continual shifts between first- and third-person narration. The changeable narrative
voice underscores once again the text's authorial complicity. This
signals the mischievous authorial command over the discourse.
Subversive narrative acts like these dictionary definitions contest
authoritarian controls. Nelly Richard comments that artistic and
literary movements that responded to dictatorship "retorcía[n]
alfabetos para comunicar su sospecha hacia las verdades re-
absolutizadas" (61). Futoransky invents dictionary fragments to
undermine European cultural symbology in Paris and to subvert
dictatorial discourse at home.

    The narration never clarifies who provides the definitions, and
for the benefit of whom. The author may be intervening, or the
narrator could provide them for the character or reader. Alterna-
tively, the character may be appropriating the discourse with the
inclusion of definitions for the reader. Perhaps Paris itself "authorizes" these definitions, just as it gives out other media and visual
messages. The narrator(s) yields authority to the other texts (Paris,
dictionaries, advertising, newspapers) that collectively constitute
this one. The collage offers only blurred and contradictory notions
of its possible editor/compilor.

    While the definitions provide some solace, they are not sufficient
to resolve Laura's disorientation. She looks to extralinguistic signs—
tarot cards, tattoos—to combat her precarious and defenseless position in this textual quagmire that is Paris. She only hopes that
some of her intensive observation will help as she continues to
search for clues: "Si alguno de tanto gurú como tienen suelto le
hubiera ido descifrando los mensajes . . ." (70). Laura gropes for all
kinds of systematic coping and interpretive strategies to apply to
her Parisian life. Her story catalogues the random assortment of
methods she comes across (personal advertisements, sorcery, and

magic) as well as those in which she participates (psychoanalysis and the Rajneesh ashram). Even her search for coping mechanisms requires her to read through the city as a printed text of newspaper classifieds, window advertisements, and neon storefront signs.

The narrator enumerates an array of occult practices available in Paris that Laura considers potentially helpful resources for reading the urban realm. However, their abundance and transnational nature only add to the plethora of sign systems. Horoscope magazines, astrologers, readers, seers (*videntes*), and ashrams occupy a chapter that begins and ends with reference to Laura's psychoanalysis. One of the two visual texts of the novel is included here as well (71), a collage of signs and advertisements publicizing spiritual mediums, magic, romantic encounters via computer or telephone, and religious symbols (see figure 5). The collage is a visual intrusion on the verbal text, another breach in the fictional contract that forces the reader to decipher the signs that the character/narrator arranges.

The occult introduced in Futoransky's Paris intertext revises the Latin American associations of Paris with the divine and mythological (see chapter 1). While the *modernistas* praised Paris as a divine manifestation, Futoransky's Paris advertises its spiritual practices as commercial antidotes to the character's disillusionment and bafflement with the city. The references to seers and readers of the occult also resonate with Breton's *Nadja* and the surrealist protagonist's bizarre link to Paris.[12] *De Pe a Pa* recontextualizes the discourse of religion and myth and its connection to urban space with these popularized practices. Laura's sequel converts the sacred readings from Eastern spirituality incorporated in *Son cuentos chinos* into contemporary consumer options. In *De Pe a Pa*, Laura takes yoga classes, has tarot card readings, and visits ashrams in her search for spiritual answers to Paris's alienation.

De Pe a Pa concludes with a list of potential endings for each character of the proposed opera "Cuarentena de la Dama." The narrative voice emerges from the notes of a "director" or "producer," reminding the reader of the novel's fictional status. An outline suggests to the reader how we "podríamos abandonar" Laura, UNESCO, and a series of stylized comical names (Ché Conde del Herault, Don Américo Longo) that satirize the social, institutional, and political networks that compose Paris (123). The narrative breaks down, as in the dictionary definitions, into alienating alphabetized entries. The outline proposes leaving one of the characters, the journalist Tili, to the task of writing "una serie de notas muy

Figure 5.1
Collage from *De Pe a Pa* (p. 71) by Louisa Futoransky.

emotivas . . . sobre queridos desaparecidos recientes" (124) for several Southern Cone newspapers. Among the alleged to have recently disappeared are Cortázar and Scorza. The next to the last entry, "e) etcétera" (124), underscores the scattered diffusion of Futoransky's ending.

The novel even concludes with the intertextualization of its main character. Laura's middle name, Falena, is only revealed in the last two pages. This personal information, an added piece of her identity, is converted into a dictionary definition that closes the novel:

> f) FALENA f. (gr. *phalaina*) Nombre de diversas mariposas crepusculares o nocturnas llamadas igualmente *geómetras*. (124)

Laura has performed the roles of novelistic character, operatic character, narrator, and reader in Futoransky's two novels, and for her finale she is cast (off) as a definition. She has an active role in the intertextual construction of her narrations and even participates in their decoding. That she is reduced to a dictionary definition in the last lines of *De Pe a Pa* represents simultaneously her semiotic triumph and her cathartic failure. The novel catalogues her just as she so yearned to have her own worlds catalogued. Her hard-fought campaign to affirm herself against marginalization—as a woman, an exile, an artist, a Third-World foreigner, a Jew—gives way. The dictionary definition of "Falena" makes her individuality into a generic species that lacks specificity. The novel "disappears" her as the definition concludes the story of an "abandoned" character, reduced like a sinister bureaucratic file to an alphabetized entry. She is thrust back into the teeming moths which are all drawn toward the City of Light.

In the same chapter in which a rash attacks her skin, her last defense, and causes her to begin to peel away, the text attacks her status as a fictional character. Laura's verisimilitude as a character diminishes as she acquires a conscious textual, fictional status. Her narrative control over the discourse in *Son cuentos chinos* protects the intimacy of her writing, while the ambivalent narrative decision making in *De Pe a Pa* circumscribes Laura in one text after another. She is a struggling semiotician ("geómetra") who becomes a victim, physically, of the very signs she tries to decipher. The systematized language of geometry would be a comforting antidote to the barrage of signs from Laura's many worlds. The dissolved borders between fiction and "reality," the fluid layers of performative staging in *De Pe a Pa*, announce the breakdown of the binary division between inner and outer worlds in gender formation.[13] Laura's rash testifies to the public invading the private, as the city of Paris seems to overrun her body as it raids all of her signifying practices.

Laura searches for a coherent structure for her urban itineraries, spiritual readings, and transnational tourism, and she expects Paris to furnish it. Ultimately she seeks a coherent self-definition within the gendered confines of transnational citizenship. However, as Butler explains, that coherence is just a surface effect.

> According to the understanding of identification as an enacted fantasy or incorporation, however, it is clear that coherence is desired, wished for, idealized, and that this idealization is an effect of a corporeal signification. In other words, acts, gestures, and desire produce the effect of an internal core or substance, but produce this *on the surface* of the body. (Butler 136, emphasis in original)

These surface inscriptions, during the process of Laura's self-definition, like the illusions of the Paris construct prove very tricky. As a consumer of the city's signs, she falls prey to their allure and ultimately allows them to cover her in a rash. The gender codification of her search transfers the city's tombstone dedications or historic plaques onto her body. She wears them like so many patterned imprints, oversized and in foreign code. The languages of Laura's many international and intertextual worlds confound her. Her numerous acts of semiotic prowess still leave her groping for more definitions, better interpretation, and clearer answers. However, her name and its definition separate her from the fictional truth of the novel, while they underscore her self-conscious (textual and emotional) conflicts of identity. The spatial, corporeal figure of a body covered in a rash responds to the invasive messages of the Paris construct on Latin American cultural consciousness.

Sidonie Smith concludes her study of marginality in women's autobiographical fiction by calling it "heretical" (176). This heresy threatens not only the boundaries of male discourse and patriarchal genres, it also directly challenges political and spiritual principles, institutions, and their practices. In the context of exile, the already politically and culturally marginal (gendered) stance is displaced at an even greater distance. More acute forms of cultural dissonance, structured by geographical, linguistic, and cultural differences, pervade exile novels such as *Son cuentos chinos* and *De Pe a Pa*. Futoransky's heretical defiance reacts against Jewish, Christian, and Asian worldviews, as well as against Third-World authoritarianism and European bourgeois values. She positions her narrator/protagonist in the liminal zone of the transitory exile whose spiritual and sensual quests become essential to her economic and political survival.

Liminal, spiritual, and exiled states of being then become analogous conditions that often converge in these novels. Gender marginality underscores these liminal states in narrators who combat patriarchal dogma through transnational displacement. However, their placelessness does not escape the grounded conceptions of cultural behaviors that impinge on their expressive freedom. In *Son cuentos chinos*, Laura's authorship of her own journal emerges from between the citations of sociopolitical doctrine and world religious masters. *De Pe a Pa* affirms its textual status from among the citations of the city itself. The narrators' most heretical move desecrates the Paris construct. These two novels infect Paris with a rash, convert it into a tragicomic opera, and bury it first under displaced desire and then under an urban palimpsest of inscriptions. Futoransky desacralizes Paris until the body of sacred readings is transformed through deterritorialized illusions.

Paris becomes a space for internal confrontation that explores intimately transcultural readings. These novels stage Paris as a site for sorting out the vast material of those readings and for challenging the gender constructs traditionally associated with it from Latin America. Paris is Futoransky's theater of cultural and textual productivity where Chinese, Zen, Talmudic, popular, occult, and touristic discourses meet. These two novels approach Paris from regional, national, and international perspectives and then display it against the spiritual, aesthetic, and sensual permutations of transcultural urbanity. *Son cuentos chinos* ends as Laura leaves Peking for Paris, and its sequel closes with an operatic finale. Futoransky admits that "me interesan las ciudades que desconozco, porque los podés observar, y al mismo tiempo, cuando te hacen mucho mucho mucho mal, podés bajar la cortina, pretender que no entendés" (interview). The curtain comes down on Paris once the city has lettered all of Laura's readings and has even inscribed her skin.

Figure 6.1
Antonio Seguí figure

Epilogue

❖

A voyeuristic gentleman frequently appears in Antonio Seguí's Parisian paintings. Rather than have him stroll through the streets like a *flâneur*, Seguí catapults his interloper over the Moulin Rouge or leaves him hovering above the Arc de Triomphe. The figure's gaze often dwarfs the city's monuments in these urban portraits. Seguí's irreverent but affectionate vision of Paris counters the city's imposing heritage for Latin America. The artist's distortion offers a contemporary critique of Latin America's aesthetic relationship with the French capital. His Eiffel Tower (see Figure 1) overtakes the canvas and crowds the edges of the frame, as though the city's expansion into the transnational imagination suddenly had reached its limit. The erotic irony of Paris as phallic (as opposed to the image of the city as wanton woman open to foreign penetration) reverses some of the complex issues of desire, urban identity, and cultural control problematized in Latin American writing.

The desiring eye of urban fiction, like the voyeuristic gaze of Seguí's figure, privileges the visual. The voyeurism of the window display, the exhibit, the arcade, and the photographer's lens casts the reader as a *flâneur* who steals glances and consumes visions. In Latin American writing, Paris projects a series of illusions that blind, seduce, disorient, or transform. The politics of gender confront the politics of cultural production in the subway cars' window reflections and the camera lens's seduction. Even the jungle is transmitted through an urban filter of literary commodification. The city is built out of sightings: patriotic plaques and metro maps, museums and mausoleums, arcades and exhibitions.

Architecture, like writing, offers icons for transnational consumption through its occupation of cultural space. Architecture *writes* the territory it inhabits by inscribing upon it a series of images and shapes, by configuring it spatially. An imaginative urban planning transposes architectural meaning onto literary space. Latin American writing's configuration of Parisian city space—its

145

subway system, bridges, and streets—relies on a codified system built into various forms of cultural expression. In Seguí's architectural reconstructions, a newsprint underlayer often peeks through his diluted oils as a reminder of Paris's inscription in Latin American culture. This printed palimpsest reveals the borrowed foundation of New World urban space. The fiction discussed in this book, under the guise of travelogs or personal memoirs, reflects a textualized city that Latin America periodically redesigns. Cortázar's stories manipulate the city's physical structures, Bryce Echenique remaps neighborhoods, Futoransky quotes the city's walls and signs, and Scorza critiques Paris's institutional edifice as cultural and literary capital.

Parisian fictions from Latin America envelop their protagonists in an architectonic world that offers a view of its own metafictional artifice. The photographic enlargement in Cortázar's "Las babas del diablo," the neighborhood mapped into Bryce Echenique's diptych, the urban itineraries of Futoransky's *De Pe a Pa*, Scorza's *La danza inmóvil*, and Cortázar's *Libro de Manuel* all portray spaces of creativity. The emergence of these creative venues makes the city a blueprint for the text's fictional design. Scattered citations, fragmented discourse, and autobiographical stances in Parisian fiction trace the protagonists' dislocated mental maps. These narrative strategies, like Seguí's distortion and caricature, demolish mimetic illusion and uncover a self-conscious function in urban fiction. Characters' names parody France's historical and literary associations for Latin America. Parisian institutions (parks, museums, cafés, universities) offer sites for reading and writing from which the texts invent paintings in motion, fantastical gravestones, and subversive political maneuvers. Love stories challenge urban social politics to remap gender roles and class distinctions. The city writes these stories while the stories simultaneously rewrite the city in mutually transformative discursive exercises. Paris and these texts provide one another with armatures for creative redefinitions.

Contemporary urban fiction from Latin America demonstrates historically many of the same preoccupations as other Western urban writing. Several pivotal moments in European aesthetics confirm the relationship between an emerging conception of urban modernity and Latin America's fictionalization of Paris. New European industrialism in the nineteenth century fueled urban expression in such writers as Baudelaire and Rimbaud, whose work furnishes central intertexts for much of the fiction studied in this book. After the placeless alienation of postwar writing, late twentieth-century fiction embraces a global and transnational cultural consciousness. Bio-geographical itineraries such as migrations, emigrations, and exile only partially account for this global sensibility. The intersections of the global economy have shaped an awareness of transnational cultural dynamism. Big cities no longer hold the exclusive rights to where culture "takes place," as international publishing exposi-tions, multinational cinema production, and electronic informa-tion technology reinterpret the arenas of local cultural negotiation. The phenomenon of Parisian space in Latin American writing, a locus of conflicting cultural and social meanings, forms part of this global cityscape. Recent urban fiction's political and aesthetic strat-egies enmesh territories or zones of confrontation so that tradi-tions, places, signs, and desires merge and overlap.

Paris's presence in Latin American fiction continues an innova-tive urban planning that extends literary space beyond local, re-gional, and continental dimensions. Paris is simultaneously intimate and sociopolitical, equally familiar and foreign. Latin American writing traces the city's iconic and discursive continuum through Proust and Hemingway, the Louvre's paintings, and the *métro's* graffiti. Their perspective takes in the end of the French colonial empire as well as Latin America's postcolonial condition. From both sides of the Atlantic, they challenge the matrices of Euro-American cultural space in order to dispute their dichotomization. Contemporary transnational writing reinscribes Paris in interstitial passageways, on subway walls, or around sculpted monuments. Latin America's urban invention becomes a self-portrait of desire and critique that rewrites the postcolonial lettered city.

Notes

❖

INTRODUCTION

The City as Text and Paris as Fiction

1. See Darío's *A. de Gilbert. Biografía de Pedro Balmaceda.*

2. From Raymond Williams to Néstor García Canclini, cultural critics have been problematizing the relationship between supposedly oppositional structural stances such as center/periphery, global/local, and foreign/indigenous. The dialogical and hybrid theories of cultural criticism in recent years question these categories' oppositionality and view them in more dynamic interrelationships.

3. Mignolo's definition of postcolonial discourse encompasses the ambivalent embracing of Western culture in the New World:

> resistencia a la occidentalización y la globalización—por un lado, y producción creativa de estilos de pensar que marquen constantemente la diferencia con el proceso de occidentalización. Esto es, la constante producción de lugares diferenciales de enunciación ("Occidentalización" 32).

4. My definition of "postcolonial" coincides somewhat with Mignolo's term *posoccidentalismo*: "concebido como proyecto crítico y superador del occidentalismo que fue el proyecto pragmático de las empresas colonizadoras en las Américas desde el siglo XVI, desde el colonialismo hispánico, al norteamericano y al soviético" ("Posoccidentalismo" 685).

5. Alberto Filippi describes Spanish America's marginal double bind: "[a]lienados frente a una cultura colonial (la cultura hispánica) en la cual eran colonizados, los latinoamericanos tendrán que compararse muy pronto con otra cultura . . . frente a la cual no se sentirán menos extraños, o en todo caso menos alienados, y precisamente porque esta cultura históricamente era más *adelantada*. . . ." See his "Notas sobre las relaciones entre cultura latinoamericana y cultura europea" (quoted in Chacón 149-69). The citation above is found on page 151.

6. Mignolo refers to the historical implications of Latin America's project of "independence": "liberarse de un imperio decadente y entrar en negociaciones con imperios emergentes" ("Posoccidentalismo" 680).

7. For a discussion of the political impact of the Atlantic trade networks in the period leading up to Latin American independence, see Peggy Liss, "Atlantic Network" (in Lynch 263–77).

8. "Urbanity was not ancillary to the Revolution," states Priscilla Parkhurst Ferguson in *Paris As Revolution* (11). Her adept interpretation of nineteenth-century French writers locates Paris as the intersection of revolution and urbanization. Her study discusses fiction writing along with the semiotics and ideology of street naming and map making in Paris during specific revolutionary periods.

9. Alonso's first chapter makes a convincing argument for the link between modernity and rhetoric. He analyzes the "relationship between this contradictory rhetorical inscription within the modern and the relentless, long-standing inquiry into the special nature of Latin American cultural expression" (24).

10. Carlos Fuentes's novel *Una familia lejana* (1980) reverses the Latin American gaze toward Paris with a French character who contemplates the otherness of the New World as a sort of parallel to French political upheaval from the French Revolution through the First World War. This novel offers a curious twist on France's imperial history in Mexico in the nineteenth century, and Paris's monumental urban design as a map of that history. See Julie Jones, chapter 5.

11. See Clifford and Marcus's *Writing Culture* for provocative discussions of writing and its historical and political implications across the disciplines. Along with the essayists they include in their volume, the Latin American narrators discussed in this book are part of a long tradition that confronts "the changing history, rhetoric, and politics of established representational forms" (25) through their incorporation of Paris as a *written* space into their fictions.

12. Kristin Ross's *The Emergence of Social Space* analyzes Rimbaud's esthetic relationship to the Paris Commune. She discusses the Commune as a reoccupation of the streets by citizens who had been displaced and contextualizes the aesthetic of bricolage that countered official monuments. Her book presents a lucid interpretation of the geographical reconceptualization—landscapism versus urban industrialization—that took place just before the next wave of European colonization.

CHAPTER 1

Desiring Paris: The Latin American Conception
of the Lettered City, 1840 to 1960

1. Mary Louise Pratt's interpretation of Sarmiento's visit to Paris contradicts Viñas's. She claims that despite his "catalogue-laden descriptions"

he presents "the metropolitan paradigm minus one dimension, however, that of acquisition . . . the *flâneur* has no capital and accumulates nothing. He does not buy, collect samples, classify, or fancy transforming what he sees" (192). He does, nevertheless, seek to transform *himself*. He spent most of his budget on clothing, in an effort to collect and copy Parisian gestures and appearances.

2. Adrian Rikfin intersperses references to popular street festivals in *Street Noises* and skillfully interprets the ambivalent images of desolation and nostalgia in French popular culture associated with the marginal areas on the outskirts of Paris. Cristóbal Pera discusses the fascination of working-class Paris for Sarmiento as a significant component of the city's mythology in the nineteenth-century. See his chapter, "Una incursión en la modernidad: Sarmiento en París," 43–68.

3. Sarmiento's portrait of Quiroga as a critique of the Rosas regime in *Facundo, o civilización y barbarie* (1845) includes simultaneously seductive and repellent descriptions of the *caudillo*. Sarmiento's civilization versus barbarism model masks these contradictions. The book's loose structure and poetic tone also undermine its very argument. Sarmiento refused to revise or tighten the book despite many contemporary readers' recommendations. He insisted on maintaining unformed spontaneity in his plea for "civilizing" order for Argentina. See Julio Ramos's "Saber del *otro*: escritura y oralidad en el *Facundo*" in his *Desencuentros de la modernidad en América Latina* 19–34.

4. The terms and images of other chroniclers resemble Sarmiento's frame of frivolity and prestige. Pedro Paz Soldán y Unánue (Peru, 1839–1895), for example, spent two years in Paris, from 1859 to 1861. He refers to the city as a literary mecca in a perfect civilization. Paris offers enchantment, glory, the "perpetuo torbellino" of a "gran feria," the artifice and pleasure of continuous festivities (100).

5. See Doris Sommer's *Foundational Fictions* for a thorough discussion of the localization of Latin American "national" narratives. She stresses the "erotic rhetoric that organizes patriotic novels" (2) after independence and demonstrates their allegorical sensuality. A similar swing away from European models that underscored American landscapes and autonomy occurred in the 1920s and 1930s with the regional *novela de la tierra*.

6. "La crónica sirvió de vehículo diseminador de nombres de autores, interpretaciones de obras e 'ideas estéticas,' y funcionó, en consecuencia, como una suerte de 'tejido conectivo' que fomentó la idea del modernismo como un movimiento. . . ." (González 63). See chapter II, "Arqueologías: orígenes de la crónica modernista," 61–120, for a thorough discussion of the genre's emergence in Latin American *modernismo*. See also Rotker.

7. On columns celebrating Paris in Latin American journalism, see also Amos Segala's introduction in Asturias *París 1924–1933*. On journalism in French that covered Latin American cultural issues, see Molloy 69–84, Patout (in Asturias 748–87), Cheymol (in Asturias 29–45), and Eve-Marie and Claude Fell's article (in *Revista de crítica literaria latinoamericana*).

8. See his *Obras completas* vol. 4, 1165–1394.

9. Jorge Schwartz *Vanguarda e Cosmopolitismo* 14. Schwartz has a number of insightful references to Darío and his "esquizofrenia cultural" (16) continually negotiated between Europe and Latin America.

10. Paris has continued to exert its power as a literary capital over Latin American letters through the twentieth century. The so-called international "boom" in Latin American fiction in the 1960s and 1970s was largely orchestrated by European publishing centers, notably Barcelona and publisher Carlos Barral. The Parisian journal, *Mundo Nuevo* (1966–1968), edited by the Uruguayan Emir Rodríguez Monegal, was also instrumental in launching the "boom" fiction of writers such as Fuentes, García Márquez, and Cortázar. French publishers such as Flammarion and Gallimard also initiated special collections dedicated to Latin American writing during this period.

11. See Adolfo Prieto's *El discurso criollista*... on reading, literacy, and the immigration policies of Argentina from 1880 to 1910.

12. Carlos Alonso situates the emergence of the regional novel within the "relationship between this contradictory rhetorical inscription within the modern and the relentless, long-standing inquiry into the special nature of Latin American cultural expression" (24).

13. Esteban Echeverría was educated at the Sorbonne, Isaac's main character in *María*, Efraín, leaves Colombia to study in London, and Güiraldes wrote *Don Segundo Sombra* while in Paris.

14. Allusion to popular and cabaret songs that evoke Paris form a significant corpus of the city's textual construction. See Rifkin's *Street Noises* for a lively discussion of the working class base of "Parisianism" in the city's cabaret and variety artists, song lyrics, posters, photography, and film.

15. *La vida breve*, Juan Carlos Onetti's 1950 novel, also relies on popular songs to weave into its underworld of drugs and crime reminiscences of Paris. The novel takes its title from the French cabaret song "La vie est brève" sung by Mami, a middle-aged French prostitute living in Onetti's ficticious (Latin American) Santa María. She recalls her French past through nostalgic cabaret lyrics and vicarious trajectories traced on a map of Paris. Her character embodies the ambivalent back-and-forth journey between Paris and Río de la Plata. When her lover takes her back to Europe, it is an "agridulce excursión al pasado, tan parecida a esta que realizaba ahora de pie junto al piano... mediante la repetición de *chansons* y de posturas ancestrales" (154).

16. Ana María Shua's *La sueñera* offers a more recent example of this Parisian metaphor:

> En un lugar que a veces es París me tienen secuestrada. En vez de correr hacia la derecha o la izquierda, las calles giran en redondo. Hay un notable exceso de escaleras.

Elijo siempre las que van hacia arriba. Sin embargo, por
más que subo, no consigo emerger de abajo de la frazada.
¡Es tan duro París para los inmigrantes pobres! (46)

17. A decade later, Julio Ramón Ribeyro's story "La juventud en la otra
ribera" (*La palabra del mudo* III [1973]) adds to this constellation of fiction
that paints Paris as a treacherous underworld. In Ribeyro's tale, a Peruvian
physician lives out all of the codified Parisian fantasies. He seduces a
French woman, stays in a bohemian Left Bank flat, and meets artists in
Montparnasse, only to end up exploited, robbed, and killed. The Paris
myth backfires, turning into "la trampa cuyas dos riberas se cierran sobre
el pobre consumidor de una mitología tardía" (Ortega 140). See Jones's
chapter, "Dreams of a Golden Age: *La juventud en la otra ribera.*"

CHAPTER 2

The Interstices of Desire: Paris As Passageway in
Julio Cortázar's Short Fiction

1. See chapter 3 for a brief discussion of *Libro de Manuel* and Cortázar's
revolutionary urban politics.

2. For a discussion of Cortázar as a modern rather than postmodern
writer, see Santiago Colás, "Beyond Western Modernity? *Rayuela* as Cri-
tique" and "Toward a Latin American Modernity: *Rayuela*, the Cuban
Revolution, and the Leap" in his *Postmodernity in Latin America: The
Argentine Paradigm*. Although his analysis almost entirely concerns
Rayuela, Colás's positioning of Cortázar's ideological and aesthetic stance
is relevant to the short fiction as well. He states that *Rayuela* proposes a
Latin American modernity that is "critical but still within the logic of
European modernity" (75). Cortázar's often ironic and other times tran-
scendental incorporation of Paris reveals one of his critical strategies for
sorting through the heap of postcolonial models from European modernity.

3. See chapter by Julie Jones and article by Jean Franco (in Loveluck)
for mappings of Breton's *Nadja* and surrealist esthetics in *Rayuela*.

4. See Benjamin, "On Some Motifs in Baudelaire" (in *Baudelaire* 107–
54).

5. See Josephine Diamond, "Paris, Baudelaire and Benjamin: The Poetics of Urban Violence" in (Caws 178).

6. A recent article on *Libro de Manuel* stresses that "Cortázar crea un
tipo de escritura que apunta hacia una realidad más compleja y busca
revolucionar no sólo la novela sino los mecanismos de lectura del hombre
americano" (Fernández Utrera 229).

7. Although the novel does not employ directly Cortázar's frequent
use of the fantastic as in the short fiction, it offers a novelistic version of

many of the narrative and thematic structures evident in the short stories. The dichotomy of Europe (= Paris) and Latin America (= Río de la Plata) suggests the vacillating anguish of protagonists caught between separate worlds. The connotations of la Maga's name indicate esoteric powers and intuition that defy conventional rationality. Ironically, la Maga is the most grounded of the group in Paris.

8. See Standish's article, "Los Compromisos de Julio Cortázar," for a discussion on the connection between his literary and political revolutionary ideals.

9. See Parkinson Zamora's article, "Voyeur/Voyant," for a thorough discussion of Cortázar's visual aesthetic in "Axolotl" and other texts.

10. The story never specifies the protagonist's national or linguistic identity. See Levinson's article, "The Other Origin: Cortázar and Identity Politics," for a sophisticated discussion of the lexicon and the character's ambiguous identity in "Axolotl."

11. For a discussion of botanical gardens as extensions of European imperialism of the "tropics," see Daniel R. Headrick, "Botany, Chemistry, and Tropical Development," and Camille Limoges, "The Development of the Muséum d'Histoire Naturelle."

12. See Limoges, "The Development of the Muséum d'Histoire Naturelle" 236–37.

13. See Levinson's detailed analysis of the spelling and translation of the axolotl among Nahuatl, Spanish and French (5–6). See also Fischer's article on zoological description in colonial chronicles with a substantive discussion of axolotls (468–72).

14. According to anthropologist Arjun Appadurai, "Natives are not only persons who are from certain places, and belong to those places, but they are also those who are somehow *incarcerated*, or confined, in those places." His argument about the "ecological immobility" of the "native" might account for the material metamorphosis that suffers an incomplete spiritual or intellectual transformation ("Putting Hierarchy in Its Place" 37). The human in "Axolotl" cannot escape the Western, hegemonic discourse (of Paris), regardless of his form.

15. I am indebted to Laura Beard's comprehensive chapter, "The Mirrored Self" in "Writing the Female Self: Identity and Authority in Contemporary Latin American Fiction" (22–90).

16. Margrit (a variation on Margret) is one of the first young women Faust seduces and ruins in Goethe's *Dr. Faustus*.

17. Without belaboring the obvious, it is important to note similar motifs between *Rayuela* and the short fiction such as unexpected erotic encounters and playful mappings of coincidence. From its first interrogative line, Horacio's search for la Maga and their "chance" meetings mark *Rayuela*. In the first chapter, Horacio states that "Andábamos sin buscarnos pero sabiendo que andábamos para encontrarnos" (9). Chapter 6 is devoted

to an explanation of Horacio and la Maga's game in which "[l]es gustaba desafiar el peligro de no encontrarse . . . el problema de las probabilidades . . . procurando explicarlos [itinerarios] telepáticamente. . . . " (31–32).

18. The story superimposes the Pasaje Güemes and the Galerie Vivienne in a sort of reverse chronology. Although the protagonist first encounters and writes of the Pasaje Güemes, architecturally and aesthetically it was modeled *after* the Parisian arcades. The Galerie Vivienne was designed by J. F. Delannoy as an extension of the Palais Royal, and it opened in 1823 (Geist 69). The Pasaje Güemes was designed by the Italian architect Francisco Teresio Gianotti (1881–1967) in 1915. Its precise address is the arcade between 175 Florida and 176 San Martín, just off Avenida de Mayo, where the financial district is located. See Ortiz, *La arquitectura*.

19. The epigraphs from Lautréamont that introduce each of the story's two parts emphasize the visual in their reference to eyes and the gas lamps. The first epigraph at the beginning of the story, "Ces yeux ne t'appartiennent pas . . . où les as-tu pris?" (*Cc* 2, 590), also furthers the issue of appropriation and otherness that the story elaborates. The second epigraph, "Où sont-ils passés, les becs de gaz? Que sont-elles devenues, les vendeuses d'amour?" (*Cc* 2, 598), continues the visual image by evoking the gas lamps. The quotation associates prostitution with the innovation of artificial light, both "illicit" sources. The epigraphs clearly orient the story's search for erotic pleasure at the expense of danger and, in this context, postcolonial appropriation.

20. Geist's seven characteristics include: 1) access to the interior of a city block, 2) public space on private property, 3) symmetrical street space, 4) skylit, 5) a system of access, 6) a form of organizing retail trade, and 7) a space of transition (12).

21. See Jones's chapter, "The City As Text: Reading Paris in *Rayuela*," in *A Common Place* for a pertinent discussion of Paris as woman in the novel and the intertextual relationship with Breton's *Nadja*.

22. For a stimulating discussion of the political and psychoanalytical implications of this element of the story, see Bernard McGuirk, "New Lack or Old Lacan? Julio Cortázar's 'El otro cielo.'"

23. See Rodríguez Monegal for an astute analysis of the spectral relationship among the Cortázar-Lautréamont figures in "El otro cielo."

24. "Notre héros s'aperçut qu'en fréquentant les cavernes, et prenant pour refuge les endroits inaccessibles, il transgressait les règles de la logique, et commettait un cercle vicieux" (Lautréamont 231).

25. *Les chants* concludes with a hanging from the obelisk of the Place Vendôme. Maldoror's finale also is viewed publicly, staged in a neighborhood that is separated from those mentioned in the rest of the last *chant*. The beginning of the sixth and last *chant* meanders through the arcade neighborhood, starting from the rue Vivienne (where Lautréamont lived). The last *chant* maps out other trajectories, crossing various bridges, moving

along the *quais*, following the rue de Rivoli until reaching the Place Vendôme. Curiously, an arcade called Passage Vendôme exists in Paris as well, not far from the neighborhood of Cortázar's final guillotining scene. See Lautréamont 227–61.

26. Lautréamont's second *chant* particularly dramatizes Maldoror's dismembering fantasies and activities, as in the god chewing on the armless and legless trunk of a man, and Maldoror himself tearing off a victim's arm (Lautréamont 100, 105).

27. Cortázar's "Autopista del sur" exemplifies the transformative role of travel and Paris. An exagerrated traffic jam along the highway from the south of France leading to Paris produces a temporary society among the cars and their passengers. Once the accident causing the prolonged interruption is cleared away, the cars continue on their journeys. The social organization that emerged out of this interstitial situation disperses due to the "aperturas que los personajes destruyen [porque] no pueden romper con sus tradiciones." See Martha Paley Francescato, "El viaje: Función, estructura y mito en los cuentos de Julio Cortázar" (in Lagmanovich *Estudios* 130). The traffic's sudden movement at the end of the story does not allow the characters any transition back to their "normal" existence. That jolt underscores the abrupt intrusion of "other" realities associated with Paris in Cortázar's fiction.

28. The intertextual mention of the song *Out of Nowhere* that Bruno hears in a Latin Quarter café underscores Paris as a portal to alternative realms of understanding (*Cc* 1, 253–54).

29. For a stimulating discussion of the social geography of the multi-layered city, see Trevor Boddy, "Underground and Overhead: Building the Analogous City" (in Sorkin's *Variations on a Theme Park: The New American City and the End of Public Space* 123–53). Geist also mentions underground tunnels and overpasses for pedestrians in his analysis of the evolution of the arcade in twentieth-century cities (79–90).

30. Colás situates *Rayuela*'s Horacio in a similar inconclusive crossroads: "the triple crisis of modern alienation, modernism's alienating responses to it, and the postcolonial's cultural alienation" (62).

31. Gyurko, in his article "Narcissistic and Ironic Paradise in Three Stories by Cortázar," imposes on Cortázar's stories a misread fantasy/reality polarity. Gyurko reduces the world of the Parisian arcades to the protagonist's imaginative fantasy, diminishing the actual dominance of this part of the plot in the narrative and overlooking the Cortazarian imperative of metaphysical exploration. Alejandra Pizarnik also suggests relegating the arcade world to a "situación imaginaria del narrador-protagonista," but still responsibly admits that this probability (to her) "no compromete su autonomía literaria." See "Nota sobre un cuento de Julio Cortázar: 'El otro cielo'" (in Jitrik *La vuelta a Cortázar en nueve ensayos* 55).

CHAPTER 3

The Immovable Feast: Paris and Politics
in Manuel Scorza's La danza inmóvil

1. The most commonly recognized *novelas de la tierra* include *Don Segundo Sombra* (1926) by the Argentine Ricardo Güiraldes, *Doña Bárbara* (1929) by the Venezuelan Rómulo Gallegos, and *La vorágine* (1924) by the Colombian José Eustasio Rivera. See Carlos Alonso, *The Spanish American Regional Novel.*

2. *Redoble por Rancas*, the first part of *La guerra silenciosa*, has been translated into French, Italian, Czech, Portuguese, Romanian, Russian, Finnish, Norwegian, German, Danish, Polish, Bulgarian, Swedish, Turkish, Hebrew, Hungarian, Dutch, English, Slavic, Albanian, Greek, and Icelandic, in that order. See Schmidt (1991) 275–76 and Escorza 361, 363.

3. The novels of *La guerra silenciosa* include: *Redoble por Rancas* (1970), *Historia de Garabombo, el invisible* (1972), *El jinete insomne* (1977), *Cantar de Agapito Robles* (1977), and *La tumba del relámpago* (1979).

4. Cornejo Polar situates Scorza in "el cruce de esta doble inserción . . . de una parte, está obviamente condicionado por la nueva narrativa hispanoamericana; de otra; se refiere a una tradición anterior, en gran parte discutida y negada por el *boom*, como es la novela indigenista y más específicamente la novela indigenista de intensa motivación social" ("Sobre el neoindigenismo y las novelas de MS" 553–54).

5. The pages cited earlier delineate Escajadillo's identifying characteristics for neoindigenism with examples from Ciro Alegría, José María Arguedas, and others. The second section of the book, "Notas acerca de la narrativa 'neoindigenista' posterior a 1971," continues from where his original doctoral thesis concluded, and begins with a useful discussion of Scorza (104–20). See also his article, "Scorza antes del último combate."

6. La Coupole is famous for hosting notable writers and artists such as Picasso, Giacometti, de Beauvoir, and Buñuel.

7. Scorza states that his novels are "máquinas de soñar, donde más importantes que los niveles reales son los horizontes oníricos" (quoted in Escajadillo "Scorza" 72). Roland Forgues also insists that Scorza's use of magical realism or "superrealidad" has a "papel de subversión del orden vigente" (*Estrategia mítica* 148).

8. According to Siegle, the term *metafiction* implies only aesthetic concerns, while novels such as *La danza inmóvil* comment on much more than fiction itself. He uses reflexivity to describe "something that turns back upon itself in the very process of its getting out again to where it was pointing before it started" (2). His semiotic approach to reflexivity in fiction supplements and politicizes the all-too psychological, arty, or metaphysical approaches that rely on the labels "self-conscious" or "metafictional."

9. "Latin American intellectuals have served as the local agents of the continent's ongoing ideological importing frenzy. . . . Traveling the globe, seeking out ideologies on the market, they assimilated them and packaged them for shipment and local consumption" (180).

10. Castañeda supplies a convincing analysis of this shift from the party's all-encompassing power to popular grassroots movements (chapter 6): "the trend in Latin America is away from this 'party'-based left to a more movement-inspired one" (202).

11. Cortázar consistently exploits Paris's "underworld" as a zone of sexual otherness (Emanuelle, the *clocharde* in *Rayuela*; the prostitutes in "El otro cielo"). The voyeuristic scenes around the Place de Clichy in *Libro de Manuel* unmask the local, multicultural theater of sexuality that coexists with the international tourist commodification of Pigalle.

12. For insightful discussions of Cortázar's collage aesthetic in *LM*, see Parkinson Zamora's article "Movement and Stasis, Film and Photo" (especially 59–63); and Santiago Juan-Navarro's chapter on Cortázar and Doctorow, the section entitled "Political Collage and Montage in *LM*."

13. "El que te dije" is paralyzed by the politics of his role as compiler/editor/chronicler of the group's events: "vuelvo a escribir y me da asco . . . quisiera ser cualquier otra cosa, cobrador de impuestos o ferretero, le tengo una envidia bárbara a los novelistas puros o a los teóricos marxistas o a los poetas de escogido temario . . . me siento tan pampeano, tan peludamente criollo con mi mate a las cuatro y mi literatura llena de palabrotas" (*LM* 249).

14. "Canon," in this study, refers to the range of literary works that a particular culture produces and legitimates over time. As Charles Altieri defines them,

> Canonical works are expected to provide knowledge of the world represented, to exemplify powers for making representations that express possible attitudes or produce artistic models, and to articulate shared values in a past culture that influences the present or to clarify means of reading other works we have reason to care about. (41)

15. Many critics and literary historians consider Barcelona publisher Carlos Barral the originator of the "boom" with the Barral literary prize for new fiction first awarded to Mario Vargas Llosa in 1963 for *La ciudad y los perros*. The French publishing house Gallimard initiated its own translation series called "Le monde entier," which included Latin American writers. The journal *Mundo nuevo*, edited in Paris by Emir Rodríguez Monegal from 1966 to 1968, propagated the "boom" by advertising soon-to-be-published novels with interviews and excerpts by Carlos Fuentes, Gabriel García Márquez, and Vargas Llosa.

16. On Scorza's Populibros project, see the interview with Ortega and the biographical chapter in Aldaz.

17. Abelardo Oquendo, personal interview, Lima, Perú, 15 June 1989.

18. Olver Gilberto de León, personal interview, Paris, France, 27 December 1989.

19. Mentioned by Daniel Moyano, personal interview, Madrid, 11 November 1989.

20. The anthropologist Arjun Appadurai's theoretical work on commodities in the global economy clarifies central aspects of the book trade as it is presented in *La danza inmóvil*. His redefinition of the Marxian concept of commodity exchange incorporates the agency of desire and the politics of social and cultural context. In the global cultural marketplace, there is a "constant transcendence of cultural boundaries by the flow of commodities," particularly evident in the European marketing of Latin American writing (15). While Appadurai states that transcultural networks of producers, distributors, and consumers indicate creativity or crisis (26–27), Scorza's presentation of transnational literary networks of Latin American fiction indicates both. Extensive literary recognition gains Latin American writing expanded avenues of distribution, but the local economies cannot support foreign editions.

21. Scorza is not alone in examining this transnational cultural mechanism. Cristina Peri-Rossi (in her short story "La influencia de Edgar Allen Poe en la poesía de Raimundo Arias" and her novel *La nave de los locos*), José Donoso (in *El jardín de al lado*), and Alfredo Bryce Echenique (in *La vida exagerada de Martín Romaña*) all incorporate characters who struggle to write, publish, and gain acceptance in the European cultural sphere.

22. "Self-erasing narratives . . . violate linear sequentiality by realizing two mutually-exclusive lines of development at the same time" (108). See his chapter 7, "Worlds under Erasure" (99–111).

CHAPTER 4

On the Border: Cultural and Linguistic Trespassing in Alfredo Bryce Echenique's La vida exagerada de Martín Romaña *and* El hombre que hablaba de Octavia de Cádiz

1. Wolfgang Luchting's study of *Un mundo para Julius, Alfredo Bryce/ Humores y malhumores*, begins with a quote from Jean-Yves Tardié's study, *Proust et le roman* (15), and includes the frequently cited interview about narrative influences. Bryce Echenique states, "La influencia de Proust puede haber llegado a través de mi madre que lo leía muchísimo y me leía largos párrafos en voz alta" (109).

2. Cornejo Polar discusses the Proustian intertext in his brief review of *MR*. While he recognizes the presence of Proust in the novel, I believe he underestimates its impact by ignoring the relevance of *La recherche* to

the construct of Paris, along with Bryce Echenique's Proustian manipulation of memory and time that so directly shape the two novels. The review diminishes Proust's significance by dismissing it due to a lack of
biographical commonalities: "[t]al filiación no va mucho más lejos, sin
embargo, pues los mundos rememorados por ambos escritores no tienen
nada en común y las actitudes de uno y otro son tan incompatibles como
la mesura y la exuberancia...." It is precisely the characters' *divergent*
backgrounds that allow the intertext to function as a social and cultural
disjunction. The review is reprinted in Ferreira and Márquez 181–84; the
phrases quoted are on page 182.

   3. Juan Angel Juristo's introduction to his edition of selected Bryce
Echenique stories and novelistic excerpts traces these Proustian stylistic
tendencies to *Un mundo para Julius*. He considers the novel's temporal
complexity and nostalgic digressions among the writer's most significant
contributions. Bryce Echenique pioneered "una representación del tiempo
con retrocesos y anticipaciones temporales que en su día produjo grata
sorpresa entre los lectores y que se cuenta como una de las aportaciones
más originales del modo de hacer literatura de Bryce Echenique" (32).

   4. The adjective "Peruvian" will refer to the expressions in Bryce
Echenique's work that insist on Peruvian settings or are etymologically of
Quechua origin. Martha Hildebrandt defines *peruanismo* as "todo uso
linguístico—fonético, morfológico, sintáctico—vigente en el Perú pero
excluido del *español general*" in her *Peruanismos* (9). However, she also
recognizes that *peruanismos* may have a variety of origins (not only indigenous), and that many terms and expressions are no longer exclusive to
Peru but have been assimilated into other Spanish American national uses
of Spanish (15–16). Although the *peruanismos* studied here are used in
other northwestern South American countries as well as in Peru, referring
to them as *peruanismos* in this analysis will distinguish them from other,
more widely used Americanisms.

   5. "Hay en la narrativa de Bryce una búsqueda de un estado de
convalescencia, de una cura o reparación, que no sólo se manifiesta
temáticamente en las continuas visitas a médicos y psiquiatras de los
protagonistas bryceanos, sino que se convierte en una suerte de ideología
literaria. Escribir y leer, pero en especial escribirse y leerse ... se ven como
la vía hacia una reintegración psíquica y física del protagonista bryceano"
(Aníbal González, "La nueva novela sentimental de Alfredo Bryce
Echenique," in Ferreira and Márquez 209).

   6. Helen Tiffin defines postcolonial counterdiscourse as an operation
that "does not seek to subvert the dominant with a view to taking its
place, but ... to evolve textual strategies which continually 'consume' their
'own biases' at the same time as they expose and erode those of the dominant discourse" (in Ashcroft, Williams, and Tiffin 96). Counterdiscourse
does not only "write back" to a colonizer's canonical text, "but to the
whole of a discursive field within which such a text operated and continues to operate in post-colonial worlds" (98).

7. Ashcroft catalogs six types of "devices of otherness": direct gloss-ing, syntactic fusion, neologisms, untranslated lexicon, ethnorhythmic prose, and transcription of dialect or variants (72). I believe Bryce Echenique in *MR* demonstrates all six categories.

8. Grutman defines literary bilingualism as "communication en deux ou plusieurs langues au moyen d'oeuvres littéraires qui fonctionnent de manière analogue ou divergente à l'intérieur de systèmes littéraires unilingues" (203).

9. Bhabha continues his discussion of cultural translation in this chapter whose central focus is Fredric Jameson's theories of late capitalism and their relevance to Salman Rushdie's *The Satanic Verses*: "[t]he complementarity of language as communication must be understood as emerging from the *constant state of contestation and flux caused by the differential systems of social and cultural signification*" (227, emphasis added).

10. According to Santamaría, the expression is an *afronegrismo*, used in Peru, meaning antiquated, "del tiempo de Maricastaña" (339). The same definition is given in Morínigo (427).

11. The guaranís are an indigenous South American community mostly located in the area that is now Paraguay. The name of the fictional Pari-sian establishment underscores Bryce Echenique's focus on Latin Ameri-can postcolonialism transferred back to Europe.

12. Octavia (d. 11 b.c.) was Augustus Caesar's half-sister and served as a mediator between her brother and Mark Anthony. Sarah Fielding's bio-graphical essay on Octavia stresses her sacrificial virtue that frustrated her attainment of passionate love: "I dreaded from my Youth that I should be sacrificed to political Views, and be disposed of in the solemn tie of Mat-rimony to some Man, whose Ambition alone would lead him to take me . . ." (Fielding 179). Bryce Echenique includes some parodic reminis-cences of the classical heroine in his Octavia's unsuccessful resistance to European aristocratic social class determinacy.

13. Octavia's cousin Leopold is not only a reference to European aris-tocracy but also to the history of colonialism. King Leopold II of Belgium started the partitioning process in Africa by claiming extensive territory in the Congo Basin during the period 1879–1880. He ruled the Congo as a personal colony from the period 1885–1908, during which the population declined drastically from brutal conditions of forced labor in rubber and ivory extraction. His notoriously abusive reign drew international atten-tion that eventually pressured him to transfer the colony to the Belgian state.

14. Mistaking the Aulnoye sign for Octavia herself serves to highlight the slippery identity issues surrounding Octavia as a character. The novel's hermeneutical intertextuality uncovers the eighteenth-century Madame d'Aulnoy (165?–1705), best known for her collections of fairy tales. Marie-Catherine Le Jumel de Barneville, Baroness of Aulnoy, was a longtime conspirator and fugitive who published memoirs of the French and Spanish court, as well as two volumes of fairy tales, *Les Contes des Fées* (1697) and

Contes nouveaux ou les Fées à la mode (1698). See Elisabeth Lemirre's edition, *Le cabinet des Fées*, 1988.

CHAPTER 5

Paris under Her Skin: Luisa Futoransky's Urban Inscriptions of Exile

1. In my analysis of Futoransky, my definition of gender takes its point of departure from Judith Butler. Gender is a system and a "project" with "laws" that govern sexual behavior within the production of social values: "gender is a project which has cultural survival as its end . . . a strategy of survival within compulsory systems" (Butler 139). In the case of the novels studied here, cultural survival is clearly not only biological reproduction. Futoransky's female protagonists are not mothers, nor is their search motivated by maternal desire. Rather, their survival requires an overhaul of the gender system to enable it to correspond to their transnational disjunctions.

2. Luisa Futoransky, personal interview, Paris, 21 December 1989.

3. Futoransky's third novel, *Urracas* (1992), focuses less on Paris and therefore will not be discussed in depth here. However, the novel does exploit metafiction to underscore displacement, along with her previous novels. *Urracas* is framed within a repeated scene in a Parisian bird market. This repetition envelops the rest of the plot in an experimental metanarrative. The narrator's and protagonist's roles often coincide in self-conscious commentaries on language, writing, and fiction. Futoransky also intertextually incorporates transnational popular culture and urban nomenclature. See my review in *Hispamérica*.

4. The first edition of *Son cuentos chinos* (Madrid: Albatros, 1983) was published after being awarded first prize in the "Premio Antonio Camuñas" novel competition. The third edition was published in Buenos Aires by Planeta in 1991. All references in the chapter will be to the second edition (Montevideo: Trilce, 1986).

5. Futoransky comments on the obstacles for foreigners who want to be integrated culturally in France: "pienso que afincándote en España, te puedes asimilar, el *establishment* cultural español te puede absorber a un lugar mediano hasta cierto punto. Pero acá no te absorbe nadie" (interview).

6. Père Lachaise is the Parisian cemetery where a number of recognized literary and cultural figures, such as Proust and Piaf, are buried.

7. For a more complete discussion of Paris in Cortázar's *Libro de Manuel*, see the section "Paris in the Literature of Latin American Leftist Activism" in chapter 3.

8. García Canclini calls graffiti "una escritura territorial de la ciudad, destinada a afirmar la presencia y hasta la posesión sobre un barrio. . . . Su trazo manual, espontáneo, se opone estructuralmente a las leyendas políticas

o publicitarias 'bien' pintadas o impresas, y desafía esos lenguajes institucionalizados cuando los altera" (*Culturas híbridas* 314).

9. Parkhurst Ferguson describes an analogous disorientation for Parisians themselves in the postrevolutionary program of renaming the city's streets. The utopian impulses hoped that written language would fix the urban text and inscribe space with new political values. The volatile effort, however, produced only confusion and undermined any possibility of a system. "The chaos and uncertainty introduced by myriad namings and renamings brought dissatisfaction all around . . . prompting amazing proposals for extensive reform of street nomenclature. . . . The inherent heteroglossia of the urban text won out" (27–30).

10. Jean Rhys was born on August 24, 1894, in Dominica, West Indies, and she died in 1975. She migrated to England in 1910 and lived in Paris between the wars. Some of her best-known novels include *After Leaving Mr. Mackenzie* (1931), *Good Morning, Midnight* (1939), and *Wide Sargasso Sea* (1966).

11. McHale elaborates on the ontological paradox of linguistic catalogues:

> On the one hand, they can appear to assert the full presence of a world . . . one so rich in objects that it defies our abilities to master it through syntax. . . . Yet at the same time, the decontextualization of words through the catalogue structure can have the opposite effect, that of evacuating language of presence, leaving only a shell behind— a word list, a mere exhibition of words (153).

12. The urban surrealist novel is a recognized intertext in Cortázar's *Rayuela* and in the textual construction of Paris for Latin Americans. Nadja visits fortune tellers and moves through the city according to mysterious intuitive motivations. See Julie Jones's chapter and Jean Franco's article for thorough discussions of surrealism in Cortázar's version of Paris.

13. "What constitutes through division the 'inner' and 'outer' worlds of the subject is a border and boundary tenuously maintained for the purposes of social regulation and control" (Butler 133).

Bibliography

⸻ ❖ ⸻

I. LITERARY TEXTS

Andrade, Oswald de. *Poesias reunidas. Obras completas* vol. 7. Rio de Janeiro: Civilizaçao Brasileira, 1972.

Asturias, Miguel Angel. *París 1924–1933. Periodismo y creación literaria.* Ed. Amos Segala. Paris: Archivos Université de Paris-X-Nanterre, 1988.

Aulnoy, Madame d'. *Le Cabinet des Fées.* 1697–98. Ed. Elisabeth Lemirre. Marseille: Philippe Picquier, 1988.

Baudelaire, Charles. *Petits poèmes en prose (Le spleen de Paris).* 1862. Paris: Garnier-Flammarion, 1967.

Borges, Jorge Luis. *Obras completas.* Buenos Aires: Emecé, 1974.

Breton, André. *Nadja.* 1928. Paris: Gallimard, 1974.

Bryce Echenique, Alfredo. *Crónicas personales.* Barcelona: Anagrama, 1988.

⸻. *El hombre que hablaba de Octavia de Cádiz.* Bogotá: Oveja Negra, 1985.

⸻. *Para que duela menos.* Ed. Juan Angel Juristo. Madrid: Espasa Calpe, 1995.

⸻. *La vida exagerada de Martín Romaña.* 1981. Bogotá: Oveja Negra, 1985.

⸻. *La vida exagerada de Martín Romaña.* 1981. Intro. Fernando Sanchez Dragó. Barcelona: Círculo de lectores, 1983.

Cortázar, Julio. *Las armas secretas.* Ed. and intro. Susana Jakfalvi. Madrid: Cátedra, 1986.

⸻. *Buenos Aires, Buenos Aires.* Buenos Aires: Sudamericana, 1968.

⸻. *Cuentos completos.* 2 vols. Madrid: Alfaguara, 1994.

⸻. *Libro de Manuel.* Barcelona: Bruguera, 1973.

⸻. *Paris: ritmos de una ciudad.* Barcelona: Edhasa, 1981.

⸻. *Rayuela.* 1968. Prólogo y cronología Jaime Alazraki. Caracas: Ayacucho, 1980.

Darío, Rubén. *Obras completas.* Madrid: Aguado, 1950.

⸻. *Prosas profanas.* 1896. Madrid: Austral, 1944.

———. *A. de Gilbert: Pedro Balmaceda Toro.* Madrid: Biblioteca Rubén Darío, 1924. [*A. de Gilbert. Biografía de Pedro Balmaceda. Obras completas.* Vol. VI. Eds. Alberto Ghiraldo y Andrés González-Blanco. Madrid: Bibilioteca Rubén Darío, 1924.]

Donoso, José. *El jardín de al lado.* Barcelona: Anagrama, 1981.

Fielding, Sarah. *The Lives of Cleopatra and Octavia.* New York: Garland, 1974.

Forgues, Roland. *Bajo el puente Mirabeau corre el Rimac.* Grenoble: Det Tignahus, 1987.

Fuentes, Carlos. *Una familia lejana.* Mexico: Era, 1980.

Futoransky, Luisa. *Son cuentos chinos . . .* Madrid: Albatros, 1983. Montevideo: Trilce, 1986.

———. *De Pe a Pa.* Barcelona: Anagrama, 1986.

———. *Urracas.* Buenos Aires: Planeta, 1992.

Gache, Roberto. *París, glosario argentino.* Buenos Aires: Babel, 1928.

García Calderón, Ventura. *Cantilenas.* Paris: América Latina, 1920.

———. *Frivolamente . . . (sensaciones parisienses).* Paris: Garnier, 1908.

Gasch, Sebastiá. *Paris, 1940.* Barcelona: Selecta, 1956.

Gelman, Juan, and Osvaldo Bayer. *Exilio.* Buenos Aires: Legasa, 1984.

Gómez Carrillo, Enrique. *Páginas escogidas.* Paris: Garnier, n.d..

———. *Vistas de Europa. Obras completas.* Vol. 4. Madrid: Mundo Latino, 1919.

Gomez de la Serna, Ramón. *París.* Ed. and prologue Nigel Dennis. Valencia: Pretextos, 1986.

Green, Julien. *Paris.* Paris: Champs Vallon, 1983.

Güiraldes, Ricardo. *Don Segundo Sombra.* 1926. Madrid: Consejo Superior de Investigaciones Científicas, 1988.

———. *Raucho. Momentos de una juventud contemporánea.* 1917. Buenos Aires: Losada, 1949.

Hemingway, Ernest. *A Moveable Feast.* New York: Scribner, 1964.

Lautréamont, Comte de. *Les chants de Maldoror.* 1869. Paris: Garnier-Flammarion, 1969.

Leon, Olver Gilberto de, ed. *Cuentistas hispanoamericanos en la Sorbona.* Montevideo: Ediciones de la Plaza, 1984.

Murger, Henri. *Scènes de la vie de bohème.* 1850. *Oeuvres complètes.* Vol. VIII. Geneva: Slatkine, 1971.

Onetti, Juan Carlos. *La vida breve.* 1950. Barcelona: Edhasa, 1977.

Paz Soldán y Unánue, Pedro. *Memorias de un viajero peruano; Apuntes y recuerdos de Europa y Oriente 1859–1863.* Lima: Biblioteca Nacional, 1971.

Peri-Rossi, Cristina. *La nave de los locos.* Barcelona: Seix Barral, 1984.

———. *La tarde del dinosauro.* Barcelona: Plaza y Janés, 1984.

Ribeyro, Julio Ramón. *La palabra del mudo.* Lima: Milla Batres, 1973.

Salazar Bondy, Sebastián. *Pobre gente de París.* Lima: Juan Mejía Baca, 1958.

Sarmiento, Domingo Faustino. *Facundo, o civilización y barbarie.* 1845. Caracas: Ayacucho, 1977.

———. *Viajes por Europa, Africa i América 1845–1847. Obras.* Vol. 5. Paris: Belin, 1909.

Scorza, Manuel. *Cantar de Agapito Robles.* Caracas: Monte Avila, 1977.

———. *La danza inmóvil.* Barcelona: Plaza y Janés, 1983.

———. *Historia de Garabombo, el invisible.* Barcelona: Plaza y Janés, 1972.

———. *El jinete insomne.* Barcelona: Plaza y Janés, 1977.

———. *Redoble por Rancas.* Caracas: Monte Avila, 1970.

———. *La tumba del relámpago.* Mexico: Siglo XXI, 1979.

Shua, Ana María. *La sueñera.* Buenos Aires: Minotauro, 1984.

Vallejo, César. *Desde Europa: Crónicas y artículos (1923–1938).* Prologue and notes Jorge Puccinelli. Lima: Fuente de Cultura Peruana, 1987.

Vásquez, Ana, Ana Luisa Valdés, and Ana María Araujo, eds. *Las mujeres del Cono Sur escriben.* Stockholm: Nordan, 1984.

Vitor, Nestor. *A obra crítica de Nestor Vitor.* Vol. III. Rio de Janeiro: Fundaçao Casa de rui Barbosa, 1979.

II. CRITICISM, CULTURAL THEORY, AND INTELLECTUAL HISTORY

Abellán, José Luis. *París o el mundo es un palacio.* Barcelona: Anthropos, 1987.

Achugar, Hugo. "El exilio uruguayo y la producción de conocimientos sobre el fenómeno literario." *Ideologies and Literature* 4.16 (1983): 224–41.

Afinidades: Francia y América del Sur. Montevideo: Uruguaya, 1946.

Aguiar, César A. *Uruguay: país de emigración.* Montevideo: Banda Oriental, 1982.

Aínsa, Fernando. *Los buscadores de la utopía.* Caracas: Monte Avila, 1977.

———. *Identidad cultural de Iberoamérica en su narrativa.* Madrid: Gredos, 1986.

Alazraki, Jaime. *En busca del unicornio: Los cuentos de Julio Cortázar.* Madrid: Gredos, 1983.

Aldaz, Anna-Marie. *The Past of the Future: The Novelistic Cycle of Manuel Scorza.* New York: Peter Lang, 1990.

Alfredo Bryce Echenique. Special issue *Co-textes* 9 (1985).

Alonso, Carlos. *The Spanish American Regional Novel: Modernity and Autochthony*. New York: Cambridge UP, 1990.

Altieri, Charles. *Canons and Consequences: Reflections on the Ethical Force of Imaginative Ideals*. Evanston: Northwestern UP, 1990.

Alvarez Ríos, Claire. "Les lettres européennes dans la revue argentine *Sur*." D.E.S. thesis. Paris: Institut d'Etudes Hispaniques, 1962.

Amérique Latine/Europe: Contacts, echanges, lectures. Centre de Recherches et d'Etudes Comparatistes Ibéro-Francophones. Paris: Sorbonne Nouvelle, 1984.

Les Années 20: Les écrivains américains à Paris et leurs amis. Paris: Centre Culturel Américain, 1959.

Appadurai, Arjun. "Putting Hierarchy in Its Place." *Cultural Anthropology* 3.1 (1988): 36–49.

———. *The Social Life of Things: Commodities in Cultural Perspective*. New York: Cambridge UP, 1988.

Ara, Guillermo. *Los argentinos y la literatura nacional*. Buenos Aires: Huemul, 1969.

Arona, Juan de. *Diccionario de peruanismos*. 2 vols. Lima: Peisa, 1974.

Ashcroft, W. D. "Constitutive Graphonomy: A Post-Colonial Theory of Literary Writing." In *After Europe: Critical Theory and Post-Colonial Writing*. Eds. Stephen Slemon and Helen Tiffin. Sydney, Australia: Dangaroo, 1989, 58–73.

Ashcroft, Bill, Gareth Williams, and Helen Tiffin. *The Post-Colonial Studies Reader*. London and New York: Routledge, 1995.

Bachelard, Gaston. *La poétique de l'Espace*. Paris: Presses Universitaires de France, 1958.

Bakhtin, Mikhail M. *The Dialogic Imagination*. Trans. Caryl Emerson and Michael Holquist. Austin: U Texas P, 1981.

Barrenechea, Ana María. *Cuaderno de Bitácora de Rayuela*. Buenos Aires: Sudamericana, 1983.

Barthes, Roland. *Mythologies*. Paris: Seuil, 1957.

———. *S/Z*. Paris: Seuil, 1970.

———. *Writing Degree Zero and Elements of Semiology*. Trans. Annette Lavers and Colin Smith. Preface by Susan Sontag. Boston: Beacon, 1970.

Beard, Laura J. "Writing and the Female Self: Identity and Authority in Contemporary Latin American Fiction." Diss. Johns Hopkins U, 1994.

Beeson, Margaret E., et al. *Hispanic Writers in French Journals: An Annotated Bibliography*. Boulder, Colo.: Society of Spanish and Spanish-American Studies, 1978.

Benjamin, Walter. *Charles Baudelaire: A Lyric Poet in the Era of High Capitalism*. Trans. Harry Zohn. London: Verso, 1983.

———. *Illuminations*. Ed. Hannah Arendt. Trans. Harry Zohn. New York: Schocken, 1968.

Benstock, Shari. *Women of the Left Bank: Paris: 1900–1940.* Austin: U Texas P, 1986.

Bernoussan, Albert. Interview with Alfredo Bryce Echenique. *Insula* 308–09 (1972): 22.

———. Interview with Bryce Echenique. *Insula* 408 (1980): 1.

———. "Necesito estar lejos de lo que cuento." *Textual* 1 (1971): 5–7.

Bhabha, Homi K. *The Location of Culture.* London and New York: Routledge, 1994.

Blanchot, Maurice. *L'espace littéraire.* Paris: Gallimard, 1955.

Bocaz, Luis. "Le roman latino-américain comme production culturelle." *Amérique Latine* 3 (1980): 31–35.

Boggio, Philippe. "Coupole: Where the Customer Is King." *Guardian Weekly* 22 December 1991: 12.

Brunel, Pierre, coord. *Paris et le phénomène des capitales littéraires*: Actes du premier congrés international du CRLC. Paris: Université de Paris-Sorbonne, 1986.

Buell, Frederick. *National Culture and the New Global System.* Baltimore: Johns Hopkins UP, 1994.

Burns, E. Bradford, and Thomas E. Skidmore. *Elites, Masses, and Modernization in Latin America, 1850–1930.* Austin: U of Texas P, 1979.

Butler, Judith. *Gender Trouble: Feminism and the Subversion of Identity.* New York: Routledge, 1990.

Caillet-Bois, Ricardo R. "El Río de la Plata, la Ilustración y la revolución francesa." *Etudes latino-américaines* II (1964): 53–62.

Campra, Rosalba. "Destinazione il nulla: 'El otro cielo' di Julio Cortázar." *Letterature d'America* 1 (1980): 67–81.

———. "Manuel Scorza" (interview). *América Latina: La identidad y la máscara.* Mexico: Siglo XXI, 1987, 173–87.

Cândido, António. "Literatura y subdesarrollo." *América Latina en su literatura.* Ed. César Fernández Moreno. Mexico: Siglo XXI, 1972.

Carafa, Brandan. "Secretos de la Torre Eiffel." *La revue argentine* 1.5 (1935): 33–34.

Castañeda, Jorge. *Utopia Unarmed: The Latin American Left after the Cold War.* New York: Vintage, 1993.

Castelar y Ripoll, Emilio. *Un viaje a París durante el establecimiento de la República.* Havana: Propaganda Literaria, 1880.

Castro-Klarén, Sara. "By (T)reason of State: the Canon and Marginality in Latin American Literature." *Revista de Estudios Hispánicos* 23.2 (1990): 1–19.

———. Interview. "Teoría poscolonial y literatura latinoamericana." By Juan Zevallos-Aguilar. *Revista Iberoamericana* 176–77 (1996): 963–71.

———. "Ontological Fabulation: Toward Cortázar's Theory of Literature." In *The Final Island: The Fiction of Julio Cortázar.* Eds. Jaime Alazraki and Ivar Ivask. Norman: U of Oklahoma P, 1978, 140–50.

Caws, Mary Ann, ed. *City Images: Perspectives from Literature, Philosophy and Film*. New York: Gordon and Breach, 1991.

Certeau, Michel de. *The Practice of Everyday Life*. Trans. Steven Rendall. Berkeley: U CA P, 1984.

Chacón, Alfredo, ed. *Cultura y dependencia, ocho ensayos latinoamericanos*. Caracas: Monte Avila, 1975.

Cheymol, Marc. *Miguel Angel Asturias dans le Paris des Années Folles*. Grenoble: Presse Universitaire de Grenoble, 1987.

——. "Les revues latino-américaines à Paris (1900–1940)." *Revue des Revues* 5 (1988): 16–17.

Chonchol, Jacques, and Guy Martiniére. *L'Amérique Latine et le latino-américanisme en France*. Paris: Harmattan, 1985.

Ciplijauskaité, Biruté. *La novela femenina contemporanea (1970–1985)*. Barcelona: Anthropos, 1988.

Clifford, James. *The Predicament of Culture: Twentieth-Century Ethnography, Literature, and Art*. Cambridge: Harvard UP, 1988.

Clifford, James, and George E. Marcus, eds. *Writing Culture: The Poetics and Politics of Ethnography*. Berkeley: U CA P, 1986.

Colás, Santiago. *Postmodernity in Latin America: The Argentine Paradigm*. Durham: Duke UP, 1994.

Collazos, Oscar, Julio Cortázar, and Mario Vargas Llosa. *Literatura en la revolución y revolución en la literatura*. Mexico: Siglo XXI, 1971.

Cornejo Polar, Antonio. Rev. of *La danza inmóvil*, by Manuel Scorza. *Revista de crítica literaria latinoamericana* 10 (1984): 190–91.

——. "Sobre el 'neoindigenismo' y las novelas de Manuel Scorza." *Revista Iberoamericana* 50.127 (1984): 549–57.

Corradí, Juan E., Patricia Weiss Fagen, and Manuel Antonio Garretón, eds. *Fear at the Edge: State Terror and Resistance in Latin America*. Berkeley: U CA P, 1992.

Cortázar, Julio. "Acerca de la situación del intelectual latinoamericano." *Ultimo round* II. México: Siglo XXI, 1985, 265–80.

——. *Argentina: Años de alambradas culturales*. Buenos Aires: Muchnik, 1984.

La cultura como empresa multinacional. Buenos Aires: Galerna, 1975.

Deleuze, Gilles and Felix Guattari. *Kafka: Pour une littérature mineure*. Paris: Minuit, 1975.

——. *Proust et les signes*. Paris: Presses Universitaires de France, 1986.

Delvaille, Bernard, text, and Robert Doisneau, photographs. *Passages et Galeries du 19e siècle*. Paris: A.C.E., 1981.

Díaz, José Pedro, and Germán Wettstein. *Exilio-inxilio: dos enfoques*. Montevideo: Instituto Testimonios de las Comarcas y del Mundo, 1989.

Donoso, José. *Historia personal del Boom*. Barcelona: Anagrama, 1972.

Escajadillo, Tomás G. "Alfredo Bryce, ese desconocido." *Oiga* 22 March 1968: 24–26.

———. *La narrativa indigenista peruana.* Lima: Mantaro, 1994.

———. "Scorza antes del último combate." *Hispamérica* 55 (1990): 51–72.

Escorza, Cecilia. "Suplemento a la bibliografía sobre Manuel Scorza." *Revista de crítica literaria latinoamericana* 19.37 (1993): 361–64.

Exilio: Nostalgia y creación. Mérida, Venezuela: Universidad de los Andes, 1987.

Fell, Eve-Marie, and Claude Fell. "Evolución del latinoamericanismo en Francia." *Revista de crítica literaria latinoamericana* 31–32 (1990): 307–17.

Ferguson, Priscilla Parkhurst. *Paris As Revolution: Writing the Nineteenth-Century City.* Berkeley: U CA P, 1994.

Fernández Utrera, María Soledad. "Julio Cortázar y *Libro de Manuel*: pensamiento y narrativa en torno al concepto de 'revolución'." *Revista Canadiense de Estudios Hispánicos* 20.2 (1996): 225–40.

Ferreira, César. "Vida y escritura: *La vida exagerada de Martín Romaña* de Alfredo Bryce," *Selected Proceedings, The Seventh Louisiana Conference on Hispanic Literatures.* Baton Rouge: Louisiana State University, 1986.

Ferreira, César, and Ismael P. Márquez, eds. *Los mundos de Alfredo Bryce Echenique: Textos críticos.* Lima: Fondo Editorial de la Pontificia Universidad Católica del Perú, 1994.

Fischer, María Luisa. "Zoológicos en libertad: la tradición del bestiario en el Nuevo Mundo." *Revista Canadiense de Estudios Hispánicos* 20.3 (1996): 463–76.

Forgues, Roland. "Entre la esperanza y el desencanto." *Palabra Viva* I. Lima: Studium, 1988, 77–90.

———. *Estrategia mítica de Manuel Scorza.* Lima: Centro de Estudios para el Desarrollo y la Participación, 1991.

Foucault, Michel. "Space, Knowledge, and Power." *The Foucault Reader.* Ed. Paul Rabinow. New York: Pantheon, 1984.

García Bryce, Iñigo. "Julius, Martín Romaña y otros marginales de Bryce Echenique." *Plaza: Revista de literatura* 12 (1987): 16–20.

García Calderón, Ventura. *Cette France que nous aimons.* Geneva: Bourquin, 1945 (and Paris: Henri Lefèbvre, 1947).

———. "Pour quoi nous sommes francophiles." *Bulletin de la bibliothèque américaine* Oct. 1915: 22.

García Canclini, Néstor. *Consumidores y ciudadanos. Conflictos multiculturales de la globalización.* Mexico: Grijalbo, 1995.

———. *Culturas híbridas: Estrategias para entrar y salir de la modernidad.* México: Grijalbo, 1990.

Geertz, Clifford. *The Interpretation of Cultures: Selected Essays.* New York: Basic Books, 1973.

Geist, Johann Friedrich. *Arcades: The History of a Building Type.* Cambridge and London: Massachusettes Institute of Technology P, 1983.

Gonzaléz, Aníbal. *La crónica modernista hispanoamericana*. Madrid: Porrúa Turanzas, 1983.

González Casanova, Pablo, coord. *Cultura y creación intelectual en América Latina*. México: Siglo XXI, 1984.

González Echevarría, Roberto. *The Voice of the Masters*. Austin: U of Texas P, 1985.

Grutman, Rainier. "Le bilingüisme littéraire comme relation intersystèmique." *Canadian Review of Comparative Literature* Sept.–Dec. 1990: 198–212.

Guerra, François-Xavier. "L'Amérique Latine face à la Revolution Française." *Caravelle* 54 (1990): 7–20.

Gutierrez, Franklin. "La problemática latinoamericana en *La danza inmóvil* de Manuel Scorza." Molina, ed., *Manuel Scorza: La sangre quemada*.

Gyurko, Lanin A. "Narcissistic and Ironic Paradise in Three Stories by Cortázar." *Hispanófila* 50 (1974): 19–42.

Hardoy, Jorge E. "Teorías y prácticas urbanísticas en Europa entre 1850 y 1930. Su traslado a América Latina." In *Repensando la ciudad de América Latina*. Comps. Hardoy and Richard Morse. Buenos Aires: Grupo Editor Latinoamericano, 1988, 97–126.

Hassan, Ihab. "Cities of Mind, Urban Words: The Dematerialization of Metropolis in Contemporary American Fiction." In *Literature and the Urban Experience*. Eds. Michael C. Jaye and Ann Chalmers Watts. New Brunswick, N.J.: Rutgers UP, 1981, 93–112.

Headrick, Daniel. R. "Botany, Chemistry, and Tropical Development." *Journal of World History* 7.1 (1996): 1–20.

Higonnet, Margaret R., and Joan Templeton. *Reconfigured Spheres: Feminist Explorations of Literary Space*. Amherst: U MA P, 1994.

Hildebrandt, Martha. *Peruanismos*. Lima: Moncloa, 1969.

Iser, Wolfgang. *Prospecting: From Reader Response to Literary Anthropology*. Baltimore: Johns Hopkins UP, 1989.

Jameson, Fredrick. *The Political Unconscious*. Ithaca: Cornell UP, 1981.

———. "Third World Literature in the Era of Multinational Capitalism." *Social Text* 15 (1986): 65–88.

Jitrik, Noé. *Las armas y las razones. Ensayos sobre el peronismo, el exilio, la literatura: 1975–1980*. Buenos Aires: Sudamericana, 1984.

———. *Producción literaria y producción social*. Buenos Aires: Sudamericana, 1975.

——— et al. *La vuelta a Cortázar en nueve ensayos*. Buenos Aires: Perez, 1969.

Jones, Julie. *A Common Place: The Representation of Paris in Spanish American Fiction 1963–1982*. Lewisburg, PA: Bucknell UP, 1998.

Juan-Navarro, Santiago. *Archival Reflections: Postmodern Fiction of the Americas (Self-Reflexivity, Historical Revisionism, Utopia)*. Lewisburg, PA: Bucknell UP, forthcoming.

Kadir, Djelal. *The Other Writing: Postcolonial Essays in Latin America's Writing Culture*. West Lafayette, Ind.: Purdue UP, 1993.

Kennedy, J. Gerald. *Imagining Paris: Exile, Writing, and American Identity*. New Haven: Yale UP, 1993.

Klor de Alva, J. Jorge. "Colonialism and Postcolonialism as (Latin) American Mirages." *Colonial Latin American Review* 1.2 (1992): 3–23.

Kristeva, Julia. *Desire in Language: A Semiotic Approach to Literature and Art*. Ed. Leon S. Roudiez, trans. Thomas Mora, Alice Jardine, and Leon S. Roudiez. New York: Columbia UP, 1980.

La Belle, Jenijoy. *Herself Beheld: The Literature of the Looking Glass*. Ithaca: Cornell, 1988.

Lagmanovich, David, ed. *Estudios sobre los cuentos de Julio Cortázar*. Barcelona: Hispam, 1975.

Lagos Oteíza, Belén, and María Luisa López Oroz. "Otra modalidad de analizar un cuento 'El otro cielo' de Julio Cortázar." *Repertorio Americano* 6.4 (1980): 18–24.

Lévêque, Jean-Jacques. *Jardins de Paris*. Paris: Hachette, 1982.

Levinson, Brett. "The Other Origin: Cortázar and Identity Politics." *Latin American Literary Review* 22.44 (1994): 5–19.

Lichtblau, Myron I., ed. *La emigración y el exilio en la literatura hispánica del siglo veinte*. Miami: Universal, 1988.

Limoges, Camille. "The Development of the Muséum d'Histoire Naturelle of Paris, c. 1800–1914." In *The Organization of Science and Technology in France*. Eds. Robert Fox and George Weisz. Paris and London, 1980, 211–40.

Locan, Enrique. "La France et Sarmiento." Series of articles. *Revue de L'Argentine* 2.15 (1936): 21–28; 5.30 (1938): 7–12; 5.30 (1939): 3–8 and 51–52.

Losada, Alejandro. *Creación y praxis: La producción literaria como praxis social en Hispanoamérica y el Perú*. Lima: Universidad Nacional Mayor de San Marcos, 1976.

———. *La literatura en la sociedad de América Latina*. Munich: Fink Verlag, 1987.

———. "Littérature et société: A la recherche d'une méthode." *Amérique Latine* 3 (1980): 36–40.

Lotman, Yuri M., and Boris Uspensky. "On the Semiotic Mechanism of Culture." *New Literary History* 9.2 (1978): 211–32.

Loveluck, John. *Novelistas hispanoamericanas de hoy*. Madrid: Taurus, 1976.

Luchting, Wolfgang. *Alfredo Bryce/Humores y malhumores*. Lima: Milla Batres, 1975.

Ludmer, Josefina. *Onetti: Los procesos de construcción del relato*. Buenos Aires: Sudamericano, 1977.

Lynch, John, ed. *Latin American Revolutions 1808–1826: Old and New World Origins*. Norman: U OK P, 1994.

Marcone, Jorge. "De *La última mudanza de Felipe Carrillo* de Alfredo Bryce Echenique o la escritura como conversación (y bolero)." In *La oralidad escrita. Sobre la reivindicación y re-inscripción del discurso oral*. Lima: Fondo Editorial de la Pontificia Universidad Católica del Perú, 1997, 249–74.

Marcus, George, and Michael Fischer. *Anthropology As Cultural Critique*. Chicago: U Chicago P, 1986.

McHale, Brian. *Postmodernist Fiction*. New York and London: Methuen, 1987.

McQuirk, Bernard. "New Lack or Old Lacan? Julio Cortázar's 'El otro cielo.'" *New Novel Review* 1.2 (1994): 49–59.

Merrell, Floyd. *A Semiotic Theory of Texts*. New York: Mouton, 1985.

Mignolo, Walter. "Colonial and Postcolonial Discourse: Cultural Critique or Academic Colonialism?" *Latin American Research Review* 28.3 (1993): 120–31.

———. *Elementos para una teoría del texto literario*. Barcelona: Crítica, 1978.

———. "Occidentalización, imperialismo, globalización: herencias coloniales y teorías postcoloniales." *Revista Iberoamericana* 170–71 (1995): 27–41.

———. "Posoccidentalismo: las epistemologías fronterizas y el dilema de los estudios (latinoamericanos) de área." *Revista Iberoamericana* 176–77 (1996): 679–96.

———. "(Re)Modeling the Letter. A Cross-Road Between Semiotics and Literary Studies." *On Semiotic Modeling*. M. Anderson and F. Merrell, eds. The Hague: Mouton, 1990.

———. "Semiosis y universos de sentido." *Lexis* 7.2 (1983): 219–37.

———. "Teorizar a través de fronteras culturales." *Revista de crítica literaria latinoamericana* 33 (1991): 103–12.

Moi, Toril. *Sexual/Textual Politics: Feminist Literary Theory*. London and New York: Methuen, 1985.

Molina, Alfonso, ed. *Manuel Scorza: La sangre quemada. Homenaje colectivo*. Lima, 1985.

Molloy, Sylvia. *La diffusion de la littérature hispanoaméricaine en France au XXe siècle*. Paris: Presses Universitaires de France, 1972.

Montalbetti, Jean, comp. "Cortázar et son double" (interview). *Magazine Littéraire* 203 Jan. 1984: 80–85.

Mora, Gabriela. *En torno al cuento: de la teoría general y de su práctica en Hispanoamérica.* Madrid: José Porrúa Turanzas, 1985.

Moraña, Mabel. "Función ideológica de la fantasía en las novelas de Manuel Scorza." *Revista de crítica literaria latinoamericana* 17 (1983): 171–92.

Morínigo, Marcos A. *Diccionario de americanismos.* Barcelona: Muchnik, 1985.

Needell, Jeffrey D. "Rio de Janeiro and Buenos Aires: Public Space and Public Consciousness in *Fin de Siècle* Latin America." *Comparative Study of Society and History* (1995): 519–40.

———. "La Sublime Puerta: la influencia francesa sobre la literatura y los literatos brasileños, 1808–1914." In Jorge E. Hardoy and Richard P. Morse, eds. *Nuevas perspectivas en los estudios sobre historia urbana latinoamericana.* Buenos Aires: Grupo Editor Latinoamericano, 1989.

Neira, Hugo. "Scorza aquí y allá: mirada limeña y mirada parisina sobre Manuel Scorza." In *Manuel Scorza: L'homme et son oeuvre.* Bordeaux: Université de Bordeaux III, 1985, 93–117.

Ortega, Julio. "Cuentos de Ribeyro." *Cuadernos hispanoamericanos* 417 (1985): 128–45.

Ortiz, Federico, et al. *La arquitectura del liberalismo en la Argentina.* Buenos Aires: Sudamericana, 1968.

Parkinson Zamora, Lois. "Movement and Stasis, Film and Photo: Temporal Structures in the Recent Fiction of Julio Cortázar." *Review of Contemporary Fiction* 3.3 (1983): 51–65.

———. "Voyeur/Voyant: Julio Cortázar's Visual Esthetic." *Mosaic* 14.4 (1981): 45–68.

Pera, Cristóbal. *Modernistas en París: el mito de París en la prosa modernista hispanoamericana.* Bern: Peter Lang, 1997.

Pratt, Mary Louise. *Imperial Eyes: Travel Writing and Transculturation.* London: Routledge, 1992.

———. "Linguistic Utopias." In *The Linguistics of Writing.* Ed. Nigel Fabb. Manchester: Manchester UP, 1987, 48–66.

Prieto, Adolfo. *El discurso criollista en la formación de la Argentina moderna.* Buenos Aires: Sudamericana, 1988.

Rama, Angel. "El 'Boom' en perspectiva." In *La crítica de la cultura en América Latina.* Eds. Saúl Sosnowski and Tomás Eloy Martínez. Caracas: Ayacucho, 1985, 266–306.

———. *La ciudad letrada.* Hanover, N.H.: Ediciones del Norte, 1984.

———. *Transculturación narrativa en América Latina.* Mexico: Siglo XXI, 1982.

Ramos, Julio. *Desencuentros de la modernidad en América Latina: Literatura y política en el siglo XIX.* Mexico: Fondo de Cultura Económica, 1989.

Reichardt, Dieter. "La lectura nacional de 'El otro cielo' y *Libro de Manuel*." *Inti* 22–23 (1985–86): 205–15.

Ribeyro, Julio Ramón. "Habemus genio." *El Observador* 21 Feb. 1982: 14.

Richard, Nelly. *La insubordinación de los signos*. Santiago de Chile: Cuarto Propio, 1994.

Riffaterre, Michael. *Fictional Truth*. Baltimore: Johns Hopkins UP, 1990.

Rifkin, Adrian. *Street Noises: Parisian Pleasure, 1900–1940*. Manchester and New York: Manchester UP, 1993.

Riva-Agüero y Osma, José de la. "Influencias imitativas en la moderna literatura peruana." *Obras completas* II. Lima: Instituto Riva-Agüero, 1941, 469–80.

Rodríguez-Alcalá, Hugo. "En el cincuentenario de *Don Segundo Sombra*." In *Actas del sexto congreso internacional de hispanistas*. Eds. Alan M. Gordon and Evelyn Rugg. Toronto: U Toronto P, 1980, 615–18.

Rodríguez Monegal, Emir. *El boom de la novela latinoamericana*. Caracas: Tiempo Nuevo, 1972.

———. "La 'Fantome' de Lautréamont." *Revista Iberoamericana* 84–85 (1973): 625–39.

Rolleston, James L. "The Politics of Quotation: Walter Benjamin's Arcades Project." *PMLA* 104 (1989): 13–27.

Romero, José Luis. "Las ideologías de la cultura nacional." *Las ideologías de la cultura nacional y otros ensayos*. Buenos Aires: Centro Editor, 1982.

———. *Las ideas políticas en Argentina*. Buenos Aires: Fondo de Cultura Económica, 1975.

Ross, Kristin. *The Emergence of Social Space: Rimbaud and the Paris Commune*. Minneapolis: U MN P, 1988.

Rotker, Susana. *La invención de la crónica*. Buenos Aires: Letra Buena, 1992.

Santamaría, Francisco J. *Diccionario general de americanismos*. Mexico: Pedro Robredo, 1942.

Sarlo, Beatriz. *Una modernidad periférica*. Buenos Aires: Nueva Visión, 1988.

———. "Modernidad y mezcla cultural. El caso de Buenos Aires." In *Modernidade: vanguardas artísticas na America Latina*. São Paolo: Memorial/ UNESP, 1990.

Sarlo, Beatriz, and Carlos Altamirano. *Literatura/Sociedad*. Buenos Aires: Hachette, 1983.

Schmidt, Friedhelm. "Bibliografía de y sobre Manuel Scorza." *Revista de crítica literaria latinoamericana* 34 (1991): 273–86.

———. "Bibliografía de y sobre Manuel Scorza: nuevas aportaciones." *Revista de crítica literaria latinoamericana* 37 (1993): 355–59.

Schorske, Carl E. *Fin-de-siècle Vienna*. New York: Random House, 1981.

Schwartz, Ellen. *Paris as Seen by Antonio Seguí*. New York: Lefebre Gallery, 1983.

Schwartz, Jorge. *Vanguarda e Cosmopolitismo Na Década de 20*. São Paulo: Perspectiva, 1983.

Schwartz, Marcy. Rev. of *Urracas*, by Luisa Futoranksy. *Hispamérica* 69 (1994): 114–17.

Seidel, Michael. *Exile and the Narrative Imagination*. New Haven: Yale UP, 1986.

Sharpe, William, and Leonard Wallock, eds. *Visions of the Modern City*. Baltimore: Johns Hopkins UP, 1987.

Shattuck, Roger. *The Banquet Years*. Toronto: Random House, 1968.

Siegle, Robert. *The Politics of Reflexivity: Narrative and the Constitutive Poetics of Culture*. Baltimore: Johns Hopkins UP, 1986.

Smith, Sidonie. *A Poetics of Women's Autobiography: Marginality and the Fictions of Self-Representation*. Bloomington: U Ind. P, 1987.

Sommer, Doris. *Foundational Fictions: The National Romances of Latin America*. Berkeley: U CA P, 1993.

Sopena, Ramón. *Americanismos: diccionario ilustrado sopena*. Barcelona: Ramón Sopena, 1982.

Sorkin, Michael, ed. *Variations on a Theme Park: The New American City and the End of Public Space*. New York: Noonday, 1992.

Sosnowski, Saúl. Rev. of *Libro de Manuel*, by Julio Cortázar. *Hispamérica* 2.6 (1974): 109–15.

Standish, Peter. "Los compromisos de Julio Cortázar." *Hispania* 80.3 (1997): 465–71.

———. "Magus, Masque, and the Machinations of Authority: Cortázar at Play." In *Structures of Power. Essays on Twentieth-Century Spanish-American Fiction*. Eds. Peter Standish and Terry Peavler. Albany: SUNY P, 1996, 75–87.

Terán, Oscar. *En busca de la ideología argentina*. Buenos Aires: Catálogo, 1986.

Tierney-Tello, Mary Beth. *Allegories of Transgression and Transformation: Experimental Fiction By Women Writing under Dictatorship*. Albany: SUNY P, 1996.

Vidal, Hernán, ed. *Fascismo y experiencia literaria: Reflexiones para una recanonización*. Minneapolis: Institute for the Study of Ideologies and Literature, 1985.

———. *Literatura hispanoamericana e ideología liberal: surgimiento y crisis (una problemática sobre la dependencia en torno a la narración del boom)*. Buenos Aires: Hispamérica, 1976.

Villegas, Jean-Claude. *La littérature hispano-américaine publiée en France 1900–1984*. Paris: Bibliothèque Nationale, 1986.

Viñas, David et al. *Más allá del boom: literatura y mercado.* Mexico: Marcha, 1981.

――――. *De Sarmiento a Cortázar: Literatura y realidad política.* Buenos Aires: Siglo Veinte, 1974.

Voyages et séjours d'espagnols et d'hispano-américains en France. Tours: Université de Tours, 1982.

Yurkievich, Saúl. *A través de la trama.* Barcelona: Muchnik, 1984.

Zabus, Chantal. "Othering the Foreign Language in the West African Europhone Novel." *Canadian Review of Comparative Literature* 17.3–4 (1990): 348–66.

Index

García Márquez, Gabriel, 152n. 10, 158n. 15
Geist, Johann Friedrich, 42, 44, 51–2, 155n. 20, 156n. 29
gender, 1, 7, 9, 12, 20, 23, 154n. 15; in Cortázar, 39–42, 45, 61; in Cortázar and Scorza, 77–80; in Futoransky, 115–16, 118, 120, 122, 125, 132, 142, 143, 145, 162n. 1
Gilbert, A. de. *See* Pedro Balmaceda Toro
Goethe, Johann Wolfgang, 154n. 16
Gómez Carrillo, Enrique, 15–17
González, Aníbal, 151n. 6, 160n. 5
Grutman, Rainier, 161n. 8
Guattari, Felix, 133
Güiraldes, Ricardo, 9, 20–22, 24, 55, 68, 135, 152n. 13, 157n. 1
Gutierrez, Franklin, 82, 84
Gyurko, Lanin, 156n. 31

Hardoy, Jorge, 19
Haussmann, Georges Eugène, 6
Headrick, Daniel, 154n. 11
Hemingway, Ernest, 93, 95, 97, 100, 103, 118, 126, 147

independence, 3–7, 12, 15nn. 6–7
indigenism, 63–66, 157n. 4
Irigaray, Luce, 40
Isaacs, Jorge, 152n. 13

Jakfalvi, Susana, 32
Jones, Julie, 150n. 10, 153nn. 17, 3; 155n. 21, 163n. 12
journalism in Paris, 15–16, 18, 151nn. 6–7, 152n. 10
Juan-Navarro, Santiago, 158n. 12
Juristo, Juan Angel, 160n. 3

Kadir, Djelal, 77
Klor de Alva, J. Jorge, 3–4

La Belle, Jenijoy, 40
Lagmanovich, David, 82
Lautréamont, Comte de, 43, 47–48, 155nn. 19, 23, 24; 155n. 25, 156n. 26
Lemirre, Elisabeth, 161n. 14
Levinson, Brett, 154nn. 10, 13
Limoges, Camille, 154nn. 11–12
Liss, Peggy, 150n. 7
Luchting, Wolfgang, 159n. 1

Marcus, George, 150n. 10
McHale, Brian, 86, 137, 159n. 22, 163n. 11
McQuirk, Bernard, 155n. 22
Mignolo, Walter, 3, 149nn. 3–4, 150n. 6
Modernismo, 2, 11, 14–20, 21, 97, 151nn. 6–7
Molloy, Sylvia, 151n. 7
Moraña, Mabel, 66
Mundo Nuevo, 152n. 10, 158n. 15
Murger, Henri, 95

Needell, Jeffrey, 19
Neira, Hugo, 87
neoindigenism, 63–66, 157nn. 4–5
novela de la tierra, 21–22, 24, 151n. 5, 157n. 1. *See also* regional novel

Onetti, Juan Carlos, 152n. 15
Oquendo, Abelardo, 81
Ortega, Julio, 159n. 16
Ortiz, Federico, 155n. 18

Paley Francescato, Martha, 51, 156n. 27
Parkhurst Ferguson, Priscilla, 5, 150n. 8, 163n. 9
Parkinson Zamora, Lois, 35, 154n. 9, 158n. 12